The Fall of the Indigo Jackal

The Fall of the Indigo Jackal

The Discourse of Division and Pūrṇabhadra's *Pañcatantra*

McComas Taylor

State University of New York Press

Art credit for Taylor/THE FALL OF THE INDIGO JACKAL

Cover art:
The jack who pronounced himself king (from the Cleveland "Tutinama")
Opaque watercolor and gold on paper, ca. 1560–1565
Mughal school, Reign of Akbar

Used courtesy of the San Diego Museum of Art (Edwin Binney 3rd Collection).

Published by
State University of New York Press, Albany

Printed in the United States of America

For information, contact State University of New York Press, Albany, NY
www.sunypress.edu

Production by Michael Haggett and Marilyn Semerad
Marketing by Fran Keneston

Library of Congress Cataloging-in-Publication Data

Taylor, McComas, 1956–
The fall of the indigo jackal : the discourse of division and Purnabhadra's Pañcatantra / McComas Taylor.
p. cm.
Originally presented as the author's thesis (Ph.D.—Australian National University, 2005).
Includes bibliographical references and index.
ISBN-13: 978-0-7914-7177-7 (hardcover : alk. paper)
ISBN-13: 978-0-7914-7178-4 (pbk. : alk. paper)
1. Purnabhadra. Pañcatantra. 2. Panchatantra. 3. Caste in literature. 4. Sanskrit literature—History and criticism. I. Panchatantra. II. Title.

PK3798.P824P3638 2007
891.2'3—dc22

2006032536

10 9 8 7 6 5 4 3 2 1

What makes power hold good, what makes it accepted, is simply the fact that it doesn't only weigh on us as a force that says no, but that it traverses and produces things, it induces pleasure, forms knowledge, produces discourse.

—Michel Foucault, *Truth and Power*

Contents

Acknowledgments

I would like to thank my friend, mentor, and colleague Dr. John Powers for the confidence and encouragement that he extended to me at the outset of this project and for his inspiration, guidance, and good humor, which have sustained me through it. My thanks are also due to Dr. Richard Barz, Dr. Adrian Burton, and Dr. Ian Proudfoot, for sharing with me their knowledge of Sanskrit, India, and literature.

Dr. Virpi Hämeen-Anttila (University of Helsinki) and Professor Patrick Olivelle (University of Texas at Austin) provided invaluable guidance and incisive criticism during the formative stages of my research.

I would also like to acknowledge the many years of friendship and support that I have received from three other generous mentors, Dr. Richard Stanley, Dr. Royce Wiles, and Dr. Primoz Pecenko.

One of the most stimulating aspects of this project has been the interaction that I have enjoyed with my colleagues in the Faculty of Asian Studies at the Australian National University. In particular I would like to thank Dr. Julius Bautista, Daryono, Mark Emmanuel, Rob Hurle, Hamdan Juhannis, Mary Kilcline-Cody, Ros Matthews, John Monfries, and Jo Pickles for their companionship.

I would especially like to thank my wife Janet for her unfailing support, and finally I would like to thank Eleanor, Annie, and Patrick for listening to all those Sanskrit stories.

Abbreviations

ĀD	*Āpastambadharmasūtra*
AP	*Agnipurāṇa*
AŚ	*Arthaśāstra*
AV	*Atharvaveda*
BAP	*Brahmāṇḍapurāṇa*
BD	*Baudhāyanadharmasūtra*
BKM	*Bṛhatkathāmañjarī*
BP	*Bhāgavatapurāṇa*
BrP	*Brahmapurāṇa*
GD	*Gautamadharmasūtra*
GP	*Garuḍapurāṇa*
Hit.	*Hitopadeśa*
KP	*Kūrmapurāṇa*
KSS	*Kathāsaritsāgara*
Mbh	*Mahābhārata*
MMW	Monier Monier-Williams
MP	*Mārkaṇḍeyapurāṇa*
MS	*Manusmṛti*
NP	*Nāradapurāṇa*
NS	*Nītisāra*
NŚ	*Nītiśataka*
OED	*Oxford English Dictionary*
PP	*Padmapurāṇa*
PS	*Pañcatantra*, textus simplicior
PT	*Pañcatantra*, Pūrṇabhadra's recension
Rām.	*Rāmāyaṇa*
ṚS	*Ṛtusaṃhāra*
ṚV	*Ṛgveda*
SkP	*Skandapurāṇa*
ŚP	*Śivapurāṇa*
ŚPB	*Śatapathabrāhmaṇa*
SPT	Southern *Pañcatantra*
ŚS	*Śukasaptati*
TA	*Tantrākhyāyika*
TB	*Taittirīyabrāhmaṇa*
TS	*Taittirīyasaṃhitā*
VāmP	*Vāmanapurāṇa*
VāyP	*Vāyupurāṇa*
VD	*Vasiṣṭhadharmasūtra*
VP	*Viṣṇupurāṇa*
VPV	*Vetālapañcaviṃśati*
VS	*Viṣṇusmṛti*
YS	*Yājñavalkyasmṛti*

Conventions

Quotations from Sanskrit Texts

The standard form for translations from the Sanskrit is as follows. The English translation is given first in quotation marks, and the source, page and line numbers follow in brackets.

> "No one had seen or heard of any as skilful as he" (PT 17.5).

> PT 17.5 = *Pañcatantra* (i.e., Hertel 1908), page 17, line 5.

Interpolations

In certain cases, I have added words to a translation to clarify the meaning. These interpolations are enclosed in square brackets:

> "You will soon see royal favor etc., which is the fruit of the honor [that you have shown me]."

Explanations in translations are given in round brackets:

> "Only the owl, seated on the throne, awaiting consecration, remained there with the *kṛkālikā* (a kind of bird)."

Numbering and Naming of Stories

I have followed Hertel's scheme for numbering and naming individual stories in Pūrṇabhadra's *Pañcatantra,* with these minor adaptations:

1. Indo-Arabic numerals are used in preference to Hertel's roman numerals.
2. The number of the *tantra* (= Hertel's "Book") is prefixed to the number of each story, for example, Hertel's "Book I, tale xxvi" becomes "Story 1-26."
3. I have incorporated the *kathāmukha* and the five frame-stories into the numbering system as Story 0-00 "*Pañcatantra* frame," Story 1-00 "Lion and bull," Story 2-00 "Dove, mouse, crow, tortoise, and deer," and so on.
4. I have modernized Hertel's spelling where necessary, for example, *brāhmaṇa* for "brahmin," *brāhmaṇī* for "brahmanee," Viṣṇu for "Vishnu."

TRANSLATION

I have adopted a translation style that is more literal than literary. The rambling, multiclause sentence structure, the strings of gerunds and the frequent use of direct speech all reflect the style and structure of the original. While this literal translation may be less pleasurable to read, I hope that it will facilitate reference to the original Sanskrit texts. All translations from the Sanskrit are mine, unless indicated otherwise.

ITALICIZATION

Sanskrit words are set in italics (see the glossary on p. 219).

OTHER LANGUAGES

For Pahlavi and Arabic terms, I have followed the orthography of Jallad (2004).

INDIAN PLACE NAMES

Where possible, I have followed the orthography of *An Atlas of India* (Delhi: Oxford University Press, 1990). For place names not found in that publication, I have followed the original orthography used in the work cited.

1

Introduction

A jackal who had fallen into a vat of indigo dye decided to exploit his marvelous new appearance and declared himself king of the forest. He appointed the lions and other animals as his vassals, but took the precaution of having all his fellow jackals driven into exile. One day, hearing the howls of the other jackals in the distance, the indigo jackal's eyes filled with tears and he too began to howl. The lions and the others, realizing the jackal's true nature, sprang on him and killed him.

This is one of India's most widely known fables, and it is hard to imagine that anyone growing up in an Indian cultural milieu would not have heard it. The indigo jackal is as familiar to Indian childhood as are Little Red Riding Hood or Snow White in the English-speaking world. The story has been told and retold by parents, grandparents, and teachers for centuries in all the major Indian languages, both classical and vernacular. Versions of the collection in which it first appeared, the *Pañcatantra,* are still for sale at street stalls and on railway platforms all over India. The indigo jackal and other narratives from the collection have successfully colonized the contemporary media of television, CD, DVD, and the Internet.

I will begin by sketching the history and development of the various families of *Pañcatantra* texts where the story of the indigo jackal first appeared, starting with Pūrṇabhadra's recension, the version on which this inquiry is based. This is followed by a review of previous scholarship on the *Pañcatantra,* including attempts to ascribe "meaning" to the text. I conclude this opening chapter with an outline of the questions that I intend to address in this study: Why did the indigo jackal fall from power, and why was his demise inevitable? What social forces are at work here? What discourses give shape and structure to this narrative? What enables these discursive statements to function effectively?

The traditional account of the *Pañcatantra*'s origins given in Pūrṇabhadra's recension begins in a city called Mahilāropya. There lived a king by the name of Amaraśakti, whose three foolish sons were averse to education. When the king asked his advisers what could be done to awaken the princes' intellectual faculties, they replied that the mastery of grammar alone took twelve years; only then could one begin to study the treatises on spiritual and worldly affairs. They added that as life was short and the obstacles to learning were many, some more expedient path should be found. Accordingly, they recommended an elderly *brāhmaṇa* by the name of Viṣṇuśarman who was famed for his learning. Viṣṇuśarman was duly summoned, and the king asked him to educate the boys in return for a grant of 100 parcels of land. The *brāhmaṇa* replied that, as an octogenarian for whom sensual pleasures no longer held any attraction, he had no desire for wealth. But he accepted the king's proposal and undertook to educate the princes in the science of worldly conduct by amusing them with stories. Asking that the date be noted down, Viṣṇuśarman declared that if he had not fulfilled his promise within six months, "then it would befit your majesty to show me your buttocks" (PT 2.9–10). Amazed at the *brāhmaṇa*'s unconventional pledge, the king nevertheless placed the princes in his care. Viṣṇuśarman took the boys to his own home, where he composed five books, or *tantras:*

1. "Separation of friends," in which a jackal manipulated the friendship between a lion and a bull to enhance his own position
2. "Winning of friends," illustrating the collaboration of a crow, a mouse, a turtle, and a deer
3. "The crows and the owls," in which a colony of owls was led to destruction by a crow who pretended to be their ally
4. "Loss of one's gains," in which a monkey, lured from a tree by a crocodile, saved himself by trickery
5. "Ill-considered actions," in which a misguided barber, expecting a miraculous reward, struck and killed some mendicant monks.

Each *tantra* serves as a frame in which numerous substories and proverbial verses are embedded. Having studied these stories, we are told, the princes gained an unparalleled mastery over worldly conduct, and "from that time onward, this treatise by the name of *Pañcatantra,* which has as its purpose the edification of the young, has spread across the surface of the Earth" (PT 2.15–16).

As we shall see, this is hardly an exaggeration.[1] By the sixth century CE the *Pañcatantra* had been translated into Pahlavi at the court of the Persian King Khusru Anushirwan (Chosroes I) at Ctesiphon in modern Iraq. The Pahlavi version was translated into Syriac, the sacred language of Christianity in the areas now incorporated in southeastern Turkey, Syria, and Palestine. The Pahlavi text, now lost, was translated into Arabic in about 750 CE by Ibn al-Muqaffaʿ, a Persian Zoroastrian convert to Islam, under the title *Kalilah wa Dimnah.* This work, the first masterpiece of Arabic narrative literature, enjoyed great popularity and is known from numerous manuscripts and printed versions. The Arabic version was of central importance to the spread of the *Pañcatantra,* because it was the source, directly or indirectly, of all further translations into the languages of the Middle East and Europe. *Kalilah wa Dimnah* spread throughout the Arabic world, and by the end of the eleventh century, the Arabic had given rise to a Greek translation known as *Stefanites and Ichnelates* by Symeon, son of Seth, a Jewish physician at the Byzantine court (Jacobs 1888: xxv; Sjöberg 1962; Condylis-Bassoukos 1995).

Persian translations of the Arabic dating from the twelfth century culminated in an important version of the tales known as *Anwāri suhailī* (later translated into English under the title "Lights of Canopus"), which spread back to India, and to Afghanistan, Georgia, and Turkey. By the twelfth or thirteenth century, Symeon's Greek version had given rise to an Old Slavonic (Bulgarian) translation. A century later, the Arabic *Kalilah wa Dimnah* had been translated into Old Spanish by the college of Jewish translators, who specialized in Arabic works of science, at the court of King Alfonso the Good in Toledo. This marks the first appearance of the text in Western Europe (Jacobs 1888: xxv).[2] In about 1270, a Hebrew version from the same or a similar source was translated into Latin by John of Capua (in southern Italy), a Jewish convert to Christianity, under the title *Directorium vitae humanae* ("Book of rules for human life").

By the fifteenth century this version had been translated into German by the cleric Antonius von Pforr of Rottenburg, near Stuttgart, as the *Buch der Beispiele der alten Weisen* or "Book of examples of the old ways." His style is said to have been "of great vigor and beauty" (Hertel 1915: ix). This, incidentally, was one of the first books in Europe to be printed with the newly introduced technology of movable type. It was highly popular in medieval times, and appeared in twenty-one editions between 1480 and 1860.

The first Czech and French versions date from the sixteenth century, and in 1552, Anton Francesco Doni's Italian translation of *Directorium vitae humanae* appeared in Venice under the title *La Moral Filosophia.* This was the source of the first English version of the tales, translated by Sir Thomas North, and published as *Morall Philosophie of Doni* in 1570. His retelling of the stories has been described as a "gem of racy Tudor English" (Lanman in Hertel 1915: ix).

An influential French translation of the Persian *Anwāri Suhailī* by G. Gaulmin and Dāwūd Sa'īd, entitled *Livre des lumières ou la Conduite des roys,* appeared in 1644, and was reprinted in 1698 as *Fables de Pilpay.* The *Anwāri Suhailī* also gave rise, via a Turkish intermediary, to another French translation entitled *Contes et Fables indiennes de Bidpai et de Lokman* (1724–1778). The name Pilpay or Bidpai found in this title, which probably first appeared in the Arabic translation as Baydaba, is the name of the ascetic who was the narrator of these tales in all subsequent non-Indian versions, occupying the role originally filled by Viṣṇuśarman in the Sanskrit *Pañcatantra.* Since the time of Benfey, there has been speculation on the meaning of this name (Benfey 1966 [1859]: 32). Scholars have repeated—uncritically—the claim that "Bidpai" might be derived from the Sanskrit *vidyāpati,* "master of knowledge," the chief scholar at a court, or perhaps from the common *brāhmaṇa* title *vājapeyi* (see, for example, Olivelle 1997: xliii). As mentioned earlier, the Pahlavi recension is no longer extant, but in the Syriac translation of that text the ascetic's name is rendered as Bīdūg, which seems even more remote from *vidyāpati.* Whatever it originally meant, the names Bidpai and Pilpay have become intimately associated with the collection in Europe.

Stories akin to those in the *Pañcatantra* reached Southeast Asia at a very early date. A stone relief in the Buddhist temple of Candi Mendut in Central Java (c. 800 CE) clearly depicts Story 1-16 "Two geese and tortoise" (Klokke 1993: 77 and 165). Laotian and Thai versions of the *Pañcatantra* were written no later than 1200 CE (Huilgol 1987: 5), and sometime between the fourteenth and sixteenth centuries, stories from the *Pañcatantra* appeared in the Old Javanese *Tantri Kāmanandaka* (Zoetmulder 1974: 438). The stories became so popular in Bali that *tantri* became the Balinese word for "fable" (Hooykaas 1929: 10). Stories from the *Pañcatantra* reached Southeast Asia by two separate paths in premodern times: first from South India in their original Hindu form, and later in Islamicized form via Persian and Arabic intermediaries as *Hikajat Kalilah dan Dimnah* (Santoso 1971: 15).

To return to the collection's later development in Europe, the basic stories from the *Pañcatantra* were at one time well known in English. The names of the various versions reflect their different genealogies and the long and twisted paths by which each reached England: *The Fables of Pilpay* (Persian and French), *Lights of Canopus* (Persian), *The Morall Philosophie of Doni* (Hebrew, Latin and Italian), and *Kalilah and Dimnah* (Arabic). Joseph Jacobs, in his introduction to North's translation, notes no fewer than twenty translations into English of the various versions of the stories (Jacobs 1888: xxviii).

The British Library catalog lists nine popular editions of the *Fables of Pilpay* published in the late seventeenth and eighteenth centuries. The tales were sufficiently well known for the essayist Charles Lamb to make a passing reference to "Pilpay, or some Indian author" in "The Wedding" (Lamb 1954[1833]: 282). But as popular literature in the English, they have since faded from sight. The British Library lists only three editions from the nineteenth century and none since 1887 (that of F. Warne and Co, publisher of *Peter Rabbit*). Perhaps the public's appetite for fables of this kind was satisfied by a diet of Aesop alone. Free from the *Pañcatantra*'s complicated narrative structure, Aesop certainly provides more digestible fare.

The stories from the *Pañcatantra* may have slipped from popularity in the English-speaking world, but they are still recognized elsewhere in Europe. Jean de la Fontaine (1621–1695) published twelve books of fables between 1668 and 1694, containing 238 stories drawn mainly from Aesop and Phaedrus, with a sprinkling of stories from "Pilpay" (La Fontaine 2001: 165). As part of La Fontaine's collection, stories from the *Pañcatantra* are still part of a living tradition in France and other parts of Europe, including Russia.

A recent English translation of a selection of La Fontaine's fables (2001) contains at least three stories which are immediately recognizable from the original *Pañcatantra*. These have reached us through French, Persian, Arabic, and Pahlavi translations of a Sanskrit original. This edition of La Fontaine represents an unbroken literary tradition stretching back at least sixteen centuries. In the process of translation and retelling, introductory chapters and individual stories have been added and subtracted, and the stories have also been tuned to local circumstances. The jackals have become foxes, and dervishes superseded *brāhmaṇas*. In spite of these changes and the stories' peregrinations through many centuries, continents and cultures, their origins in the *Pañcatantra* are often unmistakable, and some are instantly recognizable from their titles alone: "The tortoise and the two ducks," "The ass in the lion's skin," and so forth. Some of the stories in the *Pañcatantra* are also found in the narratives recounting previous lives of the Buddha known as *Jātaka* tales. As such, they have passed through Buddhist, Hindu, Zoroastrian, Christian, Jaina, Muslim, and Jewish hands.

By the end of the nineteenth century, well before the advent of modern publishing and distribution, the *Pañcatantra* as a whole, in part or as individual stories, was found in translation from Iceland to Bali, and from Mongolia to Ethiopia, in over two hundred versions and in more than fifty languages (Hertel 1914: 451–452). It is little wonder, therefore, that few writers on the subject have been able resist the cliché that the *Pañcatantra* was the most popular and widely distributed work of literature in the premodern world.[3] The *Pañcatantra*'s claim to have 'spread across the surface of the Earth' is fully justified.

THE TEXTUAL FAMILIES OF THE SANSKRIT *PAÑCATANTRA*

It is possible, but by no means certain, that there was a single, original Sanskrit text from which all other versions of the *Pañcatantra* are ultimately descended, but no such text has survived. The old doyens of *Pañcatantra* studies, the German, Johannes Hertel (1872–1955), and the American, Franklin Edgerton (1885–1963), believed that there was such an "Ur-text." They also largely agreed that the major Sanskrit versions of the *Pañcatantra* belong to four textual families: the Pahlavi, Southern, *Bṛhatkathā*, and Northwestern traditions. They disagreed on which tradition had primacy, which was closer to the "original," which most faithfully preserved the Ur-text, and they disagreed on the ways in which the various traditions were related to one another. Hertel championed a Northwestern manuscript known as the *Tantrākhyāyika* as the closest to an original *Pañcatantra*. Edgerton, in attempting to reconstruct the original from existing manuscripts, drew more heavily on the Southern *Pañcatantra*. The two competing *stammbäume* may be consulted at Hertel 1912a: 5 and Edgerton 1924: 48. This complicated debate was usefully summarized by Sternbach (1971: 30–31), and was furthered by Geib (1969) and Maten (1980–1981).

The "Core" Features Common to Most Versions

Contemporary theoretical approaches provide a productive new way of looking at the problem of textual families. In exploring the networks of motifs in Tamil folktales, Eichinger Ferro-Luzzi applied Wittgenstein's metaphor of "family resemblance" to identify stories "held together by overlapping similarities." The motifs in individual stories are "polythetic," or "multiply arranged" (Eichinger Ferro-Luzzi 1997: 111).

Previous studies of the Sanskrit *Pañcatantras* have focused on differences between the various versions. The secondary literature gives the impression that a great gulf exists between the Southern *Pañcatantra* and the *Tantrākhyāyika,* for example; that they were very different texts. I was struck, however, by the great amount that they have in common—the extent to which they share a common "core" set of stories and a similar structure. It is easy to forget that the features which are common to the many varied *Pañcatantras* and which bind them together are much more numerous than those that separate them. We may adapt Eichinger Ferro-Luzzi's approach to yield a novel way of regarding the *Pañcatantra.* It is no longer necessary to define the genre by any single uniting feature, but we may discern among its component members a "family resemblance." As the individual stories are "multiply arranged" within each collection, the *Pañcatantra* genre as a whole also forms a "polythetic network." It may be viewed as a textual system, genre or family in which shared similarities are emphasized, rather than one defined by differences.

Sternbach produced a concordance of stories for the various versions of the *Pañcatantra* in this polythetic network. He identified, in addition to the introductory story (*kathāmukha*), a total of ninety-one stories that appear in one or more of the main Sanskrit versions (Sternbach 1971: 63ff). Based on his concordance, we can readily determine which stories are found in each version. We can also identify a set of stories that occurs in most, if not all, of the early important versions. Sidestepping the debate over which stories are "original" and which are "later interpolations," I will use the term "core stories" to describe this set. These are presented in appendix 1.

While Sternbach's tables are useful for identifying stories with texts, they conceal an important fact about the structure of the stories. Not only is the basic division into five *tantras* common to all versions (except the *Hitopadeśa*); the pattern of embedding specific stories within others is also shared. For example, Story 1-06 "Heron, fishes and crab" is nearly always embedded in Story 1-05 "Crows and serpent." The level of embedding is indicated in appendix 1 by the degree of indentation from the left.

I make no specific claims for the core set, other than it constitutes the "family resemblance" that is shared by many versions. I am not suggesting that it comprises the heart of some "original" *Pañcatantra;* I am merely using this set as a productive hermeneutic device for comparing the different texts.

In the following summary, I will describe each of the main Sanskrit versions of the *Pañcatantra* in relation to the core set and to the common structure. I will also note the appearance of additional stories, and the transposition of stories from one part of the text to another. This, however, is only part of the picture. The wording and length of individual stories varies considerably from one version to another. The wording of a story, even in two closely related *Pañcatantras,* such as the *textus simplicior* and *ornatior,* may be quite different. Redactors did not always copy a preexisting text word for word. Sometimes it seems as if they intentionally set out to reword every sentence. Even though two versions may contain a similar set of stories, the actual wording of the texts may be radically different.

In all the early versions of the *Pañcatantra* the fourth and fifth *tantras* are much shorter than the first three. In the *Tantrākhyāyika,* for example, the last two *tantras* are barely one-fifth the length of the first three. Even after they were considerably enlarged in later texts such as the *textus simplicior* and *ornatior,* these two sections are still much shorter. Only in the *Hitopadeśa* are all chapters of roughly equal length, but this text is, in any event, marginal to the *Pañcatantra* genre, having abandoned the common fivefold structure in favor of a fourfold one.

Most versions of the *Pañcatantra* have an introduction similar to the one recounted at the beginning of this chapter, which describes how the five *tantras* were created by a *brāhmaṇa* for the sons of a king. As we saw above, the five *tantras* are narrative units of varying length which function as frame-stories for multiple shorter narratives embedded within them. The practice of embedding stories within a narrative framework (as in the *Decameron* or *Canterbury Tales*) is a very common feature of Sanskrit literature. While some scholars have attempted to trace this practice back to the *Vedas* (Witzel 1987, Hämeen-Anttila 2003), it is certainly common in many later genres. The *Mahābhārata,* for example, exists within two levels of framing. The inner framing device is the original recitation of the epic by Vyāsa's pupil Vaiśampāyana at the snake-sacrifice of Janamejaya. This event was witnessed by the *brāhmaṇa* Ugraśravas, who later recounted the event to the ascetics in the Naimiṣa Forest. This constitutes the second level of framing (Hiltebeitel 2001: 92). Embedding of substories within a frame is almost a *sine qua non* for *kathā* literature: the *Vikramacarita,* the *Vetālapañcaviṃśatikā* and the *Śukasaptati* all follow this pattern. In the later versions of the *Pañcatantra,* the embedding became increasingly intricate. Lanman was moved to lament that Pūrṇabhadra employed the practice with "a most objectionable freedom and complexity" (Lanman, in Hertel 1915: xiv). Keith found it "highly inconvenient" (Keith 1920: 244). Writing of the frame structure of the *Kathāsaritsāgara,* American author John Barth observed that, "like the complexity of termite tunnels or lymphatic cancer, it is more dismaying than delightful from the human point of view" (Barth 1984: 86). Barth would have enjoyed the *Pañcatantra* even less than the *Kathāsaritsāgara.*

Let us now turn from the overall structure to the individual narrative units. Most embedded stories in the *Pañcatantra* begin when one character recites a verse relevant to the situation at hand. A second character then asks "How is that?," to which the first responds with a story, concluding with the opening verse. The stories are generally humorous, irreverent, bawdy, and violent. Typically, they show how foolish characters are undone by their own stupidity or how weak characters overcome powerful adversaries by means of cunning. In addition to the *Jātakas,* many of these stories are also found in other collections such as the *Mahābhārata, Śukasaptati, Vetālapañcaviṃśatikā, Vikramacarita,* and in oral traditions.

The proverbial verses which are distributed throughout the prose sections are an important feature of the *Pañcatantra.* These are found in all Sanskrit versions of the *Pañcatantra,* except the two short "*Bṛhatkathā*" versions, which are themselves entirely in verse. The number of verses ranges from about 340 in the Southern *Pañcatantra* to over 1,000 in the *textus simplicior* and Pūrṇabhadra's recension. Sternbach undertook exhaustive research into what he termed these "*kāvya* portions" of *kathā* literature, and showed that:

> many of these stanzas were borrowed from other works of Sanskrit literature, e.g. the Mahābhārata, the Rāmāyaṇa, Kauṭilya's Arthaśāstra, etc., but it is very difficult to prove their origin. They were most often, even if found in other works of Sanskrit literature, not borrowed directly from them, but more likely from the floating mass of oral tradition. (Sternbach 1971: 27)

The Sanskrit Families of the *Pañcatantra*

We will now turn from the common features shared by most of the main versions to examine the four main textual families: the Pahlavi, Southern, *Bṛhatkathā,* and Northwestern traditions. The relationships among members of a given family are relatively clear, but the relationship between the various families is much more complex and has been the subject of an academic discussion that goes back 100 years. How are the families related to one another? Is one the descendant of another? Are some families the fraternal descendants of a common ancestor? Which is closer to the supposed "original" *Pañcatantra*? These questions are fraught with difficulty, and the answers given by Hertel, Edgerton, Geib, Maten, and Olivelle are still somewhat inconclusive. Indeed, it is no longer clear that this basically philological question is still meaningful. I will therefore restrict myself to providing an outline of each of the main textual families.

The Pahlavi Family

An early version of the Sanskrit *Pañcatantra* (or possibly a compendium of Indian stories containing the *Pañcatantra*) was, as mentioned above, translated into Pahlavi, by a physician named Barzawayh at the court of the Persian king, Khusru Anushirwan.[4] How long had the *Pañcatantra* been in existence in India before it was translated into Pahlavi? One can only guess, but long enough, we can assume, for it to have become well known, well regarded and at least moderately widespread. Khusru reigned between 531 and 579 CE, and most scholars seem to think that it would have taken at least 200 years for a text to acquire that kind of stature, so they posit a date of 300 CE as a possible *terminus a quo* for the Sanskrit *Pañcatantra.* This is obviously little more than guesswork. It has been observed that the pronunciation of the European words *denarius* and *δηνάρια* changed to *διvάρια* in the second century CE or later. Logically, *Pañcatantra* stories containing the loanword *dīnāra* must also be of the second century CE or later (Lanman's preface to Hertel 1915: x). Neither the Pahlavi text nor its Sanskrit original are extant, but we know of their existence from later translations into Syriac and Arabic, to which we shall now turn.

The Syriac

The most accessible account of the Syriac version is given by Keith-Falconer (1885). He supplies the following details about its authorship:

> ʿEbed-Jesu, bishop of Nisibis, mentions in his catalogue of Syriac writings a certain "*Būd* (or *Bōd*) *pediodeuta*" as having composed various works, principally against the Manichæans and the Markion-

> ites. This person, he says, was entrusted with the oversight of the Christians in India and Persia, and lived about 570 A.D. He further adds: "*and it was he who translated from the Indian the book of Kalīlag and Damnag.*" (Keith-Falconer 1885: xlii–xliii)

Keith-Falconer unhelpfully glosses *pediodeuta* as "a chorepiscopus." We must turn to the OED to discover that this was a "country or suffragan bishop of the early church appointed to superintend churches at a distance from the city where the bishop of the diocese resided." This is all we know about Būd, although Keith-Falconer deduced that he was a Persian who knew Syriac, rather than a Syrian who knew Persian. ʿEbed-Jesu was evidently mistaken about Būd's role, as he translated the *Pañcatantra* into Syriac from the Pahlavi, not from the "Indian" as he stated. The above quotation and the mention of King Khusru are significant because they are the only firm dates available to us in reference to any early *Pañcatantra* text.

The words *Kalīlag* and *Damnag* of the title are the Syriac equivalents of Karaṭaka and Damanaka, the names of the two jackals in the first *tantra* of the Sanskrit *Pañcatantra.*

The Syriac version is known from a single manuscript discovered in a monastery in Mardin, Turkey, in 1870. It was first edited and translated into German by Bickell (1876), and later by Schulthess (1982 [1911]). The Syriac text consists of ten chapters including the five *tantras.* Apart from the fact that these have been reordered and interspersed with material from other sources, the *Pañcatantra* material in the Syriac version closely resembles the core set. This material is similar to the *Tantrākhyāyika* in terms of stories, verses, structure, and length. The *Pañcatantra* material in Schulthess's edition has been cross-referenced with the parallel passages in the *Tantrākhyāyika.*

There is, however, one important difference between the Syriac and all the Sanskrit versions of the *Pañcatantra*: it takes the form of a discourse between a king named Dabdahram and a philosopher, Nadrab (Keith-Falconer 1885: 1). Each of the ten chapters begins with the king asking the philosopher a question, just as Yudhiṣṭhira questioned Bhīṣma on his bed of arrows in the *Śāntiparvan* of the *Mahābhārata.* Thus the whole *kathāmukha,* which is so characteristic of most Sanskrit versions, is absent. Perhaps this lack of a strong introductory frame-story enticed later authors, such as the creator of the Arabic version (see below), to supply their own. Later versions certainly exhibit a rich variety of introductory sequences to explain how the stories came into existence.

It is not clear when the arrangement of the text as reflected in the Syriac version took place. The tenth chapter, possibly of Persian origin, may have been added after the collection left India. But did Barzawayh acquire a preexisting Sanskrit work that was in effect a compendium of the *Pañcatantra tantras,* three stories from the *Mahābhārata* and the story of "Bīlār"? Did he then translate the whole into Pahlavi? Or did he compile the stories from diverse sources into their present form? These questions remain open.

The Arabic

Two centuries after Būd translated the Pahlavi stories into Syriac, ʿAdballah ibn al-Muqaffaʿ reworked the Pahlavi translation into an Arabic version under the title *Kalilah wa Dimnah.* As with the Syriac, this title is also a rendering of the names of the two jackals from the first *tantra,* Karaṭaka and Damanaka. Ibn al-Muqaffaʿ was born to a noble family in Fars in about 720. He served as secretary to various governors and amassed a considerable fortune. As the result of his involvement in a failed political intrigue in about 756, he died a terrible death: his limbs were cut off one by one and were thrown into a blazing furnace (see *E. J. Brill's First Encyclopaedia of Islam 1913–1936*, Leiden: E. J. Brill [1987]; and *The Encylopaedia of Islam New Edition,* Leiden: E. J. Brill [1971]). Ibn al-Muqaffaʿ has been described as "one of the most prominent exponents of the intellectual awakening and literary development enjoyed by Arabic prose in the period between the 8th and 11th centuries" (Jallad 2004: 14). *Kalilah wa Dimnah,* the first masterpiece of Arabic narrative literature, enjoyed great popularity and is known from numerous manuscripts and printed versions. I have based the following account on Jallad's translation (2004).

Kalilah wa Dimnah begins with four chapters of Arabic and Persian origin. The first, written by the translator Ibn al-Muqaffaʿ, serves as a general introduction, peppered with parables, on the importance of knowledge. The second chapter was written by one ʿAli ibn al-Shah al-Farisi. Like the *kathāmukha* of the Sanskrit *Pañcatantras,* it provides a fictional account of the book's origins. It describes how Alexander the Great conquered India and installed a vice-regent to rule in his stead. That appointee was overthrown by a tyrannical king known as Dabshalim. A "Brahmin philosopher" by the name of Baydaba came forward to moderate the king's behavior, but was imprisoned for his efforts. Dabshalim had a change of heart and engaged Baydaba to write a book of good counsel "to immortalize himself, and to describe the history of his reign" (Jallad 2004: 54). That book was *Kalilah wa Dimnah.* Baydaba feared that the work might be smuggled out of India to Persia, and suggested that it be locked in the royal treasury. Word of the book eventually reached the Persian king, Khusru Anushirwan, who dispatched his personal physician Barzawayh to obtain a copy.

The third chapter describes Barzawayh's mission to India. He befriended the treasurer and was permitted to translate the book into Persian. Barzawayh returned to Persia and read the precious text before the royal assembly. He would only accept one reward: that the king's vizier, Buzurjmihr ibn al-Bakhtikan, might write a chapter describing Barzawayh's mission. In fact, all Buzurjmihr ibn al-Bakhtikan wrote was a one-sentence introduction to an autobiographical essay by Barzawayh, which constitutes the fourth chapter. It is interesting to note that this chapter also contains the famous story of the "Taste of honey" from the *Mahābhārata* (11.5–6) (Jallad 2004: 76–77).

This long introductory section is followed by six chapters, five of which were the original five Sanskrit *tantras.* Then come three other Indian stories from, or also preserved in, the *Mahābhārata,* which we noted in the Syriac version above, and two of Persian or Indian origin that have apparently dropped out of the Indian repertoire altogether (Keith-Falconer 1885: xxxviii). The final three chapters consist of an Arabic story, one of the embedded stories from the *Pañcatantra* ("The traveler and the goldsmith," i.e., Story 1-09 "Grateful beasts and thankless man") and another story of unknown Indian origin. Some manuscripts include three additional chapters, of Persian and Arabic origin.

In addition to the new prefatory material and the new stories of Middle Eastern origin, a major departure from the core model is the addition of a new section dealing with Dimnah (Damanaka), in which he was put on trial and punished for his duplicity in the first *tantra.* Perhaps Ibn al-Muqaffaʿ, like Nārāyaṇa who complied the *Hitopadeśa,* felt that the jackal could not be permitted to get away with such perfidy.

The Syriac reads like a translation, but the Arabic is a very loose retelling, and includes many non-Indian elements, such as references to angels and "fearing God" (Jallad 2004: 214, 157). In other respects, the contents of the *Pañcatantra*-derived chapters are very close to the core set.

I have described the Arabic translation in some detail because it was the basis for all subsequent translations in the Middle East and Europe. Unlike the Syriac, which lay sterile and forgotten in a monastic library, the Arabic text went forth and multiplied: it exerted a huge influence through its literary progeny, which not only dispersed north and west, but reached back south and east into India and Southeast Asia.

The Sanskrit Original of the Pahlavi Translation

Despite the rearrangement of the stories and addition of new material, both the Syriac and Arabic versions contain the core set of five *tantras* and the thirty or so embedded stories common to all the older versions of the *Pañcatantra.* This suggests that both the lost Pahlavi version and the lost Sanskrit original on which it was based also contained the core stories and common structure.

As Story 4-07 "Ass in tiger skin" is missing from the third *tantra* in the both the Syriac and Arabic translations, it was therefore probably not in the original Pahlavi version or its Sanskrit precursor. The Pahlavi family is the only branch of the *Pañcatantra* from which this story is missing. The story entitled "The traveler and the goldsmith" (i.e., Story 1-09 "Grateful beasts and thankless man"), which occupies a chapter in its own right in the Arabic, is not found in the core set of *Pañcatantra* stories, but makes an appearance later in Pūrṇabhadra's recension.

The Southern Family

This family embraces the main versions of the *Pañcatantra* found in southern India and Southeast Asia. The most important member of the family is known as the Southern *Pañcatantra.*

The Southern Pañcatantra

Numerous manuscripts of this version in various scripts have been found all over southern India (Hertel 1914: 35). Artola prepared a checklist of eighty-nine such manuscripts (Artola 1957). A critical edition was published by Hertel in 1906 under the title, *Das südliche Pañcatantra: Sanskrittext der Rezension β mit den Lesarten der besten Hss. der Rezension α* (Hertel 1906). The Southern *Pañcatantra* is one of the shorter *Pañcatantras:* Hertel's critical edition is only about fifty-eight pages long and contains 341 verses.[5] The author of the southern version stated that he shortened the text intentionally:

> For the instruction of the young who have little intelligence and who may be put off by a longer composition, this work, called the Pañcatantra, is told in an abbreviated form. Even though written elsewhere, verses are introduced here where appropriate. Because they are few, this does not lead to the problem of lengthening the text. (SPT 3.3–6)

Southern *Pañcatantra* is less than half the length of the *Tantrākhyāyika,* and has significantly fewer verses than the 530 found in that text. Sternbach found that "a great number" of verses in the Southern *Pañcatantra* are also in the *Tantrākhyāyika* (Sternbach 1971: 35).

Even though the Southern *Pañcatantra* is much shorter and has fewer verses, its basic structure and content do not diverge far from the core set. It contains all the core stories with a single addition: the first *tantra* includes the story "Cowherdess and her lovers," which is not found in the other families. In the southern *Pañcatantra* the king is called Sudarśana, and his court is in Pāṭaliputra, the name of city in Northern India. In the northwestern versions of the *Pañcatantra,* the court of King Amaraśakti is, as we shall see, located in the "southern lands" in a city called Mahilāropya. One other minor difference is that the monkey's adversary is not a crocodile, but a porpoise in the fourth *tantra* of the Southern texts. I know of no translation of the Southern *Pañcatantra,* other than a very early French one by Dubois (1826).

Edgerton maintained that the Southern *Pañcatantra* contained three-quarters of the prose of the "original" *Pañcatantra* and preserved the original text "more accurately than the Tantrākhyāyika," the candidate championed by Hertel. Edgerton held that "Nearly the whole of the text may be regarded as representing the contents of the original Pañcatantra" (Edgerton 1924: 18–19).

Nepalese Verse Version

This manuscript from Nepal, which contains most of the verses from a text similar to the Southern *Pañcatantra* but lacks the prose sections, is described briefly by Hertel (1914: 37–38). The wording of individual verses in the Nepalese version differs from the Southern recension, but both Hertel and Edgerton agree that the version from which the verses were extracted and the Southern *Pañcatantra* were offshoots of a common archetype. This archetype apparently also served as the basis for the *Pañcatantra* stories included in the *Hitopadeśa.* Olivelle makes the interesting point that "The connection between Nepal and south India, revealed also in the case of manuscripts of other works, was facilitated by the employment of south Indian Brahmins in the royal temples of Nepal" (Olivelle 1997: xlii).

The Hitopadeśa

The *Hitopadeśa* ("good counsel," "appropriate advice") is a substantial reworking of the *Pañcatantra* by an author called Nārāyaṇa, who probably lived between 800 and 1373 CE (Hertel 1914: 39). Edgerton said, "This is a version connected especially with Bengal, where it is very popular, and where it presumably originated. At any rate it has supplanted all other Pañcatantra versions in popular favor there" (Edgerton 1924: 20). I assume by "very popular" he means that many manuscripts were found there. The author Nārāyaṇa says of the *Hitopadeśa* that it "was written, having drawn on the *Pañcatantra* and another work" (Hit. 18). As mentioned above, the *Hitopadeśa* shows some influence of the Southern *Pañcatantra*. The king who commissioned Viṣṇuśarman to teach his sons was named Sudarśana, not Amaraśakti, and his court was in Pāṭaliputra. The *Hitopadeśa*, like the Southern *Pañcatantra*, also contains the story of the cowgirl and her lovers.

I have referred to the editions of the Sanskrit text by Johnson (1864), Peterson (1986 [1887]) and Kale (1998 [1896]). The latter contains a serviceable translation.

The *Hitopadeśa* is much tidier than most versions of the *Pañcatantra*: it has four chapters of similar length (about forty pages), each of which contains between nine and twelve embedded stories. The first chapter, "Acquisition of friends" (*Mitralābhaḥ*), is similar to the second *tantra* in the *Pañcatantra*. The second, "Separation of friends" (*Suhṛdbhedaḥ*), is the equivalent of the first *tantra*. The third chapter, "War" (*Vigrahaḥ*), which describes a battle between geese and peacocks, bears many similarities to the third *tantra*, "Crows and owls." The final chapter, "Peace" (*Saṃdhiḥ*), describes the end of that conflict, a frame-story which has no parallel in the *Pañcatantra*. There are about 660 verses spread evenly among the four chapters. Sternbach traced the sources of these verses to the *Pañcatantra* and other *nīti-* and *dharmaśāstras* (Sternbach 1960: 20).

Of the seventy-one motifs in the *Hitopadeśa*, fifty-six are found in the *Pañcatantra* (Sternbach 1960: 20). In some cases even the order in which they appear is the same. Where stories are common to both, they appear to have been substantially rewritten in the *Hitopadeśa*, that is, the wording in the *Hitopadeśa* differs radically from that of the various *Pañcatantras*. In spite of this, the general thrust of the stories remains the same.

Offshoots of the Southern Pañcatantra

Like the Arabic *Kalilah wa Dimnah*, the Southern *Pañcatantra* was a particularly prolific parent. Its numerous offspring have been studied by Artola (1957): some are direct translations into vernacular languages, others are abridgements, expansions or reworkings of *Pañcatantra* materials. Artola has identified two Malayalam, three Tamil and four Telugu recensions dating from before the end of the sixteenth century, and two Kannada editions (Artola 1957: 235–261).

A detailed discussion of the offshoots of the Southern *Pañcatantra* lies beyond the scope of this book, but there are two points that I would like to make. First, the Tamil *Tantropākhyāna* has a "thousand-and-one-nights" type introduction, in which a servant-girl narrated a story every night to save a minister's daughter from the king's bed (Huilgol 1987: 22). This version was the basis for the later Thai, Laotian, and Javanese *Pañcatantras* (see Venkatasubbiah 1934, 1965, 1967, and 1969). For an exhaustive investigation of all the offshoots of the Southern *Pañcatantra,* see Hertel 1914: 250–337.

"*Bṛhatkathā*" Versions

Most scholars (e.g., Lacôte 1908) accept without question the existence of a collection of stories called *Bṛhatkathā* ("The great story"), attributed to Guṇāḍhya, and written in a Prakrit dialect called Paiśācī (MMW: *paiśācī:* "belonging to the Piśācas . . . , a sort of jargon spoken by demons"). It is thought that the original *Bṛhatkathā* did not include the *Pañcatantra,* but that material was added in a later version, which was created in northwestern India or Kashmir (Edgerton 1924: 23). Neither the original *Bṛhatkathā* nor its northwestern derivative are extant.[6]

The fact that the "original," complete *Bṛhatkathā* was supposed to be a vast work in an obscure language, of which we now have only two shortened relics, sounds to me like a deliberate attempt to mythologize the text's origins. I suspect that the original *Bṛhatkathā* may never have existed, and we should at least treat such "truth claims" with some skepticism.

There are, however, two collections of stories, both written in Sanskrit verse, both containing abbreviated versions of the *Pañcatantra,* and both claiming descent from an original lost *Bṛhatkathā:* these are the *Bṛhatkathāmañjarī* ("A bouquet from the *Bṛhatkathā*") by Kṣemendra (c. 1037 CE), and the *Kathāsaritsāgara* ("An ocean of rivers of stories") by Somadeva (c. 1063–1081 CE). Both are from Kashmir, which at that time was an active centre of Sanskrit learning and literature (Speyer 1908: 21; Pollock 2003: 92).

The versions of the *Pañcatantra* in these two texts have much in common: they are much shorter than all the others; they are composed entirely in verse; they contain no additional verses; they lack the *kathāmukha* set in Amaraśakti's court; and they launch straight into the first *tantra.* Despite these peculiarities, the basic structure of all five *tantras,* and to a large extent the embedded stories and the order in which they appear, approximate the core set. A comprehensive description of these two versions is found in Tawney (1926, vol. 5: 210–216).

The Kathāsaritsāgara

I have referred to the text of the *Kathāsaritsāgara* edited by K. N. Śarmā, which was published by Bihāra-rāṣṭrabhāṣā-pariṣad in Patna, 1960. The only complete English translation is that made by C. H. Tawney, under the title, *The Ocean of Story,* in ten volumes, edited with introductory material and appendices by N. M. Penzer, published in London, 1924–1928. A selection of stories from the *Kathāsaritsāgara* was translated by Sattar (1994).

The *Pañcatantra* as it appears in the *Kathāsaritsāgara* is narrated by a minister named Gomukha to a prince, Naravāhanadatta, to illustrate the proposition that:

> [A] man who displays prudence is never harmed. Even in the case of animals prudence produces success, not valour. (Tawney 1926, vol. 5: 41)

As mentioned above, this version of the *Pañcatantra* is very short and contains only 569 verses (40 pages of Sanskrit text), with twenty-seven embedded stories.

Comparing the *Kathāsaritsāgara* version with the core set, the structure of the first and third *tantras* are similar; that is, the same embedded stories appear in roughly the same order, but it lacks the *kathāmukha* and the three "self-inflicted injuries" (Stories 1-04a, b and c) of the first *tantra.* The fifth *tantra* consists of the frame-story alone, and lacks Story 5-00 "Barber who killed the monks" and Story 5-07 "*Brāhmaṇa* builds air-castles." Only the simplest outlines of the plots of the five frame-stories and the embedded stories are given.

Another peculiarity of the *Kathāsaritsāgara* is that the five original *tantras* from the *Pañcatantra* are interspersed with numerous stories from other sources. The whole *Kathāsaritsāgara,* in keeping with the oceanic theme of its title, is divided into eighteen sections known as *lambaka* ("surges"?), which are further divided into *taraṅgas* ("billows"). The five *tantras* of the *Pañcatantra* form the fourth to the eighth *taraṅgas* of the tenth *lambaka.* The first *tantra,* Story 1-00 "Lion and bull," constitutes an entire *taraṅga* itself. The four remaining *tantras* have been kept intact, but in each case, the *taraṅgas* are "padded out," before and after, with up to twenty-two short stories that illustrate the downfall of fools. These are not found in the *Pañcatantra.*

The Bṛhatkathāmañjarī

I have referred to the text of the *Bṛhatkathāmañjarī* edited by M. M. Shivdatta and K. P. Parab, first published in 1931 by Nirnaya Sagar Press in Bombay and reprinted in 1982 by Panini in New Delhi. Levi published a French translation of the first *lamkaba* (Levi 1886), but I know of no other translation of this work. Mankowski published a study of the *Pañcatantra* section of the *Bṛhatkathāmañjarī* (von Mankowski 1892).

The version of the *Pañcatantra* in the *Bṛhatkathāmañjarī* is even shorter than the one in the *Kathāsaritsāgara.* In total, the five *tantras* of the *Pañcatantra* are summarized in 312 verses. They extend to twenty-seven pages of Sanskrit text and contain thirty-five embedded stories (BKM 16: 256–567, pp. 561–587). Despite its brevity, the *Bṛhatkathāmañjarī* still conforms closely to the core set in terms of structure and content. It includes five additional stories not found in the core, all of which are found in the *Tantrākhyāyika,* suggesting that the complier of the *Bṛhatkathāmañjarī* may have had access to a text resembling the *Tantrākhyāyika* as it is known to us. Several core stories, including the three examples of self-inflicted injury in the first *tantra* and Story 3-01 "Birds elect a king," are not found in the *Bṛhatkathāmañjarī.*

Western scholars have been highly critical of the *Bṛhatkathāmañjarī Pañcatantra:* the stories "are so condensed that they can hardly be understood"; they have "lost all their flavour"; and are but "a sapless remnant" (Speyer 1908: 18). Edgerton described them as "drastically abbreviated," "mangled," and "cut to the bone (to the great detriment of the result, artistically speaking)" (Edgerton 1924: 24–25). Kṣemendra "seems to have been as brief as possible" and in doing so, "castrated" the stories (Tawney 1926, vol. 5: 212). An alternative way of looking at these short versions is as forerunners of the modern condensed book from *Reader's Digest,* or as a student's crib sheet from Sparknotes.com. Speyer is correct in saying that some of the references to stories could hardly be understood by a reader who is unfamiliar with the original. The essence of Story 1-02 "Jackal and drum," for example, is captured in a single verse (BKM 16.275). On the other hand, the text may serve to jog the memory of readers who already know the stories, prompting the pleasures of the longer versions.[7]

The Northwestern Family

The Tantrākhyāyika

The *Tantrākhyāyika* ("Little *tantra*-stories") from Kashmir is a significant member of the Northwestern family, because the *textus simplicior,* the *textus ornatior* and the later mixed recensions are all ultimately derived from it or from a text like it. Hertel published the incomplete Deccan College manuscript of the *Tantrākhyāyika* under the title *Über das Tantrākhyāyika, die Kaśmīrische Rezension des Pañcatantra* (Hertel 1904). This was followed by an introduction to the *Tantrākhyāyika* with notes and a translation into the German: *Tantrākhyāyika: die älteste Fassung des Pañcatantra* (Hertel 1909). His critical edition of the *Tantrākhyāyika* was published in 1915, under the title *The Panchatantra: a collection of ancient Hindu tales in its oldest recension, the Kashmirian, entitled Tantrakhyayika* (Hertel 1915). This was published without further introduction or notes and under dramatic circumstances.[8]

The basic features of the *Tantrākhyāyika* are as follows: taking Hertel's main text of the *Tantrākhyāyika* and the additional material in the appendices from the manuscript he called β, there are about 140 pages of Sanskrit text, including about 530 verses. In addition to the thirty-four core stories, nine further stories are given, including, significantly for this inquiry, the first appearance in a *Pañcatantra* collection of Story 1-11, "Blue jackal."

How is the *Tantrākhyāyika* related to the other versions of the *Pañcatantra*? Edgerton maintained that when Hertel first discovered the *Tantrākhyāyika,* he "hailed it as the genuine, original 'Urtext' of the Pañcatantra itself," but that Hertel later moderated this view (Edgerton 1924: 14). Edgerton also quoted Hertel as saying that the *Tantrākhyāyika* "is the only version which contains the unabbreviated and not intentionally altered language of the author" (Edgerton 1924: 14). Irrespective of how much of the "original" *Pañcatantra* was preserved in the *Tantrākhyāyika,* Hertel regarded all other versions of the *Pañcatantra* (except the Sanskrit original of the Pahlavi) as "revisions" (*Überarbeitungen*) of the *Tantrākhyāyika* (Hertel 1914: 26). He accordingly placed the *Tantrākhyāyika* and its supposed antecedents at the head of his textual *stammbaum* for the whole *Pañcatantra* corpus (Hertel 1912a: 5). Edgerton disputed the preeminence that Hertel gave to the *Tantrākhyāyika,* saying that the difference between the *Tantrākhyāyika* and the other versions, in their relations to the original, "is a difference of degree and not a difference of kind" (Edgerton 1924: 16).

It would be impossible to prove that Hertel was biased in favor of the *Tantrākhyāyika* because he was its discoverer, editor, and translator, but it would be equally impossible to prove that such facts did not color his enthusiasm for the text.

Offshoots of the Tantrākhyāyika

All the versions we have considered so far—the Pahlavi, Southern, *Bṛhatkathā*, and *Tantrākhyāyika*—conform to the core set, in terms of both form and content. Despite their differences, they are all closer to one another than they are to the offshoots of the *Tantrākhyāyika,* which we will now consider. The versions that are derived from the *Tantrākhyāyika,* namely, the *textus simplicior,* the *textus ornatior* (Pūrṇabhadra's recension) and their descendants, are much longer and more complex than any of the earlier versions, and contain many more stories and verses. This point is clearly evident from Sternbach's tables of correspondence (Sternbach 1971: 63ff).

One major structural change that unites these later versions is that the frame-story of the fifth *tantra,* "*Brāhmaṇa* and the mongoose" and the embedded story, "Barber who killed the monks," have been transposed. In the older versions, the former is the frame for the latter. In the newer ones, it is the other way around. The later descendants of the *Tantrākhyāyika* typically have a total of about eighty embedded stories (more than double the number in the core set), and contain more than a thousand verses.

The two main offshoots of the *Tantrākhyāyika,* the *textus simplicior* and the *textus ornatior,* are sometimes called the "Jaina recensions" because the redactors of both are thought to be adherents of that tradition. This is obvious in the case of Pūrṇabhadra, as we will see below. The evidence that the author of the *textus simplicior* was a Jaina is less clear-cut. In any case, as Sternbach rightly observed, neither text reveals any particularly Jaina tendencies (Sternbach 1971: 33).

Textus Simplicior

The *editio princeps* of this version was published by Kosegarten in Bonn in 1848 (Edgerton 1924: 27). He coined the term "*textus simplicior*" because it was "simpler" than Pūrṇabhadra's recension, the "*textus ornatior.*" Kosegarten's text was translated into German by Benfey (1966 [1859]). The most accessible (but noncritical) edition is that of Kielhorn and Bühler (Kielhorn 1885, Bühler 1885 and 1886). Their version was translated into German by Fritze (1884). Sternbach states that the *textus simplicior* has been translated into "almost all Western languages and many Indian languages" (Sternbach 1971: 33).

The author of the *textus simplicior* must have lived after the middle of the ninth century CE because he quoted a verse from Rudraṭa, a Kashmiri rhetorician of that period. Further, he must have lived before 1199 CE, because that was when Pūrṇabhadra used the *textus simplicior* as a source for his version. As is the case with all earlier versions, the name of the author of the *textus simplicior* is unknown. As mentioned above, Hertel supposed that he was a Jaina, but Edgerton found Hertel's arguments on that point "perhaps not absolutely compelling" (Edgerton 1924: 27).

The *textus simplicior* appears to be an amplification of an earlier version of the *Tantrākhyāyika*. It is not based directly on the version of the *Tantrākhyāyika* that is available to us, as our version of that text includes some stories not found in the *textus simplicior*. The *textus simplicior* is about 236 pages long with over 1,000 verses, compared with the *Tantrākhyāyika* which has only 140 pages and 530 verses. Comparing the individual *tantras* of the *textus simplicior* with the *Tantrākhyāyika*, the first is nearly twice as long, with the addition of many verses and six new stories. The second *tantra*, by contrast, has changed little in terms of overall length. It includes two new stories, but omits the account of the deer's former captivity. The third *tantra* is about the same length, but has many fewer stories. Nearly half of the narratives from the third *tantra* of the *Tantrākhyāyika* have been moved to the fourth and fifth *tantras* of the *textus simplicior*, both of which have been further bolstered with many additional stories from other sources. The fifth *tantra* now contains the rambling Story 5-02 "Four treasure-seekers," which contains a further twelve embedded stories, many of which are new.

The net result of all these changes is a substantial increase in the length of the first, fourth, and fifth *tantras*. The first *tantra* is now about ninety pages long, and the other four are now all of approximately equal length, being between thirty and forty pages long. This is a major change, because in all earlier versions of the *Pañcatantra*, as we have seen, the last two *tantras* were invariably much shorter. I agree with Hertel that the wording has been altered throughout, but it is unclear why he stated that the purport of stories has been changed (Hertel 1912a: 11).

According to Edgerton, the *textus simplicior* is the version of the *Pañcatantra* that became popular in western and central India. It and its descendants have "virtually crowded out all other Pañcatantra recensions in those regions" (Edgerton 1924: 27). The *textus simplicior* "is the most prevalent in India and this text is generally considered as the text of the 'genuine' Pañcatantra" (Sternbach 1971: 33). Many contemporary retellings of *Pañcatantra* stories in modern vernacular languages are based loosely on the *textus simplicior* and its descendants. As such, they may be said to constitute the *Pañcatantra* vulgate.

Later Descendants

Hertel described many "mixed recensions" (Hertel 1912a: 15–21; Hertel 1914: 104–121), which are combinations of material from the *textus simplicior* and *ornatior* (see below). Some are in Sanskrit; others are in vernaculars. Sternbach described thirteen such recensions, but noted that they were "only a few of the many" (Sternbach 1971: 37–38).

Further mixed descendants comprise the whole vast contemporary *Pañcatantra* "industry" with its proliferation of versions and forms: long, short, framed, unframed, classical, and modern. Vernacular versions are on sale at street stalls and on railway stations all over India. The stories have passed from text into other media. They provide themes for schoolchildren's art exhibitions; television puppet shows in Bengali; multimedia versions in English on CD; and the hundreds of selections, adaptations, and retellings that abound on the Internet.

PŪRṆABHADRA'S *PAÑCATANTRA*

This long, slow excursion through the history and development of the *Pañcatantra* family has delivered us at last to Pūrṇabhadra's recension, the version of the text on which this study is based. In the following section I will introduce the critical edition, translations and contents of Pūrṇabhadra's recension, and I will discuss the reasons why I chose it as the basis for my study.

Pūrṇabhadra entitled his work *Pañcākhyānaka,* which may be translated as "Little [collection of] five stories," adding that this was "another name for the *Pañcatantra*" (PT 289.15). The *editio princeps* of the Sanskrit text of Pūrṇabhadra's *Pañcatantra* was published by Hertel under the title *The Panchatantra: a collection of ancient Hindu tales in the recension, called Panchakhyanaka, and dated 1199 A.D., of the Jaina monk, Purnabhadra* (Hertel 1908). Four years later, Hertel published a comparison of eleven manuscripts of the text in *The Panchatantra-text of Purnabhadra: critical introduction and list of variants* (Hertel 1912a). In a further publication, *The Panchatantra-text of Purnabhadra and its relation to texts of allied recensions as shown in parallel specimens,* he compared extracts from Pūrṇabhadra's recension with the *Tantrākhyāyika,* the Southern *Pañcatantra,* the *textus simplicior* and the *"Bṛhatkathā"* versions, and showed how

Pūrṇabhadra's version was "contaminated" by the *Tantrākhyāyika* and *textus simplicior* in particular (Hertel 1912b: viii). Hertel believed that the manuscripts on which his critical edition was based "differed very little from the text as written down by Pūrṇabhadra himself" (Hertel 1908: xv).

Pūrṇabhadra's recension is unique among the Sanskrit *Pañcatantras* as it is the only version for which any bio-bibliographical information is available. Not only do we know the author's name, but we also know the date on which the text was completed, the luminary at whose behest it was written, and something of the process by which it was cobbled together. As the result of Hertel's detective work, we also know roughly where Pūrṇabhadra lived. There is a comprehensive account of all this information in Hertel's critical introduction (Hertel 1912a: 21–36).

The *praśasti* ("eulogistic inscription" or colophon) of Pūrṇabhadra's *Pañcatantra* states that the text had been written at the behest of a minister named Śrī Soma. The name of the author is given as Śrī Pūrṇabhadra, and he is described as both a *guru* and a *sūri* (PT 289.20 and PT 289.23). Pūrṇabhadra observed that the entire Pañcatantric *śāstra* had become corrupted (PT 289.18–19), and in the process of revising the text, he corrected every letter, word, sentence, story and verse (PT 289.22–23).

The *praśasti* gives the following as the date of the composition: *śarabāṇataraṇivarṣe* ' *ravikaravadi phālgune tṛtīyāyām* | (PT 290.11). The year of composition is *śara-bāṇa-taraṇi-varṣa*: *śara* and *bāṇa* both mean "arrow" and stand for the number five (from the five arrows of Kāmadeva), *taraṇi* means "sun" and represents the number twelve (from the twelve months in the solar year). In the Bhūtasaṃkhyā system, numbers are read from right to left, *śara-bāṇa-taraṇi-varśe* means "in the year 5–5–12," i.e., 1255. The compound *ravi-kara-vadi* apparently means "in the dark-fortnight-day (*vadi*) of the sun (*ravi*) and the [lunar mansion] *hasta* (*kara*)." The phrase *phālgune tṛtīyāyām* means "on the third lunar day of the month of Phālguna." Thus the whole date may be read as "the third day of the dark half of the month of Phālguna in the year 1255." Bhandarkar informed Hertel that this corresponded to Sunday 17 January 1199 CE (cited in Hertel 1912a: 21–22). Dr. Martin Gansten kindly informed me (pers. comm.) that he felt Tuesday 19 January 1199 CE to be more accurate.[9]

Turning from the date of the work to the identity of its writer, Hertel noted that an author by the name of Pūrṇabhadra composed a text called *Dhanyaśālicarita* in Jaisalmer at about the same time that the *Pañcatantra* was written. Hertel was able to prove that this person and the author of the *Pañcatantra* were almost certainly the same individual. He inferred from this that Pūrṇabhadra must "no less certainly have lived in north-western India" (Hertel 1912a: 26), a region of thriving Jaina culture in the twelfth and thirteenth centuries.

How do we know that Pūrṇabhadra was a Jaina? We saw in the *praśasti* that he is referred to as a *sūri,* a title given especially to Jaina teachers. Hertel also cited internal evidence from the stories. Pūrṇabhadra must have been of the Śvetāmbara tradition, for no Digambara monk would have told Story 1.22 "King, minister and false monk," in which the fraudulent ascetic of that tradition was burnt alive by the clever minister (Hertel 1912a: 26). This last point may be debatable, but the *praśasti* of the *Dhanyaśālicarita* gives the lineage of Jaina teachers, and leaves no doubt as to the Jaina affiliations of the author of that work, and who was almost certainly also the author of this one (Hertel 1912a: 24–25).

What is the significance of the date and the Jaina authorship? Are the Jain influences important in distinguishing this variant from others? In the liberal humanist tradition of literary criticism, it is assumed that authors writing at a given time and place and within a certain intellectual milieu will inevitably leave traces of their temporal, political, or intellectual environments in their work. Perhaps if we read closely we may discover things about the contexts in which the work was written, and perhaps even learn something of the psychology of the authors themselves.

Pūrṇabhadra, indeed, was not an author, but a complier and editor. From Hertel's textual criticism, we know that he combined two preexisting manuscripts into a new whole. To this whole, he may also have added other material of his own choosing. We cannot say exactly what the preexisting sources were, nor can we say with certainty what his actual input to the text was. I am unable to point to anything that would suggest a "Jaina influence" in his redaction, no more than Hertel's redaction shows Germanic influences or Edgerton's shows American ones.

Can this recension tell us anything specific about the milieu in which Pūrṇabhadra worked? The *Pañcatantra* developed as a corpus of narratives over at least seven centuries from its earliest known appearance in about 500 CE until 1199 CE when this version was compiled. During this long period, multiple recensions passed though many pairs of editorial hands, stories were added and subtracted, and they traveled the length and breadth of India. The *Pañcatantra* corpus developed continually at different times and in different places. It is not attributable to a given time or place. It was not the product of a singular, identifiable Indian society, and cannot be connected with actual social structures. This book is about ideas, rather than social actualities, and I will attempt to demonstrate how the ideas of the *Pañcatantra* relate to the ideas of the other normative texts in the Brahmanical archive.

Even when we know the biographical details of an original Sanskrit author, Sanskrit literature tends to be so formulaic, stereotyped and impersonal, that it tells us little about the society of the day. It often seems to be nourished and informed by the archive, much more than by the social realities in which it was produced. The *Pañcatantra* is a text with no clearly definable spatial or temporal context, and yet it has a very real intellectual context, which is the focus of this study.

Translations

Schmidt published a German translation of an unpublished manuscript of the *textus ornatior* (Schmidt 1901). Hertel stated that Pūrṇabhadra's *Pañcatantra* was translated by Paul Elmer More, "Associate Editor of *The* (*New York*) *Nation*, and formerly a pupil and assistant of Professor Lanman at Harvard" (Hertel 1908: xiv), but I do not believe that this translation was ever published. I found Ryder's translation (1925) useful and reliable for the prose sections of the text, but his translations of the verses are free and fanciful. The opposite is the case with Rajan (1993): her prose translations tend to be verbose, but her rendering of the verses is more accurate than Ryder's.

Structure

Pūrṇabhadra's *Pañcatantra* is by far the longest of the recensions under consideration. It is nearly 290 pages in length and contains just over 1,000 verses. In addition to the five frame-stories, there are about eighty embedded narratives.[10] The stories found in Pūrṇabhadra's recension and summaries of each are given in appendix 2. In the following section, I will compare Pūrṇabhadra's text with his two main sources, the *textus simplicior* and the *Tantrākhyāyika*.

Pūrṇabhadra's first *tantra* contains all but one of the stories found in the *textus simplicior* (Story 4-09 "Ape and officious bird," which appears in his fourth *tantra*). There are some minor changes in the order of the stories, but more significantly, nine new stories not found in the *textus simplicior* have been added. The result is that this *tantra* is nearly half as long again as the first *tantra* of the *textus simplicior*.

In Pūrṇabhadra's second *tantra,* there are also minor changes in structure: for example, Story 2-05 "Mr. What-fate-ordains," which was embedded in the frame-story 2-00 in the *textus simplicior,* was "demoted" and is now embedded in Story 2-02 "Mouse and two monks." Story 2-01 "Bird with two necks" was moved from the fifth *tantra* of the *textus simplicior* to Pūrṇabhadra's second *tantra.* Story 2-09 "Deer's former captivity," which occurs in both Pūrṇabhadra's recension and the *Tantrākhyāyika,* is not found in the *textus simplicior.*

Pūrṇabhadra seems to have followed the general structure of the *Tantrākhyāyika* for his third *tantra,* but enlarged it with a number of stories from the fourth *tantra* of the *textus simplicior.* He further expanded his third *tantra* with at least five new stories not found in our version of the *textus simplicior* (but I note that they appear in Kosegarten's recension of that text). The net result is that Pūrṇabhadra's third *tantra* is at least half as long again as either of its precursors.

The structure of the fourth *tantra* follows the *simplicior* again, minus the stories that now appear in the third *tantra.* Pūrṇabhadra added one new item, Story 4-06 "Nanda and Vararuci as slaves of love" (also found in Kosegarten). As a result of moving stories to the third *tantra,* Pūrṇabhadra's fourth *tantra* is actually a little shorter than the fourth *tantra* of the *textus simplicior.*

His fifth *tantra* follows the *textus simplicior* very closely, but lacks Story 2-01 "Bird with two necks," which was moved to the second *tantra.* The story of the "Crab as life-saver," which is in *textus simplicior,* does not appear in Pūrṇabhadra's work. It may of course have been a later addition to the *textus simplicior.* The fifth *tantra* of Pūrṇabhadra's recension and the *textus simplicior* are about the same length.

Even though there are many more stories in Pūrṇabhadra's recension and the text is much longer than the *textus simplicior,* both have about one thousand verses. A quick glance over Sternbach's concordance suggests that when Pūrṇabhadra took a story from the *textus simplicior,* he generally took the verses with it.

On the basis of the above summary, I would have to agree with Edgerton when he observed that Pūrṇabhadra's text is:

> a mosaic of the texts of the Tantrākhyāyika and Simplicior—or of texts closely resembling these two as we have them. . . . It appears that Pūrṇabhadra kept before him copies of these two main sources, and for the most part literally followed one or the other, as seemed best to him. (Edgerton 1924: 31)

Edgerton felt that Pūrṇabhadra generally followed the plan of the *Tantrākhyāyika* for his first and second *tantras*, but followed the *textus simplicior* for the last three (Edgerton 1924: 33–34). In fact, I believe that only Pūrṇabhadra's third *tantra* follows the *Tantrākhyāyika:* the other four are all closer to the *textus simplicior.* One other significant point suggested by the above comparison is that, on closer investigation, Pūrṇabhadra's copy of the *textus simplicior* may have been more like Kosegarten's than the editions of Bühler and Kielhorn that were used by Hertel and Edgerton. Finally, Edgerton speculated that Pūrṇabhadra may have used a third source as well, and he made the following curious remark:

> But it seems not humanly probable that he used many more than the three versions [i.e., *Tantrākhyāyika,* the *textus simplicior* and a possible third source] which we have now assumed as his sources,— simply because to do so would have given him more trouble than a Hindu redactor is likely to have taken. (Edgerton 1924: 38)

The first four *tantras* of Pūrṇabhadra's recension function as integrated narrative units: each has a beginning, a middle, and an end. The fifth *tantra* inherited a structural peculiarity from the *textus simplicior* and the *Tantrākhyāyika* before it, that is, it seems to finish in midair. The last embedded item, Story 5-11 "Ogre-ridden *brāhmaṇa,*" ends abruptly, with no further reference to the three higher levels of stories which frame it. These are left hanging, although we can guess the conclusion in each case. I wonder if the nesting structure had become so complicated that even its author lost the plot. After all, the final story in the fifth *tantra* is embedded in no fewer than five layers of framing narrative.

Why Choose Pūrṇabhadra's *Pañcatantra*?

The philological approach to textual criticism evolved in part under the influence of the "Homeric question" that occupied many minds during the nineteenth and twentieth centuries: Who composed the *Iliad* and the *Odyssey,* by what means, and at what time? The influence of nineteenth-century biblical exegesis, in which the role of textual criticism sought to reveal the true Word of God, is also in evidence. From a philological point of view, the oldest, most original, purest, least contaminated, least interpolated texts are the most desirable. This is what Pollock has dubbed the "ideology of antiquity," the idea that the more archaic a text, the purer it was thought to be (Pollock 2003: 4).

A huge amount of scholarly ink has been expended in identifying and reconstructing the "original" *Pañcatantra,* and in the quixotic attempt to ascribe a date, location, worldview and motivation to its putative author. The "Ur-text" and its offshoots have been privileged to the detriment of all other versions of the text. The philologists regarded the author's own text (presuming that these are both singular entities) as the "genuine" text:

> The lack of critical spirit, which is so characteristic of the old style paṇḍits, was the reason why the more complete, i.e. the interpolated and contaminated MSS. of celebrated works, were always copied, whereas the old genuine texts disappeared. (Hertel 1912a: 15)

Further, Western scholarship has privileged a text like the *Tantrākhyāyika,* which exists only in a single manuscript, and whose influence and readership must have been relatively small, over the later "vulgate" versions, which have been read by countless millions of individuals and accepted by them, we assume, as the "actual" *Pañcatantra.*

For the philologists, the crux was to determine the "original" author's intention, to access his thoughts and opinions, to read his true words. Indeed for Edgerton, the "best" *Pañcatantra,* the "original" one for which ironically no actual manuscript exists, was the one he "reconstructed." He stepped back from his completed canvas and pronounced it "to have been a finer work, artistically, than any of its descendants" (Edgerton 1924: 10). As early as 1925, the validity of attempting to reconstruct such a text was questioned (Hocart 1925: 468). Maten recognized that there was a "justifiable question whether there is any point in reconstructing the original *Pañcatantra,* or in postulating its qualities and even its perfectness" (Maten 1980–1981: 242), but promptly side-stepped it. Blackburn alone has identified the "restrictive grip" of Edgerton's reconstruction, which has excluded other Sanskrit and vernacular *Pañcatantras* from consideration (Blackburn 1996: 504).

The actual versions of the *Pañcatantra* that were read and circulated widely were the ones that philologists have regarded as "corrupted," "contaminated," and "interpolated." As far as their vast readership is concerned, these would be the "real" *Pañcatantras.* What these versions say, and how they say it, must count for something. Such an audience might well regard the much-vaunted Western reconstructions as "unreal," artificial and impoverished.

We have learned to appreciate the many *Rāmāyaṇas* (Richman 1991; Thiel-Horstmann 1991) and the "hundreds" of *Mahābhāratas* (Sumitra Bai and Zydenbos 1991; Doniger 2004: 7), but we have not yet really begun to appreciate the fact that there are multiple *Pañcatantras.* Indeed, there may never have been a single unitary *Pañcatantra.* Multiple versions have coexisted in India and elsewhere in many languages. Rather than thinking of the *Pañcatantra* as a single original text which now exists in a variety of corrupted and contaminated versions, it is perhaps more fruitful to regard the *Pañcatantra* as a *genre* or as a form, a point which brings us back to Eichinger Ferro-Luzzi's "polythetic networks."

To date, the task of Western scholarship has been to reduce the existing chaos of manuscripts, recensions and versions in the search for an origin or an essence. In India, of course, this has never been a problem: there have always been multiple versions of the stories, every region and every language having its own. Versions exist in many varied forms and media; all of which manage to coexist under the general rubric of "*Pañcatantra.*"

Why choose Pūrṇabhadra's *Pañcatantra* for a study such as this? First, as the curious and evocative story of the indigo jackal initially caught my eye, it was natural that I would be attracted to the texts of the Northwestern family, which contain this story. Pūrṇabhadra's version is by far the longest of the principal recensions and I saw it as the richest potential source of comparative data. While my close readings of the text are based on this recension, I have supplemented these readings with reference to other versions from time to time. Second, for the reasons outlined above, I did not feel constrained to seek out the oldest or most "original" *Pañcatantra,* when this recension has its own originality and reality for its readership. Third, Pūrṇabhadra's version has received comparatively little scholarly attention.

As this research project unfolded, it transpired that the issues I sought to address were so fundamental to the nature of the stories that ultimately the choice of recension was of little significance. The basic processes and dynamics with which this study is concerned appear to be similar in all versions of the *Pañcatantra.* Whether a given version of a story is long, short, or intermediate, and in many cases, irrespective of the actual wording of the text, the nature of the social discourse that informs the narrative remains consistent. Even if a story is reduced to its bare bones—"jackal rises, jackal falls"—it is still possible to describe the discourse that shapes it and its attendant set of truth-effects.

ASSIGNING MEANING TO THE *PAÑCATANTRA*

The Sanskrit authors of the *Pañcatantra* regarded their text as a *nītiśāstra,* that is, a specialist treatise (*śāstra*) on the subject of conduct (*nīti*), or more specifically, kingly conduct (*rājanīti*) (see for example PT 2.17 and PT 289.15). The opening line of Pūrṇabhadra's text, following the conventional invocation of Sarasvatī, effectively allies the *Pañcatantra* to the *arthaśāstras* (PT 1.02), a family of treatises on governance, which are closely related to the *nītiśāstras.* The idea that the *Pañcatantra* is a *nītiśāstra* is further demonstrated in the *kathāmukha,* which tells how the stories were used for the education of King Amaraśakti's sons. We will return to examine the relationship of the *Pañcatantra* and the *nītiśāstras* at a later point in this study, but in the meantime, we may discern the creators' overall intention for their work from the *kathāmukha.* Here the cardinal purpose of the *Pañcatantra* is to enable a person to avoid defeat:

> In general, one who reads or listens to this *nītiśāstra* will never be defeated, even by Śakra [Indra]! (PT 3.17–18)

The traditional Indian meaning ascribed to the *Pañcatantra*—that it is, as it claims, a textbook of political wisdom for princes and kings, a *nītiśāstra,* or a guide to conduct—runs long and deep. From the earliest Arabic translations through the length and breadth of its Middle Eastern and European peregrinations, this concept has never been seriously challenged, and has colored *Pañcatantra* scholarship in the West from Benfey to Olivelle. No one, it seems, can resist remarking that the *Pañcatantra* was originally a *Fürstenspiegel* or a *Mirror for Magistrates* (e.g., Edgerton 1924: 4; Hertel 1908: xiii; Hertel 1909: 8). Winternitz said that there "can be no doubt that the work was intended from the start to be a Nītiśāstra, that is a 'text book' of political and practical wisdom" (DLZ. 1910, Sp. 2762 cited in Edgerton 1924: 186; see also Olivelle 1997: x). "The reconstructed text is unquestionably a text-book for the instruction of kings in politics" (Keith 1920: 248).

Let us now turn from the traditional attempts to categorize the work, to more contemporary views on its meaning. According to Hertel, the intention of the *Pañcatantra* was to "convey precepts for the clever conduct of life" (Hertel 1908: xiii; Hertel 1914: 10). He went so far as to translate the word *tantra* as *Klugheitsfall* "case of cleverness" and *List* "cunning" (Hertel 1909: 8; Hertel 1914: 10). Edgerton was generally in agreement with Hertel on the nature and function of the work:

> Most of the stories remain true to the key-note of the book, its Machiavellian character; they are generally unmoral, and at times positively immoral, in the political lessons they inculcate. (Edgerton 1924: 5)

Having accepted, I think too eagerly, this overall idea of the *Pañcatantra*'s intent, the Western philological project generally remained aloof from the messy, subjective business of assigning a meaning to the text. This is perhaps a symptom of what Pollock calls "a pervasive indifference in Indology itself to the social in Sanskrit literary discourse" (Pollock 2001: 199). Edgerton, for example, was preoccupied with his mission "to follow the streams of Pañcatantra tradition in the hope of finding their source" (Edgerton 1924: 4). In doing so, he consciously adopted the language of the colonialist explorer. He had little or no further interest in the content or meaning of the stories: "For my present purpose, the contents of the versions of the Pañcatantra are of interest only in so far as they may throw light on the ultimate source of them all" (Edgerton 1924: 4).

Hertel thought of the *Pañcatantra* as consisting of "examples of cleverness," and believed, perhaps wishfully, that the "original" *Pañcatantra,* for which he sought, was a pure, unsullied work, containing only stories concerning *nīti.* He examined the meaning of each story in later recensions to filter out those that did not fit this definition. He thereby aimed to exclude all later "interpolations" in order to recover the Ur-text. He was interested in the content only in so far as it could support his thesis.

While the philological project (Hertel, Edgerton, Geib, and Maten) had little time for content, more recent researchers such as Ruben, Falk, and Olivelle have looked at other ways of assigning meaning to the text. They have attempted to identify the "political and moral philosophy" of the *Pañcatantra.* Like Olivelle, they ask, "What is the point of the *Pañcatantra*?" (Olivelle 1997: xxxi). The general assumption is that the text must indeed have a "point," a "message," or a "larger purpose."

Keith claimed that the intention of the "author" of the *Pañcatantra* was not unmoral: "he had no desire to establish the doctrine that dishonesty was the best policy; his concern was to give advice of a useful character, and it is by no means essential that such advice should be immoral" (Keith 1920: 249).

Ruben is the only researcher to set out specifically to identify the moral lessons of the *Pañcatantra,* basing his analysis on the *Tantrākhyāyika.* For him, the point of the *Pañcatantra* is that friendship enables small, weak individuals (like the animals of the second *tantra*) to withstand and overcome their tyrannical adversaries (e.g., hunters). Ruben interpreted all this within a Marxist historiography: Viṣṇuśarman was sympathetic to the practical, rising merchant class, and was against the decadent slave-owing classes of tyrants and their *brāhmaṇas* (Ruben 1959: 290–293).

To what extent does Pūrṇabhadra's recension reflect that writer's thinking, ideology, or worldview? An important aspect of the liberal humanist tradition of literary scholarship has been sketching of psychological portraits of authors on the basis of their writings. The first problem with this approach is that Pūrṇabhadra was not an author but an editor. We cannot take the whole text as a reflection of his inner self, because he rewrote, rearranged, and complied a new edition from existing works. Can we say anything about him on the basis of the material he added to his sources or subtracted from them? We know that he used the *textus simplicior* or something like it as a source. Again, we cannot be certain whether the material in his recension that is not derived from the *textus simplicior* was created by himself or whether it came from some other unnamed source. Even if we could identify with certainty those elements that he added to the text, what could we learn from them? Does a narrative like Story 1-03 "Merchant and king's sweep" reflect his sympathy for a rising mercantile class, for example? It is impossible to draw any conclusions from such a story. We cannot say whether it reflected his thinking or not, or whether he agreed with its "morality." All we could say, and even this only with reservations, is that he saw fit to include it in his manuscript. What Stoler Miller says about the position of the author in relation to epics applies equally well to the author the *Pañcatantra:*

> The notion of a "book" or "text" in the context of Indian epic must be clarified. Both classical and folk epics have a certain unbounded quality. Neither the author as an individual with intention nor the written manuscript has authority over the text and its transmission. (Stoler Miller 1991: 787)

On the basis of his recension alone, and in the absence of any further documentary evidence, Pūrṇabhadra, the "individual with intention," is unknown to us, and is likely to remain so.

Falk identified a number of stories in the *Pañcatantra* that he maintained were originally from the *Mahābhārata* and the *Jātakas.* He suggested that their original meanings had been "reversed" in the *Pañcatantra:* "Viṣṇuśarman demonstrates for the sake of the good the behavior of the wicked with the intention of teaching them how to oppose their foes with the method invented by the latter, Nīti" (Falk 1978: 192). Olivelle observes that, "According to this line of reasoning, all the cheating and deception that goes on in the *Pañcatantra* is merely intended to show how the other half lives, with the message, 'don't be like them'" (Olivelle 1997: xxxii). Olivelle argues successfully, I believe, that this is highly unlikely.

Olivelle, basing himself on Edgerton's reconstruction of the text, took up the baton that goes right back to Benfey, if not earlier, to the effect that the *Pañcatantra* has a singular, unified meaning as a political textbook:

> It seems to me clear, therefore, that the central message of the *Pañcatantra,* with the possible exception of Book II, is that craft and deception constitute the major art of government. (Olivelle 1997: xxxv)

I have three issues with this approach: first, I question whether the *Pañcatantra* does indeed have a "central message." I favor a polyphonic reading of the text that will allow many voices and many themes to be heard. The possibility of a multitude of diverse and sometimes contradictory morals, philosophies, approaches, and dicta from all the different layers of the text should be recognized.

Second, if the text did have such a single "central message," it would not be that cleverness pays off. There are many more stories in Pūrṇabhadra *Pañcatantra* in which characters suffer as a result of their foolishness (e.g., Story 3-04 "*Brāhmaṇa,* goat and three rogues") or false cleverness. These outnumber the stories in which small, clever characters succeed against powerful adversaries with cunning, or as it is called in the text, with *buddhi* ("intelligence"). Often, of course, both phenomena, being two sides of the one coin, are found in the same story: a clever, weak character may overcome a strong, foolish one (e.g., Story 1-07 "Lion and hare"). Accepting the limitations of this highly subjective process, there are about fifty instances of foolish losers and only about thirty cases of clever winners. This ratio is not confined to Pūrṇabhadra's *Pañcatantra,* however. A quick survey of Edgerton's reconstruction, on which Olivelle based his study, reveals that foolish failures outnumber successful schemers by about two to one. If we have to identify a single "meaning" on this basis, then it must be that fools must suffer.

My third qualm with Olivelle's assertion concerns the hoary assumption these stories are really related to the "major art of government." I am suspicious of all claims that the *Pañcatantra* was "a textbook for princes," a *nītiśāstra,* and so on, and I will examine these claims and the "truth-effects" that they exert on the discourse in chapter 3.

The foregoing attempts to reduce the *Pañcatantra* to a single "meaning"—to define it as a political "how-to" handbook, a practical guide for everyday life, whether it is moral, immoral, amoral, or unmoral—are all reductionist approaches that tend to essentialism the text. They are what Hiltebeitel would term "excavative scholarship" (Hiltebeitel 2001: 2). As I noted above, essentialization of the texts hides the fact that there are multiple possible meanings, and tends to stifle their chaotic, sprawling, joyous, and mutually contradictory nature. It seems preferable to remain open to a variety of readings, which permit, validate and encourage the fact that texts mean different things to different people.

It is better to think, as Olivelle does elsewhere, in terms of multiple themes and discourses permeating the narrative. In this regard, he identifies a number of interesting areas: domesticity and wildness, fate and *karma,* and the importance of friendship. Recognizing that the text is not in fact monolithic, Olivelle pointed to its diversity and complexity when he observed:

> A major strength of the *Pañcatantra,* and a reason for its abiding popularity, is that it presents strong arguments for both sides of an issue, citing proverbs containing age-old wisdom and narrating illustrative stories in support of both. (Olivelle 1997: xxxiv)

His most interesting remarks pertain to the relationship between innate nature and superficial behavior. He identified the "primacy of nature" as an important theme: the proposition that, like the mouse-girl who would only consent to marry another mouse (Story 3-13), "every creature sinks back to its own nature." The proverbial enmity between the snake and the mongoose, the owl, and the crow, and the lion and the bull, are aspects of their respective innate natures:

> The principle that nature (birth, pedigree) rather than upbringing determines behavior is illustrated in the oft-repeated proverb: there can be no friendship between grass-eaters and meat-eaters, between a food and its eater. . . . [H]uman beings belonging to different social groups and strata are compared to different species of animals. It is impossible to turn a meat-eating animal into a grass-eating one; it is impossible to change the disposition of a jackal; it is impossible that a snake and a mongoose should become friends. (Olivelle 1997: xxxvi)

These stories are mentioned in the context of "legitimizing myths relating to the class/caste division" (Olivelle 1997: xxxvi), a theme he elaborates in his paper entitled "Meat-eaters and grass-eaters" (Olivelle 2002a). I will return to the important question of the naturalization of social phenomena in chapter 3.

Questions Addressed in This Study

Following Olivelle's lead, and using the story of the indigo jackal as a prism with which to refract the discourse into its constituent elements, what does Pūrṇabhadra's *Pañcatantra* tell us about the innate qualities of individuals? How do these ideas mesh with the "legitimizing myths" of the hegemonic narratives? What factors enable these ideas to be presented forcefully and effectively? Let us open this paradigmatic narrative (Story 1-11):

> There was a certain jackal, Caṇḍarava by name, who lived in a hole near the outskirts of a city. Once, while searching for food at nightfall, his throat afflicted by hunger, wandering about, he entered the city. Then, just as he was about to be torn limb from limb by the sharp tips of the teeth of the dogs who lived in the city, his heart frightened by their terrifying barks, staggering here and there, while running away he somehow entered the house of a dyer. There he fell into the middle of a great vat of indigo dye, and the pack of dogs departed just as they had come. Now, as his life had not yet run its course, having somehow emerged from that vat of indigo dye, he went to the forest. Then, having seen that his body was colored by the indigo dye, all the hosts of animals that lived in the vicinity, thinking, "What is this creature richly endowed with this unprecedented color?," their eyes darting with fear, fled and said, "*Aho!* Where has this unprecedented creature come from? Its behavior and capabilities are unknown; therefore let us flee as far as possible. For it is said, 'The wise person who desires his own welfare does not trust someone whose behavior, family and prowess are unknown.'"
>
> But Caṇḍarava, having realized that they were overcome with fear, said this, "*Bho, bhoḥ*, wild animals! Having seen me, why do you flee in terror? For having realized that the wild animals had no one as their master, Indra consecrated me, Caṇḍarava by name, as

> king. For that reason, abide in happiness within the compass of my adamantine limbs." Having heard his words, the hosts of wild animals—lions, tigers, leopards, monkeys, hares, deer, jackals and the rest—bowed down to him and said, "Master, command us: what are we to do?" He then made the lion his minister, the tiger his chamberlain, the leopard the keeper of his betel-box, the elephant his doorkeeper and the monkey his umbrella bearer. But those jackals, who were his own kind, were all seized by the throat and expelled. And while he was thus enjoying the splendor of the kingdom, the lions and the rest, having killed wild animals, laid them down before him. And he, in accordance with lordly *dharma,* having apportioned [the flesh], gave it to them all.
>
> While time passed in this way, one day, in the assembly hall, having heard the chorus of voices of jackals howling in the vicinity, the hairs on his body standing erect, his eyes filled with tears of joy, he leapt up and with a very shrill voice, he began to howl. The lions and the rest, having heard this, thinking, "This is a jackal," their heads bowed in shame for one moment, stood up and said, "*Bhoḥ!* We have been deceived by this jackal, therefore let it be killed." Hearing that, he tried to flee, but was torn to pieces by the tiger and died.

Why did the indigo jackal fall from power? What forces are at work here? Why was it inevitable that he should be brought down? Drawing on this and many other stories found in Pūrṇabhadra's recension, I will explore the ways in which the *Pañcatantra* attributes certain innate qualities and other characteristics to individuals on the basis of their birth in a particular station. What factors lend veracity to these statements concerning individuals and their position in society? What factors enable this discourse to function as "true"? To paraphrase Hiltebeitel (2001: 4), what do these stories do and how do they do it?

Central to all these questions is the concept of the division and classification of society. I must establish some conceptual limits for this inquiry by bracketing off the sociological and anthropological questions of the reality of caste/*varṇa*/*jāti* in Indian society. To ask what the *Pañcatantra* might tell us about division on the ground in Indian society is a question fraught with difficulty. First, the relationship between division as a theme in literature and the "reality" of division in society is highly problematical. Second, such a question is based on the idea that there is a single *Pañcatantra* with one "meaning" and a single unitary Indian society in which to observe the phenomenon. In fact, the text, its meaning, and society are not single transcendental entities, rising above the vagaries of time and place. They are diverse, shifting, and contingent; they are also resistant to unitary interpretations. I will be confining this inquiry to the idea of *jāti* and *varṇa* as literary tropes—as ideas, ideals, and ideologies. The scope of this study is the world of Sanskrit literature, and more specifically, the "orthodox" texts in what we might call, adapting Foucault, the "brahmanical archive." Even though I am restricting myself to division as an idea in this literary universe, I do not underestimate the potency of ideas or their significance in shaping and driving social realities. The resultant historical and contemporary social realities of *varṇa* and *jāti,* however, lie beyond the ambit of this investigation.

The word "caste" is highly problematic. In Orientalist scholarship, it has been used to define Indian society as "other" and as inherently inferior to Western societies. The word "class," on the other hand, has long been a captive of Marxist discourse and seems too Eurocentric to be applied to premodern India. The Sanskrit word *varṇa,* which originally meant "color," was the basic unit of division in idealized brahmanical society as it is reflected in the *Vedas* and the later *dharma* texts. The brahmanical archive usually speaks of four *varṇas:* the *brāhmaṇas* (priests), *kṣatriyas* (warriors), *vaiśyas* (merchants and farmers), and *śūdras* (servants). As both the words "caste" and "class" have been co-opted by other projects and are laden with historical baggage, I have elected to use the original Sanskrit term.

In addition to *varṇa,* there is another term used to describe the group into which one is born: *jāti.* In common modern usage, this describes one's occupational group or "subcaste." These human *jātis* are rarely mentioned in the *Pañcatantra,* or indeed in the normative texts as a whole. On the other hand, the *jāti* is also the basic division of the animal realm and is a key concept in these stories. The *jātis* of the animal realm that we find in the *Pañcatantra* are, as I will argue, the analogue of the *varṇas* in human society as depicted in the hegemonic texts, and have the basic meaning of "kind" or "species." Jackals, for example, all belong to one *jāti,* and lions belong to another. Much of what the *Pañcatantra* says explicitly about *jātis* in the animal realm, the way in which they function and the kinds of characteristics attributed to them, are, as we shall see, intimately bound up with ideas about the *varṇa* in human society. They are both the manifestations of the one way of seeing the world. They are both products of what I call the "discourse of division."

Although both *varṇa* and *jāti* have important anthropological and sociological implications in contemporary society, and although there are certainly parallels between their modern usage and their use in Sanskrit literature, I am confining myself in this study to these terms as they appear in the classical normative texts.

Caste, class, *varṇa,* and *jāti* are all social divisions. Ganguly remarked insightfully that these ways of dividing are also ways of uniting: divisions do not just fence others out (Ganguly 2001). They also provide a sense of unity within the groups that they define—and humans, a gregarious species, *like* to belong to groups. Nevertheless, I use "discourse of division" to refer to the social divisions in these texts, even though it may also have a uniting function. In the following section, I will explain in detail what I mean by this term.

"Discourse of Division" in the *Pañcatantra*

The "discourse of division" in the *Pañcatantra* entails everything that pertains to the ways in which societies are divided internally. It brings with it the presumption that discourse is produced by a social elite to maintain its position and privileges. Discourse is, however, largely beyond the control of individuals, and both those who benefit and those whom it may disadvantage participate in discourse more or less unconsciously. By using this term we acknowledge that the ideas relating to division are part of a power structure. Power is produced by knowledge and knowledge, in turn, induces the effects of power. Knowledge generates power in a cyclical and dialectical fashion—the two are mutually productive. We will be investigating the way in which brahmanical power is made manifest, in Foucauldian terms, in its "capillary form" in the *Pañcatantra,* and we will see how the discourse of division feeds back into brahmanical power.

A "discourse" is whatever constrains, but also enables, writing, speaking, and thinking on a given social object or practice within a specific historical period (McHoul and Grace 1993: 31). The discourse provides the external boundaries for its subject, but it also provides internal structure: how statements on a given subject are to be constituted, ordered, and validated. Yet practitioners within the discourse are so inured to the governing procedures that they may cease to be conscious of them. The problem is not to determine whether discourses are valid or not, for they "are neither true nor false" (Foucault 1977: 118). They are essentially neutral, and our interest lies first in describing the discourse of division, using the story of the indigo jackal as our starting point. We will examine Pūrṇabhadra's *Pañcatantra* more broadly, and then investigate the ways in which the discourse functions within a "regime of truth."

A given discourse is usually ascribed to a particular epoch. It is more difficult, or perhaps even unnecessary, to define a historical period for this particular discourse of division, which is reflected in a literary medium. If we were to attempt such a definition, we would be concerned with the period during which a specific cultural hegemony prevailed—the orthodox, brahmanical, "Hindu," Mīmāṃsic, Sanskritic tradition of Indic culture. The discourse permeates the great, long brahmanical literary tradition, and is found in all systems of thought whose foundations lie on the authority of Vedic bedrock. As we shall see, the discourse makes its earliest textual appearance in the *Puruṣasūkta* of the *Ṛgveda,* c. 900 BC. To the extent that the *Pañcatantra* is still popular, and a similar discourse of division still functions in contemporary society, the effective historical period of our inquiry is not yet at an end. Irrespective of whether caste, *varṇa,* or *jāti* are treated as religious, political, or economic constructs, social division is an ongoing process and this discourse is still in operation.

The discourse of division, as I use the term, is the grand corpus of all that may be said, written, or thought about *varṇa,* or *jāti* within this Sanskritic episteme in general, and in Pūrṇabhadra's *Pañcatantra* in particular. While several stories in this collection deal explicitly with the concepts of *varṇa* and *jāti,* I argue that the discourse of division is much more pervasive than this alone would indicate. It provides the background against which many of the narratives are played out. It provides a set of unspoken assumptions; the "natural" and barely perceptible ground rules that govern societies, real and fictional. The first major objective of this book is to describe these ground rules, as I read them, in Pūrṇabhadra's *Pañcatantra.* In the following chapter, I will outline three aspects of the discourse of division, specifically the ways in which *jāti*—the station at birth of the animal characters in the narratives—determine the following aspects of the individuals' being:

- "essential nature" or *svabhāva*
- social status, especially one's position in the social hierarchy
- permissible social relationships in terms of "natural" enmity and amity.

No discourse can operate in a vacuum: it can only be effective if it appears to be true. Discourse requires a certain infrastructure to lend it authority, veracity and credibility. In the third chapter, I will explore five factors that constitute the "regime of truth," which enables the discourse of division to function:

- the role of the authoritative voice with which the discourse is enunciated
- the process of universalization of the discourse, which induces the impression that it is applicable to all times, places, and audiences
- the process of naturalization in which contingent social phenomena are projected on to the natural world
- the "śāstric paradigm" as it pertains to the *Pañcatantra*
- the way in which the *Pañcatantra* functions as a node in a network of intertextual references.

In the fourth chapter, I will explore ways in which the discourse of division in the *Pañcatantra* accords with the broader brahmanical archive of "hegemonic texts," including the *Vedas, Brāhmaṇas, Purāṇas,* epics, *Dharmaśāstras,* and *Dharmasūtras,* with particular emphasis on traditional descriptions of the origins and nature of the *varṇa* system. This will provide the cultural background against which the discourse of division in the *Pañcatantra* was created and received and a context in which we may understand and interpret it.

In the fifth chapter, I will draw these threads together to illustrate the factors that contributed to the indigo jackal's fall from power, and show why its fall was inevitable, given the nature of the *Pañcatantra.* On the basis of these outcomes, I will suggest some future avenues of inquiry, and offer a preemptive defense of my methodology and findings. I conclude with a brief reflection on the nature of discourse and its contemporary relevance.

Now that we have established the scope and questions for this inquiry, we may begin our search for some answers. The first step in this process is to describe the discourse of division as it manifests Pūrṇabhadra's *Pañcatantra,* and this will be the object of the following chapter.

2

The Discourse of Division in the *Pañcatantra*

> Like "being" according to Aristotle, the social world can be uttered and constructed in different ways: it can be practically perceived, uttered, constructed, in accordance with different principles of vision and division. . . .
>
> —Pierre Bourdieu, *Language and Symbolic Power*

In this chapter, by undertaking a close reading of Pūrṇabhadra's *Pañcatantra,* I will examine the ways in which the discourse of division is articulated. Beginning with an overview of the concept of *jāti* as used in this text, I will then describe three aspects of the discourse: *jāti* as the determinant of an individual's essential nature, social status, and natural enmity and amity.

The Concept of *Jāti* in the *Pañcatantra*

Jāti as "Kind"

Etymologically, *jāti* is an abstract noun formed from the root *jan* "be born." A partial, edited list of the definitions of *jāti* from Monier-Williams is given below:

1. birth, production, rebirth
2. form of existence (as man, animal, etc.) fixed by birth
3. position assigned by birth, rank, caste, family, race, or lineage

4. kind, genus (as opposed to species), species (as opposed to individual), class
5. generic properties (as opposed to the specific ones)
6. natural disposition
7. character of a species, genuine or true state of anything

How do these seven points relate to one another and to our analysis of the *Pañcatantra*? For our purposes *jāti* means in the first place (1) "birth," and by extension (2) the "form of existence fixed by one's birth." The concept of immutability attendant on one's birth is evident here: the state in which one is born, one's *jāti,* cannot be changed. Contingent on one's birth is a fixed position in social space: (3) a "position assigned by birth, rank, caste, family, race or lineage." This will be of particular significance at a later point in this discussion when we examine the relationship between *jāti* and the position of the individual in social space. The fourth point applies most directly to the surface text of the *Pañcatantra* in which many of the references to *jāti* are concerned with the interactions of animals of different "kinds" (4). A major concern of the *Pañcatantra* and of this study is the metaphoric relationship that exists between the *jātis* of the metasociety of the animal realm (4) and the social divisions that exist in human societies (3). While the surface text speaks of animals, the subtext is about people. The last three aspects of the definition bear on another important aspect of this investigation: *jāti* as the determinant of one's essential nature (*svabhāva*). One's *jāti* not only fixes one's position in social space, but brings with it a set of innate propensities, inclinations, and dispositions (6); indeed, one's *habitus.* These fixed, natal qualities are the closest approximation to one's actual "true" character, or "genuine or true state" (7).

Let us now turn to the ways in which the word *jāti* is used in the *Pañcatantra.* First, in the context of human society, *jāti* is found, but only in a single instance, in the sense of an occupational grouping. In Story 5-06 "Two-headed weaver," the artisan's wife said to her husband that if he had a second pair of hands, he could weave twice as much and would win the respect of his peers: "Time will pass [for you], among your *jāti,* being praised by them" (PT 275.11).

Although this idea of *jāti* as the basic unit of division in the human world is of enormous significance in contemporary Indian societies, this sense is rarely found in *Pañcatantra,* nor is it encountered frequently in other normative Sanskrit texts (see, e.g., Halbfass 1991: 350). These texts almost invariably use the word *varṇa* to describe the primary unit of social division. As we will see in chapter 4, individuals' *varṇa* determines their role in the sacrifice, their occupation, their essential nature, their position in social space, whom they may marry, with whom they may associate, from whom they may accept food, and so on. I will not be arguing that the *Pañcatantra* is "really about *varṇa*" when it speaks of *jāti.* Perhaps there is some historical correlation between animal *jātis* of these narratives and *jātis* as we find them in the reality of Indian society that remains to be explored. However, the concept of *varṇa* in the normative texts, the concept of animal *jāti* in the *Pañcatantra,* and the *jāti* as it manifests in Indian society are, I maintain, three aspects of the same discourse of division.

The second and much more significant way in which the word *jāti* is used is illustrated in the well-known Story 1-07 "Lion and hare":

> There was in a certain forest region a lion, intoxicated with pride, by the name of Mandamati, and he continually practiced the destruction of wild animals. He spared no animal that he had seen. Now, all the deer, boar, buffaloes, wild oxen, hares, etc., born in that forest, having met together, with pitiful expressions, kneeling on the ground, heads bowed, respectfully began to request that lord of beasts: "Enough, your majesty, of your practice of destroying all the animals without cause, which is harmful to the next life and is excessively cruel." (PT 40.16–21)

The word *jāti* appears in the following section:

> "It does not befit you to practice the destruction of our families. For if you stay at home we will send one forest animal in turn as food for the master everyday. This being the case, there will be no disruption of your majesty's sustenance or of our *jātis.* Therefore, let this royal *dharma* be put into practice." (PT 41.4–7)

These *jātis* refer back to the assembled groups of animals in the first quotation above: the deer, boar, buffaloes, wild oxen, hares, and so on. In another episode (Story 1-06 "Heron, fishes and crab"), a crab reflected on the fact that a heron was "the natural enemy of our *jāti*" (PT 112.4–5), suggesting that crabs constitute a *jāti.* Similarly, a snake in Story 4-01 "Frog's revenge overleaps itself," on hearing the voice of a frog, said to himself, "This one who calls me is not one of my own *jāti*" (PT 232.1–2). The inference here, also, is that snakes constitute a distinct *jāti* with respect to frogs. We find further specific examples of the use of the word *jāti* with reference to mice, dogs, and donkeys (PT 215.22, 255.9, 272.12), often in the compound *svajātīya,* "of one's own *jāti.*"

From these examples we can see *jāti* as it is used in the *Pañcatantra* roughly corresponds to a kind. It would be imprudent, however, to attempt to map *jāti* with more precision on to any more "scientific" equivalent. For example, the words "species" and "genus" are problematic because, while cats and dogs both constitute single species, the *jātis* of frogs and snakes encompass many species. "Kind" is a more appropriate translation than either species or genus, because it is suitably imprecise, flexible, literary, and non-taxonomic.

Jāti in the Wider Sense

In addition to "kind," there is another, wider sense in which *jāti* is used in the *Pañcatantra.* In Story 1-13 "Lion's retainers outwit camel," a jackal and a lion are said to be "of the same *jāti,* on account of having claws as weapons" (PT 79.12). Later in the story, a leopard and a lion are also said to be related in the same way (PT 80.5). This idea of a taxonomic relationship based on shared physical attributes is repeated in Story 4-04 "Jackal nursed by lioness" (PT 241.16–22) to which we will return below. The ultimate point of this story is that jackals and lions do *not* belong to the same *jāti,* as the jackal later discovered. Nevertheless, this example at least demonstrates the existence of the broader concept of *jāti* introduced above: there is a super-*jāti* that incorporates "those having claws as weapons." This might be roughly equivalent to "beasts of prey," "predators," and so forth and might, in fact, be equivalent to the word "dog-footed" (*śvāpada,* PT 69.6).[1]

The third and final example of *jāti* in the broader sense is found in Story 1-10 "Louse and flea," in which the king instructs his attendants to search his bed for any creatures of the "*jāti* of vermin" (PT 68.3). The key concept here is that all insects or vermin (*svedaja,* literally, "born of sweat") are regarded as members of the one super-*jāti.*

In the above section I have shown how the word *jāti* is used in the *Pañcatantra* to express the idea of "kinds" of animals, or, occasionally, larger groupings of similar species. In all the above examples the word *jāti* and its derivatives are used explicitly. Many stories in the *Pañcatantra,* which deal with the interactions of characters and groups of characters, implicitly concern *jāti,* even though the word itself may not be used explicitly.

Of immediate relevance to our present enquiry is the role of *jāti* in the story of the indigo jackal. Three points are to be made. First, there is the universal nature of *jāti:* all animals in the narrative are members of one *jāti* or another, that is, they inhabit a world primarily divided into *jātis.* Second, there is the question of difference: the jackals and the lions, the tigers, and so on all belong to different *jātis,* roughly equivalent to their species. Third, there is commonality: all members of a given kind belong to the same *jāti,* that is, all jackals—the indigo jackal and those of his fellows whom he exiled—share common membership of the one *jāti.*

Having established the credentials of the concept of *jāti* as the basic unit—the basic division—of the forest society described in the *Pañcatantra,* and having shown that it is a real and frequently encountered concern in these narratives, I will now examine the various ways in which the discourse pertaining to *jāti*—that is, the discourse of division—manifests in the *Pañcatantra.*

Svabhāva—"Essential Nature"

In this section I will show how birth into a particular *jāti* determines an individual's essential nature (*svabhāva*). We will begin with an overview of *svabhāva* in the *Pañcatantra.* This is a compound of *sva* "own," and *bhāva* "manner of being, nature, temperament, character" (MMW). The definition for *svabhāva* itself is "own condition or state of being, natural state or constitution, innate or inherent disposition, nature, impulse, spontaneity" (MMW).

Svabhāva in the *Pañcatantra*

Story 5-05 "Ass as singer" provides important direct evidence of the relationship between *jāti* and *svabhāva.* An ass was browsing one night in a cucumber patch:

> Thereupon, the people who guarded the field, having heard the donkey's braying, grinding their teeth with rage, having raised their sticks, rushed forward. And after they arrived, while [the donkey] was beaten, it fell to the ground. And then, having tied a mortar with a hole in the middle around its neck, the field-guards went to sleep. But the donkey, its pain gone, on account

> of the essential nature of its own kind, stood up a moment later. (PT 272.8–13)

The important phrase here is "whose pain is gone, on account of the essential nature of its own kind." The donkey has a "natural" hardiness, a capacity to shake off the effects of the flogging it received and to endure the weight of the mortar. These are the manifestations of the supposed resilience of the species that arise from its essential nature and which are common to all members of that *jāti.* Just as the *jāti* of donkeys has a *svabhāva* that is characterized by hardiness, so too are the essential natures of other groups determined by their *jāti,* as we shall see below.

A jackal was searching for food in the wilderness when he heard a strange noise (Story 1-02 "Jackal and drum"). On investigation, he discovered that the sound was caused by the wind blowing dry canes against an abandoned kettledrum. The jackal, who had not seen such a thing before, wondered if it were an animal on which he might feed. He asked himself, "Does this sound arise from its own nature, or from something else?" (PT 13.14–15). Here, the jackal mistakenly attributes an essential nature to the unknown "creature" he has encountered. In the jackal's worldview, *svabhāva* is something that the strange animal and, by implication, other creatures, would possess.

A third example where *svabhāva* is mentioned explicitly comes from the *Hitopadeśa,* which, as we saw in chapter 1, is a close cousin of the *Pañcatantra:*

> It is difficult for one to overcome one's essential nature. If a dog were made king, would it not chew on a sandal? (Hit. 1923–1924)

The idea is that all dogs share a common essential dog-nature, and, irrespective of the individual's circumstances, that nature will continually reassert itself, because *svabhāva* is "difficult to overcome." That is, one's *svabhāva,* determined by one's birth, is a fixed quality that cannot be changed.

In the following paragraphs, I will present two more illustrations of how *svabhāva* is related to *jāti.* In these examples, the focus is on hostility between certain species. We will pass quickly over these now, as we will return to this question of "natural" enmity in more detail at a later stage.

In Story 3-03 "Cat as judge between partridge and hare," the bird warned the hare not to approach a cat with the words, "Surely he is our natural enemy. Therefore, standing at a distance, let us ask him" (PT 191.1–2). That is, the cat, on account of its *svabhāva,* was the enemy of both the partridge and the hare. This opinion is not based on the partridge's knowledge of the individual cat in question; rather, it is a blanket statement that applies to cats in general, to cats as a *jāti.* From the point of view of the partridge, cats as a *jāti* possess a particular *svabhāva,* one characteristic of which is their tendency to catch and kill small animals.

The same may be said of Story 4-01 "Frog's revenge overleaps itself," in which the frog-king said to a snake, "You are our natural enemy" (PT 232.16–17). The frog inferred an enmity to this snake in particular, based on what he knew of snakes in general. He had no knowledge of the individual in question, but attributed a common *svabhāva* to all members of the *jāti* of snake: that is, they eat frogs.

At this point we will observe the role of *svabhāva* in the story of the indigo jackal that we introduced above. The jackal's inherent nature reasserted itself, despite his elevated position and despite his usurpation of the trappings and perks of office. The jackal had assumed all the rights and responsibilities of kingship, but was undone as soon as he heard the howls of his fellows:

> having heard the chorus of howls of jackals howling in the vicinity, the hairs on his body standing erect, his two eyes filled with tears of joy, having stood up, with a very shrill voice, he began to howl.[2] (PT 69.18–20)

He had not changed, and was indeed unable to change, in any fundamental way. He was the superficial sovereign, one who enjoyed the betel-nut box and the umbrella and the other perks of office, but the horripilation, the tears and the howl—these were the "natural" response of one jackal to another. Suddenly all his sophisticated deceit melted away, and he stood before his erstwhile minions, vulnerable and exposed. There was not even a fight to the death; he was killed ignominiously while trying to run away. As if to seal the fate of one who attempted to deny his essential nature, the jackal was not simply killed, but, we are informed with added literary flourish, he was "torn to pieces" (PT 69.24). His *svabhāva* "naturally" precluded him from kingship. When his *svabhāva* reasserted itself on hearing the voices of his old companions, his pretensions, his power and his authority all slipped away. The sovereignty of the indigo jackal, like his marvelous new appearance, was only ever skin-deep.

At one level, the narratives of the *Pañcatantra* are about individuals: this jackal called Caṇḍarava, Saṃjīvaka the bull and so on. But one interesting feature of the text is that most of the stories are about interactions between characters of different kinds: a jackal and a lion, a cat and a hare, or a crow and a cobra. Few focus primarily on the interaction of two individuals of the same kind. We rarely see a situation in which, for example, two such animals are the protagonist and the antagonist in a given narrative. There are a few exceptions: the two jackals of the first *tantra,* the three fish of contrasting dispositions (Stories 1-17 and 5-04) and the wicked and virtuous parrots (Story 1-29 "Good makes good, bad makes bad"). In general, however, the creators of the *Pañcatantra* are not primarily concerned with comparing personality types within a given kind. Their art lies in drawing on a vocabulary of easily recognizable stereotypes that are generalized at the level of *jāti.*

To conclude this section on *svabhāva,* I have attempted to demonstrate, with examples from the text, how the concepts of *jāti* and *svabhāva* are used in the *Pañcatantra.* Individuals are divided on the basis of their birth into *jātis.* This is the basic division of the fictional forest society. Further, we have seen that every creature has an essential nature that is shared by all members of its *jāti.* An organic relationship exists between them: one's *jāti* ultimately determines one's *svabhāva.* The essential nature of all donkeys is hardiness; it is in dogs' nature to chew on sandals; and jackals will always howl in response to others of their kind.

When the creators of the *Pañcatantra* present us with the indigo jackal, it is as the Ur-jackal, the representative of particular *jāti* with a known and finite set of characteristics. The individual is a metonymy for the group. As a member of a given *jāti,* the indigo jackal was assumed to have a known, fixed *svabhāva.* For this story to work, it must be understood that the jackal will always react in a given way to a given set of circumstances. All jackals were created equal, as it were. The *Pañcatantra* is saying, in effect, that "once a jackal, always a jackal."

JĀTI AND SOCIAL STATUS

We will now broaden our examination of *jāti* to examine its role as the determinant of an individual's social status, but before proceeding, it will be useful to establish a model for the metasocieties depicted in the text. In this section I will accordingly draw on a hierarchical model of Indian society and on Bourdieu's concept of social space to produce a hybrid model. We will then employ this hybrid to map the groups and interactions that appear in these narratives.

Dumont defined hierarchy as the "principle by which the elements of a whole are ranked in relation to the whole" (Dumont 1970: 66), and he proposed a hierarchical model of Indic societies in which individuals are arranged along a vertical axis. The basic determining factor of one's position in the hierarchy was purity/impurity: "The opposition of pure and impure appears to us the very principle of hierarchy, to such a degree that it merges with the opposition of superior and inferior; moreover, it also governs separation" (Dumont 1970: 59).

Dumont's approach, in particular his Orientalist leaning, has been widely criticized. Dirks, for example, sees power, not purity, as the driving force (Dirks 1987: 7). Appadurai regarded Dumont's thesis as "an elegy and a deeply Western trope for a whole way of thinking about India, in which it represents the extremes of the human capability to fetishize inequality" (Appadurai 1986: 745). The main problem with Dumont is the "fetishizing" and the centrality that is bestowed on the idea of hierarchy, not, I believe, the concept of hierarchy itself. We may now safely move beyond Dumont's concept of hierarchy as the central, essentializing trope of Indian societies—most would agree that there is no such thing as *homo hierarchicus*—but we may still put to good use some of his ideas. The opposition of pure and impure as an ordering principle of a hierarchy is, as we shall see, one that is particularly well suited to understanding the fictional societies of the *Pañcatantra.*

In the collection entitled *Language and Symbolic Power,* Bourdieu introduced his concept of "social space," which provides, I believe, another useful framework for looking at the question of *jāti* in the *Pañcatantra.* For Bourdieu, sociology is a "social topology":

> Accordingly, the social world can be represented in the form of a (multidimensional) space constructed on the basis of principles of differentiation or distribution constituted by the set of properties active in the social universe under consideration, that is, able to confer force or power on their possessor in that universe. Agents and groups of agents are thus defined by their *relative positions* in this space. (Bourdieu 1991: 229–230)

Bourdieu's "social world" may be applied the metasocieties of the *Pañcatantra* narratives in which the "agents or groups of agents" are characters in the narrative and their respective *jātis:*

> The active properties that are chosen as principles of construction of the social space are the different kinds of power or capital that are current in the different fields. . . . The kinds of capital, like trumps in a game of cards, are powers which define the chances of profit in a given field. . . . For example, the volume of cultural capital . . . determines the aggregate chances of profit in all games in which cultural capital is effective, thereby helping to determine positions in the social space. . . . (Bourdieu 1991: 230)

One's position in social space, then, is determined by the amount of power or capital that one exercises. We will return to the question of what types of capital, in particular symbolic capital, determine the topography of social space in the *Pañcatantra.*

> On the basis of knowledge of the space of positions, one can carve out *classes* in the logical sense of the word, i.e. sets of agents who occupy similar positions and who, being placed in similar conditions and submitted to similar types of conditioning, have every chance of having similar dispositions and interests, and thus of producing similar practices and adopting similar stances. (Bourdieu 1991: 231)

The "similar dispositions" shared by members of a given set of agents provide a useful analogy for the *svabhāva* imputed by the creators of the *Pañcatantra.*

Taking Dumont's hierarchy based on purity and impurity, and Bourdieu's concept of social space together, let us now explore ways of mapping the interactions of characters and *jātis* in the *Pañcatantra.* As we will see, the jackal is usually associated in the Indic context with death and impurity, and would therefore sit squarely at the bottom of Dumont's social hierarchy. The owl is also regarded as highly inauspicious and impure, being associated with death and with the disruption of the Vedic sacrifice—but it is also strong, fierce, and frightening. Owls, therefore, are impure but powerful. These characteristics distinguish it from the jackal, which is impure but weak, and they make "low" seem to be an inappropriate status for the owl. Dumont allows only a single form of capital (purity), and provides only a unidimensional vertical axis. In this case, both the jackal and owl would be mapped on to the bottom of the hierarchy. Bourdieu, in contrast, permits multiple forms of capital. Under his scheme, jackals and owls would both rank low in terms of purity, but owls would greatly outrank jackals if their social capital in the form of power is measured. Bourdieu suggests a two-dimensional set of vertical and horizontal axes. This allows us to map jackals and owls low in terms of purity, but owls high in terms of power.

In looking for ways to extend this idea of a two-dimensional social space on which to map these groups of characters, it seems fitting to appropriate the Indic metaphor of the *maṇḍala.* On the grandest scale, *maṇḍalas* are "cosmoplans" or diagrams of the universe:

> [They] consist of an inner circle containing a principal deity (or deities), enclosed in a multilevel square palace with openings at the found cardinal directions. The palace is placed in a multitiered circle. Additional figures are generally found outside this large circle. (Leidy and Thurman 1997: 17)

Figures of lesser importance occupy a series of concentric bands stretching out toward the periphery. In the furthest reaches of the *maṇḍala* are found the charnel houses, cremation grounds and cemeteries (e.g., see Leidy and Thurman 1997: 85, 152–153).

An embryonic *maṇḍala* is perceptible in the *Arthaśāstra*'s guidelines for the construction of a fort. Here, social space and hierarchy are reflected in what is, in effect, town planning. The royal palace should be situated "in the middle of the houses of the people of all the four *varṇas*" (AŚ 2.4.6). The *brāhmaṇas, kṣatriyas, vaiśyas,* and *śūdras* are allocated to the north, east, south, and west, respectively. Outside the city walls are the burial or cremation grounds. At the outermost perimeter of the urban plan, at the very fringes of society, "heretics and *caṇḍālas* shall live beyond the cremation grounds" (AŚ 2.4.23).

The *maṇḍala* is also used as a model of social space in *Pañcatantra.* In Story 1-00 "Lion and bull," the lion was alarmed at hearing the unfamiliar bellowing of the bull:

> And having heard that, his heart was deeply perturbed, but having concealed outward signs of emotion, he positioned himself in a military formation of four *maṇḍalas* (*caturmaṇḍala*) underneath a spreading banyan tree. Now, the names of the four *maṇḍalas* of the formation are: *Siṃha, Siṃhānuyāyin, Kākaravarga* and *Kiṃvṛtta.* With reference to these, in all the cities, towns, districts, villages, markets, hamlets, wild tribes, *brāhmaṇa* land-grants, monasteries and communities, one alone occupies the position of

> *Siṃha.* Several members of the retinue occupy the position of *Siṃhānuyāyin.* The *Kākaravarga* is the middlemost group, and the *Kiṃvṛtta* occupy the edge of the forest. Thus these three represent the highest, the midmost and the lowest. (PT 4.19–24)

There are two points to be made here. First, this is notionally a military formation, but it is also a useful model for the whole metasociety of the forest, as it allocates a locus in social space for everyone from the lion/king to the cities, towns, districts, and so on. Second, according to the text, this arrangement is strictly a set of four concentric circles (*caturmaṇḍala*), not a single *maṇḍala* in the sense in which I use it. Despite this discrepancy, the model is useful, having a lion/king/power at the center, surrounded in successive ranks at increasing distances by his closest followers, the *Kākaravarga* and *Kiṃvṛtta,* representing, the "highest, the midmost and the lowest" ranks. The names of the last two divisions are problematic, particularly "*Kākaravarga.*" *Kiṃvṛtta* means "What is an event?" and suggests heroism or imperturbability: an individual or group who does not wonder at any event—I take this to mean "dread-nought." A useful concept is found in the definition of *Kiṃvṛtta*: those who "occupy the edge of the forest." The word of interest here is *anta,* which I have translated as "edge," but which also means "end" or "limit." It conveys the sense that the outermost *maṇḍala* is "at the edge" and is peripheral.

Returning now to the text, and following Bourdieu's conception of "class," it is fruitful to imagine *jātis* as "sets of agents who occupy similar positions in the social space, and hence possess similar kinds and similar quantities of capital, similar life chances, similar dispositions, etc." (Thompson 1991: 30). These are similar to Bourdieu's "classes on paper," that is, theoretical constructs "which the analyst produces in order to explain or make sense of observable social phenomena" (Thompson 1991: 30).

We have remarked on the fact that Dumont adopted purity/impurity as the "single true principle" and "fundamental conception" that underlay the hierarchical system of castes (Dumont 1970: 43). I would suggest that auspiciousness is a useful ordering principle for the ordering of social space here. While acknowledging that there is some general equivalence between purity and auspiciousness, I prefer the latter as it is the word (*śubha*) that is used in the *Pañcatantra* itself.[3]

Drawing on the schemes of Dumont and Bourdieu, then, I propose the following hybrid model. The center of the *maṇḍala* is the locus of prestige, power, and auspiciousness. Moving from the center toward the periphery, desirable qualities diminish and inauspiciousness increases.[4] I suggest, moreover, that auspiciousness, prestige, and power are linked through knowledge. We can show that auspiciousness and knowledge, while not necessarily equivalent, may go hand in hand (e.g., the *śāstra*-quoting bull of Story 1-00 was "endowed with many auspicious marks"). Auspiciousness makes one a suitable vessel for knowledge, perhaps. If, as Foucault says, power and knowledge are two sides of the same coin, and as we have shown, knowledge is linked to auspiciousness, then is auspiciousness not linked to power as well? It seems that there are also certain reverberations here of the *brāhmaṇa* identity (auspiciousness/knowledge) and *kṣatriya* identity (power). Auspiciousness is one form of "symbolic capital" that functions as an organizing principle in social space (see Bourdieu 1991: 230).

I stress that I am not attempting to model a real historical polity. Unlike Dumont's hierarchy and Milner's sociological approach, the social *maṇḍala* is not an attempt to "explain" Indian society. It is, I believe, a useful hermeneutic framework for interpreting the dynamics of the narrative. As I have said before, these texts are about ideas, ideals, and ideologies, and I feel justified in bracketing off the far more complex social realities that existed outside of the text. I am not proposing that Indian society be envisaged as a *maṇḍala;* I am merely suggesting that the *maṇḍala* is a helpful way of mapping groups in these narratives. To borrow from Bourdieu, we are dealing with "*jātis* on paper."

> This "class on paper" has the *theoretical* existence which belongs to all theories: as the product of an explanatory classification, one which is altogether similar to that of zoologists or botanists, it allows one to *explain* and predict the practices and properties of the things classified—including their propensity to constitute groups. (Bourdieu 1991: 231)

I intend to exploit the ambiguity of "on paper" in its dual senses of "in theory" and "in literature" as this is a study of ideals expressed in literature, not realities manifest in society.

There is one final observation to be made before we begin our investigation of status: there is an interesting interplay between the words outcaste, "out of caste," and outcast, "cast out"; they are similar in sense, frequently interchangeable, but are at the root, different. Both are important in this following discussion. Compared with a vertically ordered hierarchy, a *maṇḍala,* based a radial gradient of auspiciousness and prestige, is better able to accommodate both the outcaste and the outcast.

Having now established the social *maṇḍala* as a legitimate and efficacious heuristic model, in the first of the following sections, I will examine five stories in which characters of peripheral status were translated—by chance or by design—to central positions of prestige and power.

Story 1-11 "Blue Jackal"

I will begin by examining in some detail the status of the indigo jackal before and after his elevation. From the time of the *Vedas,* the jackal has been associated in Sanskrit literature with carrion, death and inauspiciousness. Just a few examples will serve to illustrate these associations. With dogs and various species of birds, it is associated with the eating of corpses:

> Do not prepare our bodies for the dog, the jackal, the *aliklavas* [MMW: type of carrion bird], the vultures and the black birds! Your insects, O Paśupati, and your birds shall not devour us. (AV 11.2.2)

> Let jackals, evil omens and dogs go far away; let those women with disheveled hair who bewail misfortune go far away. (AV 11.2.11)

The inauspiciousness associated with the corpse is transferred to the jackal and to its cries as the portent of death. The cries of the jackal are frequently used in literature to foretell great slaughter on the battlefield:

> On that terrible night, jackals crying in all directions inspired terrible fear, with their mouths that had mouthfuls of flame. (Mbh 7.129.14)

> And many kṣatriyas, eager for victory, bereft of life, fell to the ground, O king, covered with arrows. At the joyous tumult of the wolves, vultures and jackals by day, your army suffered a disaster, while your son was watching. (Mbh 9.22.74–75)

The cry of the jackal conjures up images of death and creates an inauspicious atmosphere, in which, according to Manu, the sacred syllables of the *Veda* may not be uttered:

> A *brāhmaṇa* shall not recite [the Veda] during a dust-storm, or while the sky is reddish, or while a jackal howls, or while dogs, donkeys or camels cry, or in company. (MS 4.115)

In the *Sabhāparvan* of the *Mahābhārata,* Vidura provided Dhṛtarāṣṭra with this warning about his son:

> Because, immediately after his birth, the wicked-minded Duryodhana, the family-destroyer of the Bhāratas, cried discordantly like a jackal, it was known that he would be the cause of your destruction. Knowing even that, you do not recognize the jackal in the form of Duryodhana living in your house. (Mbh 2.55.2–3)

At one of the great climaxes in the *Mahābhārata,* at the game of dice, which was ultimately to bring so much suffering into the world, the cries of a jackal were heard:

> Then, in the abode of King Dhṛtarāṣṭra, at the *agnihotra,* a jackal cried loudly. Asses were answering him, O king, and on all sides terrible birds also. Vidura, who understands the truth, and the daughter of Subala, heard the terrible sound. Bhīṣma and Droṇa and wise Gautama cried loudly, *'Svasti! Svasti!'* Then Gāndhārī and the wise Vidura, having marked the terrible omen, in great affliction then informed the king. (Mbh 2.63.22–24)

Similarly, there are numerous references to the inauspicious nature of the cry of the jackal in the *Rāmāyaṇa* (e.g., Rām. 3.55.4).

These "hegemonic" texts create a variety of inauspicious associations for the jackal. As a natural scavenger, it is associated with corpses, and through contact with the dead, it becomes "unclean," and everything about it is tainted. The *Pañcatantra* is informed by these texts, and is also part of this hegemonic tradition: it adopts the tradition's conventions, uses them, shapes them, and perpetuates them. While it is of course impossible to know the minds of the "traditional" audience of these narratives, these associations are so common and so consistent that it is hard to imagine that anyone familiar with the broader world of brahmanical literature could not bring these cultural associations to their "reading" of the *Pañcatantra.*[5]

The jackal's inauspicious howls reverberate through this particular story. Even the protagonist's name is laden with negative associations: Caṇḍarava means "whose voice is fierce" (MMW: *caṇḍa*—fierce, violent, cruel, impetuous, hot, ardent with passion, passionate, angry). In my mind, at least, *caṇḍa* conjures up another word to which it may be related, *caṇḍāla* (MMW: an outcast, man of the lowest and most despised of the mixed tribes, born from a *śūdra* father and a *brāhmaṇa* mother).[6]

The *Manusmṛti* lays down a number of restrictions on the behavior of these outcast/outcaste *caṇḍālas*, whom it declares to be the "lowest of men" (MS 10.12). It stipulates that the dwellings of *caṇḍālas* must be outside the village (MS 10.51), just as the jackal Caṇḍarava "lived in a hole near the outskirts of a city" (PT 68.14). Manu declares that *caṇḍālas* must "wander from place to place" (MS 10.52). Typical of jackals in the *Pañcatantra* as a whole, Caṇḍarava was "wandering about" in search of food (*paribhraman*, PT 68.16). Manu says of *caṇḍālas* that "their transactions should be among themselves, and their marriages with those who are of the same kind" (MS 10.53). The explicit explanation for Caṇḍarava's demise in the prefatory verse of Story 1-11 was that he broke this very injunction: he had rejected those who were his natural peers and had dealings with those who were not of his own "kind":

> One who abandons insiders and treats outsiders as insiders meets death, just like the fool Caṇḍarava. (PT 68.10–11)

Hobson-Jobson, an interesting repository of nineteenth-century pride and prejudice, provides another angle on the status of the outcast. With reference to "pariahs," it states, "As with other castes low in caste-rank they are also low in habits, frequently eating carrion and other objectionable food, and addicted to drink" (Yule and Burnell 1968 [1886]: 678). The alleged eating of carrion on the part of the "pariah" provides us with another parallel to the corpse-eating jackal.

Another similarity shared by the *caṇḍālas* and the jackal is their common association with death. Cremation-grounds are among the approved places of residence for outcastes in general (MS 10.50, AŚ 2.4.23); *caṇḍālas* may only wear clothes recovered from the dead (MS 10.52); they must carry the corpses of those who have no relatives (MS 10.55); and executioners were drawn from among their ranks: "And they should kill those condemned to death, always in accordance with the *śāstras*, at the king's command" (MS 10.56).

The final element that binds *caṇḍālas* and jackals together is their shared relationship with dogs, and, to a lesser extent, donkeys. In Manu, *caṇḍālas* appear to share the lowest rung of the social ladder with "those who cook dogs" (MS 10.51). *Caṇḍālas'* wealth is in the form of dogs and asses (MS 10.51). Jackals, on the other hand, are bound to dogs through an eternal, paradigmatic mutual enmity, but also though their common identity as wandering scavengers and perpetual outcasts. Story 5-05, "Ass as singer," illustrates an association between a jackal and a donkey. Just as the human outcasts, the *caṇḍālas,* associate with donkeys, so does the outcast jackal.

I have selected these examples to demonstrate the types of cultural stereotypes that abound in textual sources. What can nonliterary sources, specifically the plastic arts, show us about the cultural associations that pertain to the jackal.

Among the images of the Vaitāl temple (c. 775 CE) in Bhubaneswar (Orissa) is an image of a wrathful female deity, Chāmuṇḍā, with sunken eyes and the hood of a snake on her head. A jackal drags at a corpse under her feet (Panigrahi 1961: 79). Elsewhere in the same complex, a female figure is flanked by a tripod with two human heads placed on it and a jackal eating a prostrate corpse (Panigrahi 1961: 80). A late-eighteenth-century Mughal painting of a cremation ground depicts one jackal standing over a skeleton while another gnaws on a bone, while in the background, Śiva makes a garland of severed heads (Stchoukine 1929: Plate XCIV). These examples suggest that the negative associations of the jackal are more than a purely literary trope, but enjoyed currency in the broader Indic cultural world.

This leads to my final point, which is an etymological one: one of the many Sanskrit words for jackal is *śivā,* meaning "auspicious," a name it shares with that most terrible deity. Ironically, by this association with Śiva, the most auspicious of names bears connotations of death and destruction.

Such are the cultural associations that audiences might bring to their "reading" of this story. The indigo jackal, before his elevation, was at the very periphery of the social *maṇḍala,* a wanderer, a denizen of cremation-grounds, a resident of the "edge," neither in the city nor in the forest, both outcast and outcaste, associated with death and inauspiciousness, so low that even the pariah dogs despised him. Let us see how his new, elevated status is expressed.

As soon as the jackal returned to the forest and witnessed the flight of the other animals, he sensed a power vacuum into which he could maneuver himself. "Having realized that the wild animals had no king," he thrust himself forward, claiming to have been anointed by Indra, the king of the gods. The assembled animals prostrated themselves before him and addressed him as "master" (*svāmin,* PT 69.10). He established his credentials and exercised his royal prerogative by appointing various animals to official positions. Other expressions of sovereignty are apparent in his "enjoying the splendor of the kingdom" and apportioning among members of his retinue the prey that was delivered to him. All this is done "in accordance with lordly *dharma*" (PT 69.16), the disbursement of power (office) and wealth (food) being two key elements of sovereignty.

Here we have seen the jackal, the lowest of the low, usurp the highest position of authority. He moved from his "natural" position on the periphery of the social world to its epicenter. As we saw in the description of the *maṇḍala* above, "one alone occupies the position of *Siṃha*," and the *siṃha*, of course, can only ever be a lion.

Story 4-04 "Jackal Nursed by Lioness"

The indigo jackal, a social outcast and a member of a marginalized, peripheral *jāti*, intentionally and actively sought to subvert the "natural" order of things by assuming a more central position in the social *maṇḍala*. What is the role of individual volition or intention in this process? Is the intention to subvert the "natural" hierarchy the problem, or the subversion itself?

The indigo jackal tried to "become a lion" by assuming a central position of sovereignty. Story 4-04, "Jackal nursed by lioness," provides a second example of a jackal "becoming a lion," but in this case, the jackal achieved this effect incidentally by being adopted into a lion family. Everything that have I said about the peripheral status of the jackal in the preceding section also applies in this case:

> There was in a certain forest region a pair of lions. Now, one day, the lioness gave birth to two sons. The lion, having killed deer and so on always gave them to the lioness. Now, one day, wandering in the forest, when the Blessed Sun proceeded to its home among the peaks, the lion had found nothing. Now, while he was going to his own home, he found on the path a jackal cub. And thinking that it was only a cub, his compassion aroused, he gripped it between his teeth and, with care, having brought it alive, gave it to the lioness. And then the lioness said, "*Bhoḥ,* beloved! Have you brought me something to eat?" The lion said, "O beloved, today, except for this jackal cub, I found nothing. And thinking, 'He is of our own *jāti* and is an infant,' I did not kill it. . . . Now, having eaten it, be satisfied. In the morning I will bring you something else." She said, "Beloved, having thought 'It is an infant,' you did

> not kill it. Therefore how may I kill it for the sake of my own belly? . . . Therefore it will become my third son." Having spoken thus, she satisfied it fully with milk from her own teat. Thus the three young animals spent their childhood, mutually ignorant of the difference between their *jātis*, behaving and disporting themselves as one. Now, one day, there arrived a wild elephant wandering in that very forest. Having seen it, the two sons of lions were angered and desiring to kill it, drew near it. Then the son of the jackal said, "*Aho!* This elephant is the enemy of your family. Therefore do not approach it." Having spoken thus, he ran home. And the two, because of their elder brother's fear, grew faint-hearted. . . . Now, the two brothers arrived home, laughing, and told their parents about their elder brother's actions, in that having seen the elephant, he ran away a great distance. But [the jackal], having heard that, his mind filled with rage, his lower lip trembling, his eyes red, his brow knotted into three ridges, being ridiculed, spoke harshly to the two. Now, the lioness led him to one side and informed him, "Son, never speak like that. Those two are your brothers." Now he, filled with great anger by those conciliatory words, said to her, "Am I inferior to them in heroism, beauty, knowledge, learning or skill, that they may ridicule me? Therefore, I will certainly kill them." Having heard that, the lioness, desiring to preserve his life, having laughed inwardly, said, "You are a hero, you have acquired knowledge, you are handsome, son, but no elephant has been slain in the family into which you were born. Therefore, listen carefully, son. You are the son of a she-jackal, nourished by me, filled with pity, with milk from my own teat. Therefore, before these two sons of mine, because of their youth, realize that you are a jackal, go far away and live among those of your own *jāti*. Otherwise, struck down by them, you will take the path of death." And he, having heard that, his mind deeply terrified, slowly crept away and joined those of his own *jāti*.

I have already discussed in an earlier section the concept of the greater *jāti* that encompasses all those animals "armed with claws," that is, both jackals and lions in this case, and the question of the lions' and jackal's individual *jātis*. The issue here is that the jackal and lion cubs were suckled together and played together harmoniously, "mutually ignorant of the difference between their *jātis*" (PT 242.11), until the elephant appeared.

The "natural" enmity between lions and elephants is a common trope in Sanskrit literature. In the *Pañcatantra* alone, there are four battles between these rivals. In the *Ṛtusaṃhāra,* Kālidāsa refers to the "hostile disposition" (ṚS 1.27) that was supposed to exist between them. Other examples are found in the plastic arts: a Gandharan lid box from about the fifth century CE depicts a lion attacking an elephant (Lerner and Kossak 1991: 91–92), as does a ninth-century sandstone basement frieze from Gadarmal temple, Badoh, in Central India (Snead 1989: 81). Elsewhere in the *Pañcatantra,* this rivalry is mentioned by the mouse Hiraṇyaka in Story 2-00 as one of the paradigmatic "eternal" enmities "born of essential nature" (PT 131.7).

The sudden appearance of the elephant triggered an innate response in the lion cubs, a response conditioned by their *svabhāva:* they were impelled by some inborn leonine proclivity to attack it. The jackal, on the other hand, being of a different *jāti,* was not subject to the same impulses that the lion cubs experienced, and reacted very differently. In response to his own jackal *svabhāva,* his *śṛgālatvam,* he exercised discretion and ran away.

The one puzzling feature of the story is that the jackal said to the young lions that "This elephant is the enemy of your family" (PT 242.15). If the jackal were truly ignorant of the difference in their *jātis,* why did he say "your" instead of "our"? Nevertheless, the overriding sentiment of the story—the whole point of the story, in fact—is that they were of different *jātis,* but were ignorant of that fact.

The indigo jackal was undone by his essential nature, that immutable quality determined by his *jāti,* which irresistibly reasserted itself when he heard his fellows' ululations. The jackal suckled by the lioness was undone when his foster-brothers' lion-*svabhāva* came into play at the sight of the forest elephant, and they ran to attack it. At this moment, the illusion of unity and equality that existed among the siblings evaporated. The crisis came to a head when the lioness revealed the truth to the jackal: "No elephant has been slain in the family into which you were born." That is to say, the jackal's *jāti* lacked the power and prestige of the lion's, it was smaller, weaker, inferior, peripheral. The lioness' warning underscored the differences between the two animals. The jackal, though reared by a lion, was born of a jackal and remained at heart a jackal. The lioness urged it to seek out those of its own kind and live among them and it did so (PT 243.13–14). As we saw with the indigo jackal, this jackal's own *jāti*—his own kind—were his natural peers.

The lioness warned the jackal that as soon as the lion cubs realized that he was not of their own *jāti,* they would strike him down and kill him. As in the preceding story, and as we will see repeatedly in the examples that follow, such transgressive movements toward the center of the *maṇḍala* always fail. Unlike the indigo jackal, however, "lionhood" was thrust on the orphaned cub. His own volition played no role in his promotion; he did not actively seek out central status for himself, but was brought into the family by fate, through the agency of the male lion that found him in the forest. In answer to the question posed at the beginning of the section, it is not the "will to power" that is at issue, but the apparent impossibility of movement to more central positions. This principle is also at play in the following story.

Story 3-01 "Birds Elect a King"

The story of how the birds attempted to elect an owl as their king was told by the old crow counselor, Sthiravījin, to the crow-king, Meghavarṇa, in the frame of the third *tantra,* Story 3-00, "War of crows and owls." This story, which explains the perceived "natural" enmity that exists between the two species, is a mythical "just-so" explanation of the observable "mobbing" behavior exhibited by most birds in response to birds of prey. Story 3-01 hardly warrants recognition as a story in its own right, being an integral part of the frame-story's narrative, merely providing the "historical" background to the enmity between the two communities.

The story opens with an assembly of many flocks of birds, "including geese, cranes, cuckoos, peacocks, *cātakas,* owls, pigeons, turtledoves, partridges, blue jays, *bhāsas,* skylarks, *karāyikās, śyāmas* and woodpeckers" (PT 180.12–13). Together these various flocks constituted the society of birds ruled over by the bird-king, Garuḍa. That divine being, however, was preoccupied with his duties as Viṣṇu's attendant, and had become negligent in his duty of care toward his subjects. He had failed to protect those who were "afflicted by dangers of snares, entrapment, and so on" (PT 180.16–17). The society of birds decided to elect a new king, and selected for consecration an owl (PT 181.4). As the pretender sat waiting for the solemn ceremony to begin, a crow suddenly appeared and interrupted the proceedings (c.f. the interruption to the consecration of Rāma) with this pronouncement:

> *Bhoḥ!* This is improper. When these excellent geese, peacocks, cuckoos, partridge, shelduck, pigeons, cranes and the rest are available, it is my opinion that you should not consecrate this owl

> of terrible appearance, for: "Hooked bill, squinting eyes, cruel and unpleasant to behold—such is his visage when not angry. What will it be like when he is enraged?" Similarly: "Having made an owl king—whose essential nature is fierce, very terrifying and cruel, and whose cry is not pleasant—what advantage will come from it?" (PT 182.7–15)

The crow continued:

> Further, this base creature is wicked-souled, evil-minded and will be unable to protect his subjects. Not only will he fail to protect us, we should fear him. (PT 187.18–21)

And later,

> All the birds, having heard his words and having said, "[The crow] has spoken well," saying, "Having assembled again let us consult one another on the matter of the king," they departed as they had come. Only the owl, seated on the throne, awaiting consecration, sat there with the *kṛkālikā,* and he said, "Who is there? *Bhoḥ!* Why is the consecration not performed now?" Having heard this, the *kṛkālikā* said, "Good sir, the crow has taken steps to obstruct the consecration and the birds have gone in their preferred directions. Only that very crow alone for some reason remains here. Therefore stand up quickly so that I may lead you to your own abode." Having heard that, with despair, the owl said, "*Bho,* wicked-souled one! Because you interrupted the royal consecration, therefore, starting from now, there will be enmity between us." (PT 192.11–21)

According to Sanskritic tradition, owls can see in the dark but they are blind during the day. The image of the impotent, raging, blind owl-king, sitting on the throne, calls to mind that other blind king, Dhṛtarāṣṭra, whose reign also proved to be so ruinous. The enraged and humiliated owl left the scene with his sole attendant, a bird identifiable only as a *kṛkālikā*. With the departure of the owl, the historical hostility between the crows and owls was born. This enmity provides the background to the war between the two communities and is the subject of the frame-story of the third *tantra,* Story 3-00.

We have already touched on some of the cultural associations pertaining to the figure of the owl, but before we proceed to analyze this narrative, we will explore these in greater depth, just as we did for the jackal above. What preconceptions might audiences have brought to their understanding of this text? It seems that from the very earliest times, in the Sanskritic literary tradition, the owl has been the embodiment of malevolence. In the first verse of the following invocation to Indra and Soma from the *Ṛgveda,* a destructive female force transforms herself into some sort of nocturnal bird. In the second verse, *rākṣasas* take the form of night birds and threaten to disrupt the sacrifice:

> May she who wanders like an owl at night, hiding her body with guile, fall down into endless caverns. May the pressing-stones destroy the *rākṣasas* with their sounds. Spread out, O Maruts, search among the people. Seize and grind the *rākṣasas* who, having become birds, fly at night, who bring disruption to the divine sacrifice. (ṚV 7.104.17–18)

Later in that same invocation we read the following exhortation to destroy various malign forces (*yātu*): "Destroy the owl-fiend, the owlet-fiend, the dog-fiend and the wolf-fiend" (ṚV 7.104.22).

If owls are embodied *rākṣasas* and *yātus,* it is hardly surprising that their call is regarded as inauspicious. Or perhaps the reverse is the case: they were regarded as embodied fiends, because of the unearthly nature of their call. Some owls make a blood-curdling screech, not a benign hoot. In the following protective song, the call of the owl presages misfortune, possibly the sullying of the sacrifice suggested in ṚV 7.104.18 above. The reference to the pigeon stepping on or into the (sacrificial?) fire would support this interpretation. In any case, the prayer aims to prevent or counteract these inauspicious events:

> If the owl calls, may it be in vain, or if the pigeon steps on the fire. To the one who sent the messenger, to Yama, to Death, be homage! (ṚV 10.165.4)

The second interesting point here is the explicit reference to the owl as the messenger of Yama, who is Death personified. We saw above that the *Vedas* may not be recited when jackals are howling; a similar restriction applies in the case of owls. The *Āpastambadharmasūtra* requires that Vedic recitation be suspended when "dogs bark, donkeys bray, wolves or solitary jackals howl or owls call" (ĀD 1.10.19).

The inauspicious nature of the owl's call carries over into the epics. Cataclysmic events, such as defeat in battle, were heralded by their ominous cries: "And owls, unseen, were especially foretelling great terror of extreme harshness for the army of the Kauravas" (Mbh 7.129.15). Such turmoil in human society is often presaged by parallel "unnatural" events in the natural world of the epics. At the moment when disaster was about to descend on the Vṛṣṇis and the Andhakas toward the end of the *Mahābhārata,* the natural order of things—*ṛta*—was seriously disturbed: "cranes imitated the cry of owls and similarly goats imitated the call of jackals" (Mbh 16.3.5).

In Story 1-12, which I will discuss in some detail below, a goose received a visit from "death in the form of an owl" (PT 72.10–11). These closely related aspects of the owl's nature, first as the embodiment of malice, and second as the messenger or harbinger of death, find expression in the *Pañcatantra.* The "evil omen" (PT 73.17) of the owl's "discordant cry" (PT 73.16) led to the goose's death.

To supplement this textual evidence, we find supporting evidence in the realm of temple arts. In Kannauj, Uttar Pradesh, we find a representation of an "esoteric goddess (*yoginī*) on an owl" dating from about the first half of the eleventh century:

> Still feared in India, these goddesses are icons of an esoteric cult, and details of their worship were likely transferred orally from *guru* to initiate. Vidya Dehejia, in her recent study of the cult and its monuments, concludes that they are associated with the esoteric Śaiva Kaula sect, whose rites involved practices offensive to mainstream Hindu/Brahmanical society, such as drinking wine, eating flesh (human at times), and engaging in sexual intercourse leading toward the acquisition of occult powers. The *yoginīs* appear to have centred around Śiva, especially in his horrific form as Bhairava. . . . (Desai and Mason 1993: 190)

The owl's association with this wrathful deity is in accord with its inauspicious status at the periphery of the social *maṇḍala* that we have seen in the textual tradition. The appearance in this context of Bhairava is interesting, as we saw this same deity associated with jackals in the section above. It seems that the jackal, Śiva/Bhairava, this *yoginī* and the owl are linked by a chain of inauspicious associations.

In summary, then, owls may be seen in a broader cultural context as the embodiment of malignity. Their cry was regarded as inauspicious, they were associated with the disruption of the sacrifice and they were the harbingers of death.

Let us now reexamine Story 3-01 in the light of these associations. First, one puzzling aspect of the story is that the assembly of birds originally chose an owl of "pleasant countenance" (*bhadrākāram,* PT 181.4). This is surprising because, as we have seen, owls are invariably depicted in Sanskrit literature as both terrifying and ugly (see Story 3-00 in particular). Perhaps this device was employed by the creators of the *Pañcatantra* to highlight the naïveté and poor judgment of the assembled birds. Perhaps the point is that they, in their ignorance, regarded the owl as having a "pleasant countenance." They needed the crow, whom they recognized as "extremely intelligent among birds" (PT 181.19), to enlighten them.

In any case, the crow ridiculed their choice and described the owl as "one whose essential nature was fierce" (PT 182.14). The owl's innate ferocity rendered him unfit for sovereignty over the birds. A king should be the provider of protection—something Garuḍa was failing to do at that moment. The owl's *svabhāva* not only prevented him from protecting them; on the contrary, it made him their potential enemy. The crow swayed the assembly with his argument, and the consecration was aborted.

Owls may have been regarded as inauspicious and unwelcome, but how does their social standing compare with the jackal? The creators of the *Pañcatantra* made much of the fact that owls are "day-blind" (PT 192.9), in contrast to the other birds, who are said to be "night-blind" (PT 192.9). The distinction between day- and night-blindness, a literary expression of the owls' nocturnal habits, sets owls apart from the other *gaṇas* of birds. It makes them different; they are the "other," perhaps even at some primeval level at which the cultural matrix privileges day over night, light over dark. In any case, the above quote from the *Āpastambadharmasūtra* certainly locates owls among the outcastes and pariahs. Being mentioned in the same breath as dogs, donkeys, wolves, and jackals is suggestive of their peripheral status. Owls may be more powerful and more dangerous than jackals, but they are still on the outer edge of the *maṇḍala.*

The point of this narrative is not that the individual owl on the throne had particular characteristics that rendered him unfit for kingship: this is not about individuals or individual traits. The characteristics attributed to that individual are applicable the whole *gaṇa* of owls. Much is made of their "cruel" appearance and their curved bills, both of which are allusions to the fact that they are predatory and carnivorous. Owls catch and kill live prey: this is an observable biological fact. Here it is interpreted as their "nature." Owls as a *jāti* were unsuited to kingship because of their *svabhāva,* their perverse natures, their otherness, which is epitomized by their nocturnal habits and their "day-blindness." Their *svabhāva,* like that of the indigo jackal, relegates them to the periphery of the *maṇḍala,* and precludes them from ascending to the center of power.

Story 4-03 "Potter as Warrior"

In this story, we will observe what happens when another character of marginal social status approaches the center of the social *maṇḍala.* The story tells of a drunken potter, who tripped and fell on a sharp potsherd, which left a terrible scar on his forehead. Later, driven abroad by famine, he joined the retinue of a king. The king saw the formidable scar on the potter's forehead, and because such a scar is usually the mark of a hero who stands his ground, he assumed that the potter was warrior who had been wounded in battle (PT 240.16). The king honored him as a *kṣatriya* and showered him accordingly with favors and gifts, but in so doing aroused the jealousy of the other princes. One day, while reviewing his troops, the king had occasion to ask the man about his wound. The potter told the king the truth about his origins and how he had cut himself on a broken pot:

> Then the king reflected, "*Aho!* I have been deceived by this potter who is impersonating a prince. Therefore, he is to be seized by the throat." When that had been done, the potter said, "Your majesty, do not behave thus. Behold the swiftness of my hand in battle." The king said, "*Bhoḥ!* You are the abode of all qualities. But even so, you must be gone!" (PT 241.4–8)

To illustrate the point that the potter had no place among the warriors, the king told the above story of the adopted jackal (Story 4-04). There is a clear parallel between the potter and his tenuous position among the warriors and the jackal cub growing up with the lions. Both are inferiors among superiors, the adoptive positions of both are "unnatural" and unsustainable, and both are forced to withdraw. The king pressed home his point:

> "Therefore, before these soldiers learn that you are a potter, be gone as swiftly as possible. Otherwise, having earned their scorn,

> you will die." And the potter, having heard that, left in haste. (PT 243.17–19)

What is the "traditional" social status of the potter? The earliest reference that I have been able to find is in the *Taittirīyasaṃhita.* A song of homage to Rudra contains a list of occupations: doorkeepers and charioteers, carpenters and makers of chariots, potters (*kulāla*) and smiths, *puñjiṣṭa* and *niṣādas* (TS 4.5.4.8–15). The last two groups are slightly problematic; they are glossed respectively by MMW as "fisherman, birdcatcher," and "N[ame] of a wild non-Āryan tribe in India (described as hunters, fishermen, robbers, etc.)." This list certainly suggests that potters are in lowly company, as we know from elsewhere that at least the charioteers, smiths, and barbarians are all, to varying degrees, beyond the pale. It has been said elsewhere that "The unclean *shudras,* such as the potters and the tanners and the outcastes, were not permitted to enter the precincts of the temple, since their presence would pollute it" (Thapar 1966: 189).

Before the *svayaṃvara* of Draupadī, the five Pāṇḍava brothers, on arriving at Drupada's capital, took up residence in the house of a potter and adopting the lifestyle of ascetics, they lived on alms. "Nobody recognized those heroes who had arrived" (Mbh 1.176.6–7). Again, this does not prove conclusively that potters were peripheral, but if the Pāṇḍava, disguised as wandering mendicants, wished to remain incognito, then staying in the house of low social status would not attract unwanted attention.

This external evidence suggests that potters constituted at least a moderately low social grouping, somewhere toward the edge of the social *maṇḍala.* The internal evidence of the tale itself confirms this: for the story to make sense, the potter must be inferior to the warriors with whom he is confused. The fact that the king drew a comparison between the jackal among the lion cubs and the potter among the warriors suggests that the potter may be lumped together with the other outcastes. The potter and jackal are tarred with the same brush.

The king mistook the potter for a warrior, but nowhere in this narrative is it stated explicitly that the potter tried to pass himself off as a *kṣatriya* or that the king mistook him for a one. But the words used in this story, *vīra, yuddhṛ,* and *rājaputra,* all have such strong *kṣatriya* connotations that it is hard to imagine that "traditional" audiences would not bring such cultural associations to their reading. We cannot say with certainty that this is an example of a *śūdra* masquerading as a *kṣatriya,* but we can say that a member of a group located toward the periphery of the social *maṇḍala* moved or was caused to move toward a position closer to its center. The king warned the potter that if the princes learned of his lowly origins, he would certainly be killed. The potter's centripetal movement from a peripheral group to a more central one would result in his death. In the event, the king, who respected the potter's military prowess, permitted him to escape with his life.

This story is another example of how individuals' social standing is determined by their birth. The potter cannot become a warrior, because he is by his very nature a potter. Possessing the external attributes of warriorhood—the scar and the acknowledged prowess—he was able to act like a warrior for a short while, but ultimately he could never become that which he was not. Like the indigo jackal and the adopted cub in the preceding stories, the potter's *svabhāva* was fixed and immutable, as was his peripheral social position. It is unnatural, unthinkable, impossible, and undesirable that any of these could be changed as the result of volition.

Story 4-07 "Ass in Tiger Skin"

In this well-known story, a laundryman, wishing to provide fodder for his donkey at no expense to himself, draped a tiger skin over its back, and set it free each night to graze in a field of corn. One evening the donkey heard a she-ass braying in the distance and answered her. The owners of the field, realizing the beast's true nature, promptly beat it to death.

Let us begin our discussion with an exploration of the cultural connotations that the figure of the donkey might bring to this context. There are some references to donkeys with neutral or even positive associations in the earliest texts. In the *Ṛgveda,* for example, the donkey is mentioned as a draught animal (ṚV 1.162.21, 3.53.23). Paradoxically, the Aśvins' chariot was drawn by donkeys (ṚV 1.34.9, 1.116.2), a curious choice for those who "possess horses." A hundred donkeys are mentioned as a gift (ṚV 8.56.3), and much later, ten thousand donkeys are part of a tributary presentation in the *Mahābhārata* (Mbh 2.47.21).

Yet donkeys are attended more frequently with negative associations than with positive ones. They are mentioned in the same breath as dogs, worms, insects, jackals, and carnivorous animals in various contexts in the *Manusmṛti* (MS 2.201, 11.200). Any contact with a donkey or its "by-products" is polluting. It is an offense for a *brāhmaṇa* to ride a donkey or to ride in a carriage drawn by one (MS 11.202). Because donkeys are unsuitable for riding, it is doubly inappropriate that a *brāhmaṇa* would recite the *Vedas* while mounted on one (MS 4.120). The urine and, as the Victorian translations quaintly put it, ordure, of a donkey are classed with those of the pig, camel, jackal, monkey, and crow in terms of their capacity to pollute (MS 11.155). While the dust raised by carriages, horses, elephants, grain, and cows is auspicious, the dust kicked up by donkeys (and brooms, dogs, goats, sheep, and garments) is impure (BD 2.6.34).

Direct or indirect contact with a donkey is polluting for a ritually pure person, but donkeys and particularly their skins also seem to have been used as external significations of the guilt of a variety of transgressors. For example, a woman who sexually abused a young girl was forced to ride on a donkey (MS 8.370). A man who unjustly abandoned his wife was required to wear a donkey's skin with the hairy side out and beg from seven houses for six months (ĀD 1.28.19). An abortionist also had to wear the skin of a dog or a donkey with the hairy side out (ĀD 1.28.21). A student who had broken a vow of chastity had to sacrifice a donkey to Nirṛti and wear its skin for a year (GD 23.17–19).

The polluting influences of the donkey are not restricted to direct contact. Even indirect contact, for example, hearing a donkey, was inauspicious. From the very early times, braying has had exclusively negative associations. The twenty-ninth song of the *Ṛgveda* contains the following supplication: "O Indra, destroy the ass that is braying in such a discordant way" (ṚV 1.29.5). The word *pāpa,* which I have rendered as "discordant," is semantically rich: MMW gives the following gloss: "bad, vicious, wicked, evil, wretched, vile, low, . . . boding evil, inauspicious." Without overtranslating the word, it is tempting to think that the braying was regarded as inauspicious even in Vedic times. Those who "bray like donkeys" are mentioned in the context of night-wanderers, eaters of flesh and bone, and those who cause abortions in the *Atharvaveda* (AV 8.6.10). As we saw above, Vedic recitation is suspended when donkeys bray (MS 4.115, ĀD 1.10.19). In the epics, the preternatural braying of donkeys is not an uncommon omen presaging the onset of a battle:

> And the sky grew red and was [filled with] cries of donkeys, wild animals and birds. Everything was covered in darkness. One could discern nothing. (Mbh 3.153.5)

Śisupāla, the Cedi king who was killed by Kṛṣṇa Vāsudeva, was born with three eyes and four arms. At birth he brayed like a donkey and called out (Mbh 2.40.1), echoing the inauspicious circumstances attending Duryodhana's delivery.

One final piece of evidence on the inauspicious nature of the donkey's braying is etymological: the primary meaning of one of the many words for donkey, *khara*, is glossed in MMW as "hard, harsh, rough, sharp." In this sense, *khara* also means "harsh-voiced."

As we have seen, all the "by-products" of a donkey—urine, dung, touch, and sound—are inauspicious, but even in the absence of these, the donkey's malign disembodied presence foretells disaster: "Clouds resembling ruddy donkeys with rainbows and lightning, having filled the sky, rained down flesh and blood" (Mbh 14.76.19). A similar passage in which donkey-shaped clouds rained down unpleasant substances is found the *Rāmāyaṇa* (3.21.26–3.22.1).

How are donkeys treated in the *kathā* literature? Two of the asses in the *Pañcatantra* are explicitly associated with laundrymen: one in this story and another in Story 4-02 "Ass without heart and ears." As mentioned above, it is risky to take nineteenth-century opinions on the hierarchy of castes too seriously, but here is an interesting observation on laundrymen: "There are several castes in the Tamil country considered to be lower than the *Pariahs, e.g.* the caste of shoemakers, and the lowest caste of washermen" (Yule and Burnell 1968 [1886]: 678). The peripheral status of the laundrymen and that of the donkey with whom they are associated seem to reinforce one another.

The braying of the donkey is a theme shared by three *kathā* tales: this one, Story 5-05 "Ass as singer" and a tale in the *Hitopadeśa* in which a donkey refused to raise the alarm when a burglar appeared (Hit. 1024ff). In the first two narratives, braying led directly to the donkey's death or punishment. In the third, the animal should have brayed to warn of the intrusion, but failed to do so. In this case, its silence caused its demise.

We can see from the above that donkeys, and particularly their braying, have inauspicious associations in the cultural milieu in which these texts are situated. These associations also position donkeys toward the periphery of the social *maṇḍala*. In this respect, they differ little from their traditional masters, the outcaste laundrymen.

The child-molesters, absconders, abortionists, and randy students mentioned above took upon themselves the impurity of the donkey when they donned its skin as punishment. In the same way, when the laundryman in this tale cloaked the donkey in the tiger skin, it adopted some aspects of the tiger's status—its ferocity, strength, prestige, reputation, and, I suggest, its centrality. In both cases, the wearing of the skin conferred the characteristics of the skin's original owner on the wearer. The wearer became at once physically cloaked with the external attributes of the skin, and at the same time ritually or metaphorically cloaked in the intangible associations of the "peripherality" or centrality that the skin conferred.

What happened to the donkey once it took on the external manifestation and the intangible associations of the tiger? In this genre, tigers and lions represent similar things: power, ferocity, carnivorousness, and so on, and the distinction between the two species is not always clear. For example, in one manuscript of the *Hitopadeśa* (Dhano, *Hitopadeśa*, British Library shelfmark Or. 13934), a narrative that features lions is illustrated with pictures of tigers. Doniger makes the interesting point that tigers replaced lions in iconography as the latter became relatively scarce in India (Snead 1989: 11). Although the tiger does not enjoy the sovereignty that is conferred on lions, they appear to occupy a similarly central position in the social *maṇḍala.*

I suggest that the inauspicious and peripheral donkey, in taking on the physical appearance and attributes of the tiger, moved to a position of greater centrality, a position of power and prestige that inspired fear in the owners of the field. Taking advantage of this skin-deep manifestation of centrality, the donkey was able to graze in peace. On the appearance of the she-ass, however, the donkey's *svabhāva* reasserted itself, and its "true nature" was revealed. Its prestige slipped away as easily as the tiger's pelt. This infraction, which I suggest constitutes a centripetal movement from the periphery to the center, led to the animal's demise: it was "killed with blows from sticks, stones and arrows" (PT 248.5–6).

In addition to the shared pattern of centripetal movement that characterizes all the stories discussed in this section, there are several interesting parallels between this and the story of the indigo jackal. First, neither character exercised any volition to achieve its centrality: the jackal fell by accident into the vat of dye and the donkey was involuntarily clad in the pelt by the laundryman. Second, both achieved centrality through a change in their "skin," that is, their external appearance. Third, having moved toward the center, both benefited from the concomitant power and prestige: the beasts of prey brought fresh meat to the jackal and the donkey had as much grain as it could eat. Fourth, each was inevitably tied to its own kind by sound: the jackal heard his fellows howling; the donkey heard the she-ass braying. In both cases, the sounds of members of their own *jāti* resulted in the resurgence of the individual's *svabhāva* and the unraveling of their pretences.

In the end, it was impossible for the indigo jackal and the other peripheral characters above to occupy more central positions. Similarly, the donkey could never truly "become" a tiger, even though it could temporarily acquire the superficial appearance and attributes of power. The donkey's essentially base nature precluded it from any position of greater centrality.

Summary

In this section I have attempted to show how individuals' stations at birth determine their position in the social *maṇḍala.* The jackals, owls, and donkeys in these stories all belong to specific *jātis,* or in the case of the potter, to a specific *varṇa.* As we have seen, all individuals of a given *jāti* share a generic *svabhāva.* The creators of the *Pañcatantra* drew on a specific vocabulary of hoary cultural stereotypes. In each of these four cases above, the individuals' essential natures render them peripheral, inauspicious, or contaminating. The jackal, in particular, shared many characteristics with the outcaste/outcast *caṇḍāla.* Because of their *svabhāva,* centripetal movements toward the locus of power were not just undesirable, but were unnatural, unthinkable, and impossible. These themes are clearly summarized in the following verse:

> Even without wealth a steadfast person touches a lofty state with many honors. Even if surrounded by wealth, a pitiable person will be in the power of another. Even if it wears a crown of gold, a dog never achieves the lion's dignity, which is born of its own nature and has abundant attainments of the aggregate of qualities. (PT 154.27–30)

The dignity of powerful, central individuals is said to be innate. It "is born of their own natures" and it arises from their *svabhāva.* No matter how one dresses up an inferior or peripheral character, it will never achieve central status.

These stories are obviously not written to provide social advice to jackals or owls: the animal characters are metaphors for human agents ("the steadfast person," "the pitiable person"), and animal *jātis* function, I suggest, as metaphors for social groups. This discourse implies that just as the natural world is divided into *jātis,* so is the human world divided into groups, some of which are "naturally" inauspicious and peripheral. The implications of the discourse of division are unambiguous: like the jackal, owl, and ass, members of peripheral social groups, because of their low birth and because of their very natures, are unfitted to approach, let alone occupy, the center of the social *maṇḍala.* We will return to consider this proposition in detail at a later point.

Enmity/Amity

We have now seen how one's birth determines one's essential nature and fixes one's position in society. We will now examine the role of the *jāti* in determining "natural" enmity (*svabhāvavaira*) and its counterpart "natural" amity. We will begin with an overview of the concept of enmity as it is expressed in the *Pañcatantra*. This will be followed by a study of the fraught relationship between meat-eaters and grass-eaters, which is a specific subset of the relationship between predators and their prey in general. I will also discuss some "natural enmities" that do not center on predation. I will conclude this section by examining the implications of enmity and amity for our reading of the indigo jackal.

The Concept of "Natural Enmity"

How is the concept of "natural enmity" (*svabhāvavaira, sahajavaira*) used in the *Pañcatantra*? The most comprehensive treatment of this term is found in the frame-story of the second *tantra*. Here the crow Laghupaṭanaka was keen to embark on a friendship with the mouse Hiraṇyaka, but the latter was reluctant, thinking that crows and mice in general were subject to a "natural enmity." His reasoning was as follows:

> There are two types of enmity, natural and incidental. . . . "Incidental enmity instantly comes to an end through incidental kindness. Natural enmity ends only with death." . . . Incidental enmity is produced by particular causes. Therefore it may be removed by rendering appropriate friendly service. However, natural [enmity] never abates. This is the eternal enmity between the mongoose and the snake, grass-eaters and those armed with claws, water and fire, the *devas* and the *daityas,* dogs and cats, mutual rivals, lions and elephants, hunters and wild animals, crows and owls, the wise and the foolish, chaste and unchaste women, and good and bad people.[7] (PT 131.2–11)

The mouse described this inborn hostility as being *sahaja,* meaning "accompanying birth," or as MMW puts it, "congenital, innate, hereditary, original, natural." It is significant that inborn hostility is also described as *svābhāvikaṃ* (PT 131.7), which means "arising from or related to one's *svabhāva.*" That is to say, innate enmities such as these are an attribute of an individual's *svabhāva,* and as we saw above, *svabhāva* is common to all members of a given *jāti.* For this reason the entire *jāti* of lions is hostile to elephants, the *jāti* of the mongoose will always attack snakes, and so on. Innate hostility is not just a characteristic of a few individuals; it is a generalized phenomenon that may be observed in all members of a given *jāti.*

These enmities form a major trope in the *Pañcatantra.* For example, when the mongoose in Story 5-01 saw a cobra approaching a sleeping infant, he instantly recognized the snake as his "natural enemy" (*svabhāvavairiṇaṃ,* PT 260.12–13), and killed it. The elephant in Story 4-04 "Jackal nursed by lioness" was identified as the lions' "family enemy" (*kulaśatruḥ,* PT 242.15). He was their "natural," traditional, hereditary foe. In Story 1-27, the crab recognized the heron as "the natural enemy of our *jāti*" (PT 112.4–5). The cobra was the "great enemy" of the crows in Story 1-05.[8] (PT 35.23)

These enmities play an important role in many stories in the *Pañcatantra,* and provide a static, background hostility against which the drama of individual narratives is played out. For the purpose of this inquiry, the relationships of most interest are not those in which a "traditional" enmity is taken for granted and is played out to its "natural," logical conclusion, but those relationships which are attempted *despite* the existence of such an enmity. In these cases, individuals attempt to form transgressive relationships across such "natural" divides, such as that which is supposed to exist between predators and their prey, and to which we will now turn.

Meat-Eaters and Grass-Eaters

Story 1-00 "Lion and Bull"

In this story, a jackal called Damanaka, being the scion of a family of ministers, but holding no office, sought to ingratiate himself with the lion-king Piṅgalaka. He planned to win the lion's favor by encouraging his friendship with a bull named Saṃjīvaka, but when the blossoming relationship proved to be disadvantageous for the jackal, he changed tack and conspired to wreck it. For our purposes, the nature of the relationship between the lion and the bull is of central interest. Let us begin with Saṃjīvaka himself. The story starts with a lengthy virtuoso description of the bull's city of origin:

> In the southern lands was a city called Mahilāropya, vying with the city of Indra, endowed with all good qualities, forming the di-

> adem-jewel for the earth and resembling the summit of Mt Kailāsa. Its gates and watchtowers were filled with various machines, weapons and carriages. Its gates, vast as Mt Indrakīla, were furnished with broad doors, tall arched portals and stout crossbeams. Its many temples were situated on well-planned intersections and squares. It was encompassed by a ring of ramparts resembling in appearance the serried Himālaya, accompanied by moats. (PT 3.4–8)

This is more than a stereotypical flourish with which Sanskrit authors liked to begin their compositions and with which they displayed their mastery of the language. This highly idealized and poetic description provides more than an imaginary geographical setting for the narrative. The city is fine, beautiful, and ultimately civilized. Even its name, Mahilāropya, "to be ascended by women," exudes an air of genteel sophistication. In my mind, any bull that hails from such a wonderful place becomes imbued with its qualities. The beauty, sophistication, and urbanity of the city—its civilization—are assimilated by all its citizens, human and animal alike. Saṃjīvaka is described as being an auspicious bull, having the appearance of a white cloud, with golden bells adorning his chest (PT 3.25–26). Even his name, meaning "vivifying" or "animating," is alive with positive associations.

From that fine city, a merchant called Vardhamāna set out on a trading mission to Mathura with Saṃjīvaka in his caravan. While passing through a forest, the bull sank into a muddy bog and injured his leg, whereupon the merchant "descended into deepest despondence" (PT 4.6). The caravan waited for five days, but as the bull had not recovered, the merchant ordered his men to stay behind, and if the bull died, they were to cremate its remains. But the carters, fearing the forest, falsely reported that the Saṃjīvaka had perished. The merchant "was pained for a moment, and having performed funerary rites with a sense of gratitude, reached Mathura without obstruction" (PT 4.12–13). The man's emotions for the bull—sadness, respect, and gratitude—even to the extent of arranging a funeral for it, were similar to those one might feel for a fellow human. Just as the city "rubbed off" on it, the bull's relationship with the merchant serves to emphasize his genteel, urban, urbane, and civilized nature.

The bull eventually recovered from its injury and proceeded to the banks of the Yamunā River:

> There, eating the tips of grass-shoots as green as emerald, in a few days, he grew as fat, humped and strong as the bull of Śiva. Every

> day he remained there tearing up anthills with blows of the tips of his horns like an elephant. (PT 4.15–17)

The narrator does not merely allude to the bull's herbivorous nature, but stresses it with the luxuriant set-phrase describing his fodder. Thus, Saṃjīvaka, the grazing bull, a character drawn against an ornate background of the city of Mahilāropya and the merchant Vardhamāna, a creature of civilization, his strength recovered, now reached that liminal surface, the riverbank, the interface between civilization and wilderness, where creatures of the wild and civilized worlds come together to drink, and inevitably, to interact.

Just as the rich description of the city seemed to highlight the civilized nature of the bull, the description of the forest provides an untamed, threatening and violent environment for the lion:

> fascinating with its *dhava*, *khadira*, *palāśa* and *śāla* trees; densely provided with other trees of pleasant appearance; extraordinarily frightening on account of its many elephants, wild oxen, buffalo, deer, yaks, boar, tigers, leopards and bears; having various caves and abysses filled with waters which came forth from the mountain slopes. (PT 3.26–4.1)

The lion, the arch-carnivore who ruled over this wilderness, came down to the banks of the Yamunā to drink. At this point, the text provides a long and detailed description of the lion's rule, with a particular emphasis on his untrammeled, unadorned, natural lordliness. For our purposes, the following verse is of particular interest, as it accentuates the difference in the natures of the two protagonists:

> The lion, which always eats the flesh of the elephant slowly dripping ichor, lacking the food it desires, does not eat grass. (PT 5.7–8)

In spite of all this magnificent lordliness, when the lion heard the unfamiliar bellowing of the bull in the distance, he was terrified. (Remember that the bull was tearing up anthills "like an elephant" and remember too the traditional hostility between these *jātis*.) Concealing his feelings, he accepted the jackal's offer to investigate.

We have before us a picture of the urbane, sophisticated grass-eating bull and the rude, vigorous lion, sovereign of the forest, who is above all a carnivore. Let us now turn to the relationship that developed between them. The jackal, seeing the bull, devised a means to further his own position by fostering and then destroying a relationship between the two: "*Aho!* Good fortune has befallen! By means of an alliance and a battle with this [bull], Piṅgalaka will come under my influence" (PT 14.29–30). To achieve these ends, as we shall see, the jackal exploited their "natural" latent enmity.

The bull prudently requested a guarantee of safe conduct before consenting to approach the lion. The jackal won such a guarantee from the lion, and suggested to Piṅgalaka that "with fraternal love, you should pass the time together eating, drinking, working, playing and residing with him" (PT 16.10–11). The jackal further cultivated feelings of mutual admiration between the two by falsely representing the lion as the mount of Caṇḍikā (Durgā) and the bull as Śiva's attendant, Nandin. He told the lion that the bull had said "I was directed by the Great Lord, satisfied by me, to graze on grass near the Yamunā River. Why say more? The Blessed One gave me this forest for me to play in" (PT 16.5–7).

Assuming that the bull enjoyed divine protection, the lion now thought he understood how such a defenseless animal could survive in the wilderness unmolested: "Grass-eaters cannot wander without fear in this desolate forest bellowing thus, were it not for the grace of a god" (PT 16.7–8). Note how the bull's herbivorous nature is emphasized in both these passages. Finally, the two meet:

> Saṃjīvaka, having bowed to [the lion] with reverence, stood before him with decorum. Piṅgalaka raised his strong, round, long, right paw ornamented with claws that resembled diamonds, and, having honored him, said, "Are you prospering? Why do you live in a remote forest?" When asked thus, Saṃjīvaka told of his own separation from the merchant just as it had happened. And having heard that, Piṅgalaka said, "Friend, do not fear. Live as you wish in this forest protected by my limbs. Further, you must always enjoy yourself near me, because there are many dangers in the forest as it abounds with many fierce animals." (PT 21.14–20)

Thus began the friendship of the bull and the lion. Let us now examine the impacts that the relationship had on the two participants and on the members of the lion's retinue:

> Thus the time passed for the two of them, enjoying deepest mutual affection. Saṃjīvaka, who had attained intellectual proficiency

> through the study of many *śāstras,* in a few days, made Piṅgalaka wise, even though he had been simple-minded. Having been caused to abandon the way of the forest, he was enjoined to the ways of civilization. Why say more? Every day, Saṃjīvaka and Piṅgalaka did nothing but confer together. All the other subject creatures stood by at a distance. Not even the two jackals could obtain an audience.[9] Further, owing to the lion's lack of fortitude, all the subject animals and the two jackals, afflicted by hunger and disease, having assembled in one place, remained there. (PT 21.24–22.2)

This is a serious turn of events. The effete, educated bull from the city has effectively emasculated the lion. Piṅgalaka, as the jackals complained to one another, "has become fond of the words of Saṃjīvaka and has become negligent towards his own responsibilities" (PT 22.17–18). The heart of the issue lies in the statement that the lion, "having been caused to abandon the ways of the forest (*araṇyadharma*), was enjoined to the ways of civilization (*grāmadharma*)." One key aspect of *araṇyadharma* is the hunt. Under the influence of the bull, the lion gave up hunting, with the result that there was nothing for his retinue to eat. The lion's neglect of his kingly duties as provider and protector caused the breakdown of the forest society. Hunger bred discontent.

The ultimate incompatibility between the bull and the lion was a point of contention between the two jackals as they tried to decide on a course of action. Karaṭaka rebuked Damanaka with the words, "Because you brought the grass-eater and the master together, you were carrying embers in your bare hands [i.e., you brought this problem upon yourself]" (PT 22.25). Complaining about their master's new lifestyle, one jackal remarked to the other that the lion "generally behaves according to the ways of a grass-eater" (PT 34.21–22). It is significant that the jackals stressed the grass-eating nature of the bull. The close association between the grass-eating bull and the carnivorous lion perverted the normal "ways of the forest," and as the lion was behaving like a grass-eater himself and forsook his kingly *dharma,* forest society was on the brink of collapse.

We have now gone full circle from the perfect lion who "always eats the flesh of the elephant slowly dripping ichor, [and who], lacking the food it desires, does not eat grass" to one who "generally behaves according to the ways of a grass-eater."

The jackal Damanaka now resolved to put into action the second part of his scheme: to further enhance his position by driving a wedge between the lion and the bull (PT 34.22–23). He achieved this by means of a simple ruse based on his superior knowledge of the "natural enmity" that existed between them. He merely fanned that latent hostility: first, he told the lion that the bull was planning to kill him and seize his kingdom (PT 58.8). The lion lurched between rage and incredulity:

> Piṅgalaka said, "He is a grass-eater; we are meat-eaters. How can he do me any harm?" Damanaka said, "It is so; he is a grass-eater. Your majesty is a meat-eater. He is food. Your majesty is his devourer." (PT 65.28–30)

Ultimately, under the constant goading of the jackal and in spite of his initial misgivings, the lion resolved to kill the bull. In the meantime, the jackal had falsely informed Saṃjīvaka that Piṅgalaka intended to kill him to feed his retinue. The bull lamented, "Alas! *Bhoḥ!* Alas! How inappropriate for me, a grass-eater, to have an association with a meat-eating lion!" (PT 74.14). Saṃjīvaka and Piṅgalaka met and fought a battle (PT 100.7ff), from which the lion finally emerged as victor (PT 123.27ff). There ensued bitter remorse on the part of the lion and vehement disagreement between the two jackals. Damanaka assured the doubting lion that he had acted appropriately, but Karaṭaka harangued Damanaka for his perceived treachery. Karaṭaka had the last word, however, that the death of Saṃjīvaka was cruel, unwarranted and treacherous.[10]

The members of Piṅgalaka's retinue could not survive without the food provided by the lion, and the lion having adopted the "ways of a grass-eater" had given up hunting. The friendship between the bull and the lion was unsustainable. The text suggests that the death of Saṃjīvaka was cruel, but at a deeper level the subtext endorses it. How else was the forest community to sustain itself? How could it survive without food? It could not tolerate the disruptive, unnatural relationship between the urbane bull and the wild lion. The text leaves us hanging: we are unsure if Piṅgalaka was reconciled to the death of Saṃjīvaka, or whether he accepted Damanaka back into his fold. Yet the subtext is complete. With the death of the bull, the existential equilibrium in the forest was restored. The transgressive and unnatural relationship between the denizens of civilization and the wilderness, between herbivore and carnivore, was annulled. The lion endured great remorse on the loss of the erstwhile friend:

> With his paws smeared with gore, under the sway of the memory of their former affection, having wiped his eyes which were wet with tears of pity, filled with great regret, he spoke these words, "Oh,

> Alas! Great is this misdeed, for Saṃjīvaka, like my own second self, has been killed. I have harmed only myself." (PT 123.27–29)

How are we to interpret this story? One possibility is to read it as a story of broken *rājadharma:* the lion failed in his kingly duties, he permitted his subjects to go hungry, and the social order crumbled. Another approach is to view it in terms of *varṇa.* The lion, a king and therefore perhaps representing the *kṣatriya,* grew too close to the bull, a *brāhmaṇa* (white, auspiciously marked, knowledgeable in many *śāstras,* able to enlighten the dull lion-king, just as Viṣṇuśarman educated the three dull princes). But surely such a relationship had been culturally sanctioned since the earliest times. Where is a king without a *guru* or a *purohita?* Or is the bull representative of the *vaiśyas,* like his master, the merchant Vardhamāna? Is the text warning against the excessive influence of a *vaiśya* on a *kṣatriya?* In contrast, we have several examples of merchants who make exemplary royal ministers (e.g., Story 1-03, "Merchant and king's sweep"). With reference to this and similar tales, Olivelle identified:

> an underlying sociological principle: there are some groups in society that are naturally predatory, while others are by nature prey; and there can be no association, alliance or friendship . . . between them. (Olivelle 2002a: 101)

But which classes are predators and which are prey?

> The Vedic texts repeatedly call the Brahmins and especially the Kṣatriyas—that is, the unified upper crust of society consisting of the priestly and political powers—the eaters, and the Vaiśyas and the Śūdras—that is, the commoner and working classes—the food. (Olivelle 2002a: 107)

May we equate the meat-eating lion of this story with the *brāhmaṇas* and *kṣatriyas,* and the bull with the "commoner and working classes"? In one sense it is true that the "upper crust" live off the other groups—it is they who ultimately produce the agricultural surplus, which is offered up as *dakṣiṇā* and taxes. But it seems to me that the lion makes a very poor *brāhmaṇa* and the bull with his brahmanical attributes an even worse commoner. It is difficult to find a satisfactory one-to-one correspondence between the meat-eaters, grass-eaters and any particular groups within society.

In any case, there is a different way of approaching this question. The above analysis strikes difficulties because we are attempting to view the relationship between the bull and the lion in terms of a one-to-one correspondence between the animals' *jātis* and the *varṇas* of human society, or because we are looking for a natural hierarchy—who is superior: bull or lion, grass-eater or meat-eater, predator or prey? But if we set aside the linear and vertically arrayed hierarchy and return to the concept of a multidimensional, spatially arranged social *maṇḍala,* a new interpretation becomes possible. Only one further adjustment is required, and it is, admittedly, a challenging one: we need to set aside the equivalence of carnivorousness and kingship. This is difficult because the paradigmatic meat-eater in this genre is always the lion and he is also the paradigmatic king. But it is certainly not the case that every carnivore is a king—far from it—the jackals, leopards, wolves, and so on are all of varying, inferior status.

In the story of the lion and the bull, neither beast is more or less auspicious than the other. Both were auspicious in their own way: the bull bore "auspicious marks"; the lion displayed all the attributes of ideal, unfettered sovereignty. The lion was more powerful and was able to kill the bull. The bull, "knowledgeable in many *śāstras,*" was also powerful in his way, as *rājaguru.* This brings us to that old Indological chestnut: Who is superior, *kṣatriya* or *brāhmaṇa?* Temporal or spiritual authority? This question is ultimately unanswerable, but is the wrong question in any case. This story need not be viewed in terms of auspiciousness or power. We can see here the interplay of difference and incompatibility.

This brings us to my main contention: meat-eaters and grass-eaters are simply a way of representing two different, incompatible groups. Let us think of them as open, undefined, but mutually distinct and incompatible. We see the discourse of division manifesting in a new and different light: according to my reading, in these stories the *Pañcatantra* merely confirm that society is divided into groups, just as "naturally" as the animal world is divided into meat-eaters and grass-eaters. Some (not all) of these groups are natural, distinct, mutually exclusive, and fundamentally incompatible. The Vedic dichotomy between *grāmya* and *āraṇyaka* cannot be overstepped: there is an unbridgeable division between them. The bull died as the result of an impossible, unsustainable cross-*jāti* relationship with the lion. That is not to say that mutually beneficial relationships across *jāti* divides cannot occur: the second *tantra* illustrates just such a fruitful collaboration. The discourse of division holds that society is naturally divided, and that some sections of society are naturally inimical to the interests of others. When individuals fail to recognize this, and attempt to form relationships with those who are, by their very nature, hostile to their interests, they will fail. The discourse shapes narratives like this one to prove that such relationships are impossible.

Story 1-13 "Lion's Retainers Outwit Camel" and Story 1-21 "Jackal Outwits Camel and Lion"

In the preceding section, I attempted to show how the abortive relationship between the carnivorous lion and the herbivorous bull might be read as a metaphor for the division of societies into analogous irreconcilable, incompatible sectors. In the next section I will continue to explore this theme in two closely related narratives, Story 1-13 "Lion's retainers outwit camel" and Story 1-21 "Jackal outwits camel and lion." There are many obvious parallels between these stories and Story 1-00 "Lion and bull" (see, e.g., Olivelle 2002a: 102). Superficially, both deal with a jackal's cleverness in tricking a naive camel into offering itself as food for an incapacitated lion. For our purposes, it will be fruitful to examine the relationship between the camel and the lion, and we will begin by examining what the text reveals about the nature of the camel.

In the first story, a camel set out from a certain city with a caravan, but collapsed under the excessive weight of its load while passing through a wilderness. The master of the caravan, thinking that the forest was dangerous, abandoned it. The camel survived and soon recovered its strength. Thus the animal's origin in the city, its association with humans, its "otherness" in the dangerous wilderness, and its herbivorous habits—its *grāmya* nature, in short—clearly divide it from the wild animals in the forest.

How did the forest animals react to the intruder? Its comical form was previously unknown to them, and its appearance in the forest was unprecedented (PT 76.4–5). The lion commanded the crow to find out about the intruder, and the crow returned with the information that "It is a called a camel in the world" (*uṣṭro 'yaṃ loke prakhyātanāmā,* PT 76.6). Now, *loke* probably means "in popular speech," or "in common language" in this context, but could also be rendered as "in the world of men." Certainly from the point of view of the forest animals, the camel was "other." Nevertheless, when it recounted the tale of its separation from the caravan, the lion, who "understood the conferring of kindness" (PT 76.8), granted it a guarantee of safe conduct, and the camel joined the lion's retinue. There are many obvious parallels between this and the story of the lion and the bull above.

The lion was subsequently injured in a fight with an elephant, and as he could not hunt, his retinue grew hungry. When the jackal suggested to the lion that they should kill and eat the camel, the lion was outraged and cited the guarantee of safety (PT 77.9–13). The jackal, undeterred, persuaded the lion that if the camel were to offer itself voluntarily, then it would not be considered a misdeed to kill it (PT 77.20). The lion half-heartedly concurred.

All four animals then came before the lion, and the crow offered his own body as sustenance for his master, but the jackal intervened, citing a prohibition against eating crow flesh, and offered himself instead. The leopard then objected, on the grounds that, as mentioned above, the jackal and the lion were members of the same super-*jāti.* He too offered himself in the place of the jackal. At this point the camel thought,

> They have made fine speeches, but no one has been killed by the master. Therefore I will also say something appropriate, because these three will also dismiss my offer. (PT 80.1–4)

But when the camel came forward and disingenuously offered itself, the jackal and leopard tore open its belly, the crow put out its eyes, it died and was eaten by the others.

There is no need to dwell at length on the second of these two tales, as it shares many features with the first. In brief, a jackal told a camel who had joined a lion's retinue that it would get two bodies back if it offered itself as food. The camel foolishly agreed and was killed. The jackal then tricked the lion into abandoning the carcass and he ate it himself. There are only two points that I wish to make in reference to the second story: first, at its heart lies the impossibility of a sustainable relationship between the camel and the lion. Second, although Pūrṇabhadra's recension does not explain how this camel came to be in the lion's retinue, the *simplicior* recension does: a camel cow strayed from its herd to give birth and was killed by the lion in question. When he tore open her belly he found the living calf, and moved by his love for it (PS 1.77.13), took it home and adopted it. I only mention this because the calf's links to its mother and to the herd serve to differentiate it further from the wild animals.

Is it fitting for a lion to feel compassion for a camel, to guarantee its safety, or for the camel to join a lion's retinue? I suggest that it would seem most unnatural. It is a breach of the normal order of things; a perversion of *āraṇyadharma,* the "law of the jungle."

Again, I see no specific correlations between the animal *jātis* in these two narratives and particular groups in human society. It would be difficult to relate camels or lions to any definite group at a particular locus on the social *maṇḍala.* I do not believe that the creators of the *Pañcatantra* intended their audience to identify with either camels or lions, for example. The take-home message is simpler than that: in spite of *dharma,* promises, or good intentions, there can be no sustainable relationship between members of different groups whose interests and goals are mutually incompatible. According to the discourse, all societies are "naturally" divided into groups, and each group has a given set of characteristics, its *habitus.* That groups exist, and that they may be mutual incompatible, are both manifestations of the discourse of division.

Story 1-14 "Lion and Wheelwright"

The major division examined above was that which exists between meat-eaters (lions, jackals, etc.) and grass-eaters (bulls and camels). This division, I suggest, represents a special case of a more general division between predators and their prey. In Story 1-14 "Lion and wheelwright" we will encounter again some of the themes identified above. There is, for example, a continuing emphasis on food as the distinguishing feature of different groups. The twist here is that the potential prey is not a grass-eating bull or a camel, but a "grain"-eating human.

In this story, a wheelwright, who had gone into the forest with his wife to cut timber, saw a lion and "thought that he was as good as dead" (PT 81.7). In an attempt to save his life, he approached the beast, saying, "Come, come, friend! Today, you should eat my own food, prepared by your brother's [i.e., my] wife" (PT 81.9–10). The wheelwright effectively attempted to establish a familial relationship with the lion by representing himself as the animal's brother and his wife as its sister-in-law. The wheelwright sought to encompass the lion within his own family to minimize the danger to himself. The lion replied;

> "Kind sir, grain is not a means of sustenance for me, because I am a meat-eater. But, all the same, on account of your kindness, I will try a little. What kind of delicacy is this?" When the lion had spoken thus, the wheelwright satisfied the lion with various kinds of delicacies, beginning with sweetmeats, *aśokavartin* and foods flavored with sugar, ghee, raisins and *caturjātaka.* (PT 81.11–15)

Having accepted food from the wheelwright, the lion gave him a guarantee of safe conduct and granted him permission to wander at will in the forest, just like the lions in the preceding stories. The man suggested that the two should meet every day, but stipulated that the lion must always come alone. As a consequence of his daily liaison with the wheelwright and the picnic lunches he provided, this lion also gave up hunting (PT 81.20). His two meat-eating attendants (*piśitāśanau,* PT 81.5), a jackal and a crow, neglected and hungry, inquired where the lion went during the day and whence he returned so replete (PT 81.22–23). Their master admitted that he spent time with the wheelwright and accepted food from him (PT 82.1–3). The two immediately suggested killing the man, so that they might sustain themselves with his blood and flesh (PT 82.4). The lion recoiled at the suggestion, reminding them of the guarantee of safety that he had given—by now, a familiar response—but agreed they might accompany him in the expectation of receiving food from the man. As soon as the wheelwright saw the lion approaching with his "wicked retinue," he and his wife, regarding the sight as inauspicious, quickly climbed to safety in the branches of a tree (PT 82.7–10). When the puzzled lion asked the wheelwright about his apparent change of heart, the man responded with this verse:

> Because you have a jackal at your side and a sharp-billed crow, I have climbed a tree. Your retinue is not auspicious. (PT 80.23–24)

In his natural state, the lion is, as we have seen, the forest carnivore par excellence: the wheelwright assessed the lion's fundamental disposition correctly when he judged the beast to be "very frightening" and "regarded himself as finished." The lion, too, was responding to his own untrammeled nature when he said that grain was not a fit means of sustenance for him because he was a meat-eater. There is no doubt about the members of his retinue, who are explicitly described as "meat-eating" and hankering after the wheelwright's "blood and flesh."

A most "unnatural" relationship had sprung up between the two. The lion accepted food from his "brother," the wheelwright, and granted him free access to the forest in return. The lion, the ultimate devourer of blood and flesh, meekly accepted sweets and cakes from the hands of his human friend. He was softened, somehow "un-lioned," by his daily truck with the man. I am reminded of the lion Piṅgalaka in Story 1-00 who grew soft and negligent as the result of his relationship with the bull Saṃjīvaka, and of the tenderness displayed by the lions in their relationships with the camels.

When the lion approached with his retinue, the wheelwright interpreted this as an outward manifestation of some inward change. Suspecting that the lion was about to revert to his natural state of carnivorousness, he and his wife prudently removed themselves from harm's way.

I am interested in the role that the refusal and acceptance of food plays in this narrative. At first the lion distinguished himself from the wheelwright, as he, a meat-eater, could not eat "grain," that is, the wheelwright's cakes and sweets. In the preceding discussions, the *jātis* of the lion and bull and the *jātis* of the lion and camels were also defined on the basis of their respective foods, meat, and grass. In this story, the food types—meat and grain—also define and differentiate the two incompatible groups. Yet in accepting "grain," that is, human food, the lion joined metaphorically the wheelwright's *jāti* as his "brother," and thereby entered into an "unnatural" and unsustainable relationship with him. In the end, the "natural" order would reassert itself and the transient relationship between the perceptive wheelwright and the *barfi*-eating lion evaporated just as the latter's "essential" carnivorousness was about to reassert itself.

Relationships between Predator and Prey

Story 3-16 "Frogs Ride a Serpent" and Story 4-01 "Frog's Revenge Overleaps Itself"

The discourse of division that separates predators and their prey is most clearly enunciated in a dialogue in Story 2-00 "Dove, mouse, crow, tortoise and deer" between the crow Laghupaṭanaka and the mouse Hiraṇyaka whom he was trying to befriend. The mouse rebuffed the crow's overtures thus:

> You are one who feeds on another; I am an item of prey. What friendship could there be between you and me? It is said: "The deluded fool who makes friends with someone unlike himself—whether lower or higher—will become a public laughingstock." (PT 130.25–27)

The key concepts in this passage are *paribhoktṛ,* glossed as "eating, enjoying, living at another's cost" (MMW), but more literally "feeding on another" and hence "predator"; and *bhojyabhūta,* "become food," and hence "item of prey." Admittedly, a sustained and mutually beneficial relationship developed between the crow and the mouse, despite the fact that they belonged to different *jātis.* For the moment we may take the mouse's observations on the relationship between predator and prey as an axiom that colors much of the *Pañcatantra.* In this section I will investigate the ways in which this concept is articulated in two abortive relationships between frogs and snakes.

An aged snake called Mandaviṣa mischievously told some frogs that he had been cursed by a *brāhmaṇa* to provide rides for them. The frogs were delighted, and their king, Jalapāda, immediately hopped out of the lake and climbed on to the snake's back. The other frogs followed according to seniority, and even those who missed out on a ride hurried along behind. The snake amused them with "many special ways of proceeding" and the king "achieved happiness from touching his body" (PT 222.15–19).

At this juncture, a second snake, surprised to see Mandaviṣa being ridden by frogs, said, "Friend, it is repugnant that you are ridden by them who are our food!" (PT 223.12–13). There is an echo here of another incident in Story 2-00, in which the crow carried the mouse on its back to visit the tortoise. On seeing this strange sight, the tortoise asked, "Why did you bring him, your food, here on your back?" (PT 134.14–15). The bearer is inferior to the borne, as a horse is subservient to its rider. When the snake bore the frog and the crow carried the mouse, this natural order was inverted. The predator is superior to the prey, and yet both the snake and the crow debased themselves by adopting the inferior, subordinate position, thereby scandalizing the second snake and the tortoise respectively.

One day, the snake with the frogs on its back moved more slowly than usual. In response to the frog-king's inquiry, the snake replied that without food, he lacked the energy to carry them. The frog then made the ignoble suggestion that the snake should eat some of "the lowly frogs" (PT 223.1–2). In spite of the snake's ominous observation that "many kinds of frogs make for excellent eating" (PT 224.23–24), Jalapāda did not recognize his wicked intention. After feeding on frogs constantly for several days, the snake regained his strength, but before long, he had eaten them all, including the king, "so that not even their seed was left" (PT 225.5–6).

In Story 4-01 "Frog's revenge overleaps itself," a frog-king by the name of Gaṅgadatta, tormented by his kinsfolk, decided to avenge himself, and invited a snake into his well to eat his troublesome relatives. Although he knew that the snake was his natural enemy (*svabhāvavairī* PT 232.16), he steeled himself with the observation that:

> A wise person may destroy one troublesome enemy by means of another troublesome enemy, just as [removing] a painful thorn with another thorn is [conducive] to happiness. (PT 231.24–25)

When Gaṅgadatta summoned the snake near his hole, the latter reflected, "This one who calls me is not of my own *jāti*" (PT 232.1–2). The snake was naturally suspicious, and even when Gaṅgadatta explained himself, he remained incredulous:

> This is not to be believed. Does grass have bonds of affection with fire? It is said "One who is to be killed by another does not approach him, even when he is asleep." Therefore, why do you say this? (PT 232.12–15)

Eventually, the snake, being elderly and hungry, agreed to Gaṅgadatta's proposal and entered into an apparently cordial relationship with him. Gaṅgadatta told the snake that certain members of his retinue were to be spared, and he could eat only those at whom he pointed (PT 233.14–15). The snake readily agreed, and at first ate only the frog's rivals. When all the troublesome kin had been eaten, Gaṅgadatta tried unsuccessfully to persuade the snake to leave the well, saying that he had fulfilled his duty as a friend. But the snake refused and set about eating the frog's friends and family as well. In the end, only Gaṅgadatta remained. Even at that late stage, the two maintained a semblance of friendship. The frog offered to find more food for the snake, to which the snake replied "I cannot eat you who are like a brother to me. Therefore, if you do thus, then you will immediately become like a father to me!" (PT 235.13–14). Using this as a pretext, the frog fled the well.

The important feature of this story is that the enmity is so clearly and explicitly expressed in terms of *jāti.* Both protagonists acknowledged that they belonged to different *jātis* and both foresaw the enmity: the frog knew the snake was his *svabhāvavairin* and the snake observed that there could be no relationship between "grass and fire." Yet both sought an advantage from this cross-*jāti* relationship: the frog wanted to be rid of his rivals, and the snake wanted an easy meal. To the very end, the snake invoked familial ties, calling the frog first his brother and then his father. The snake sought to locate himself metaphorically within the same family, the same *jāti,* as the frog.

Jalapāda, the frog from the first story, also failed to recognize the snake's essential predatory nature, and suffered for his indiscretion. Every attempted relationship between mutually incompatible individuals (e.g., predators and their prey) represents a poor assessment of *svabhāva* on the part of at least one of the two parties. A potentially abortive cross-*jāti* relationship only arises when all those vulnerable bulls, camels, frogs, and so on fail to appreciate that by their very nature they are prey. At the same time they ignore the predatory *svabhāva* of the lions, snakes, and so forth, which will be their undoing.

In conclusion, the frog-kings in both stories welcomed the snakes, but placed restrictions on which frogs were to be eaten: in the first story, it was "lowly frogs"; in the second, the troublesome kinsfolk. In both, the restrictions were soon broken and the snakes decimated the populations. The message on unsustainable relationships is equally clear in both: frogs will never benefit from relationships with snakes. The discourse of division around predator and prey is clearly expressed here in terms of differences in *jāti,* and that natural enmity is an aspect of a being's *svabhāva.*

Other Predators and Their Prey

I want to emphasize that the theme of the abortive relationship between predator and prey is not just restricted to the few stories that I have analyzed above, but recurs throughout the text as one of its dominant motifs. I will summaries below some further examples.

The motif of the aged, infirm predator who uses deceit to compensate for failing strength is found again in Story 1-06 "Heron, fishes and crab." Here the heron, a predator, falsely informed some fish and a crab that fishermen were approaching. They abandoned caution and called on him to rescue them, using a string of injudicious epithets: "Uncle! Father! Brother! Friend!" (*māma* ' *tāta* ' *bhrātaḥ* ' *sakhe* ' PT 37.12). By "naming" him in these familial terms, it seems to me, they were blurring the lines between their respective *jātis* and were declaring him metaphorically to be one of their own. The heron, of course, carried them off and killed them all, except the clever crab who acted quickly to save himself.

The friendship between another pair of ultimately incompatible individuals in Story 4-00 "Ape and crocodile" was also characterized by familial vocabulary. The monkey repeatedly addressed the crocodile as "brother" (e.g., *bhrātaḥ,* PT 230.12, 230.16). The crocodile in return called him his "sworn brother" (*pratipannabhrātā so 'smākam* ' PT 229.3) and referred to his wife as the monkey's "brother's wife" (*bhrātṛjāyā,* PT 229.28, etc.), that is, he cast himself in fraternal relationship with the monkey. Their friendship came unstuck when the crocodile attempted to kill and eat the monkey.

In Story 3-03 "Cat as judge," as we have already seen, a partridge and a hare were locked in a dispute over ownership of a burrow. The hare suggested that they take their case for adjudication to a cat that was knowledgeable in *dharma*. The partridge was reluctant: "Surely he is our natural enemy. Therefore, let us ask him while we stand at a distance" (PT 191.1–2). The cat won their confidence with sweet words of *dharma,* lured them close under the pretext of being deaf, and caught and ate them both. The key concept here is *svabhāvaśatrubhūta*—literally, "one who is an enemy on account of his *svabhāva*." The litigants were right in their initial assessment of the cat: he was their "natural" enemy. They trusted him, approached him, and had dealings with him: enough to bring them undone.

Nonpredatory Enmity

Story 3-00 "War of Crows and Owls"

In all the relationships that we have considered so far, the creators of the *Pañcatantra* employed the concepts of "natural" predator and "natural" prey to illustrate certain insurmountable divisions between *jātis*. I will now examine a set of relationships, closely allied to these, yet rather less drastic. These relationships are also characterized by "natural enmity," but there is no suggestion of one party eating the other. They entail a nonpredatory hostility between members of two more-or-less equally matched *jātis*. The first such relationship is between the owl-king Arimardana and the crow-minister Sthirajīvin in the framing narrative of the third *tantra,* Story 3-00 "War of crows and owls."

For the reasons that were outlined in Story 3-01 "Birds elect a king," Sanskritic culture assumes a fundamental, natural enmity between crows and owls. In this story, which draws extensively on the strategic thinking of the *Arthaśāstra,* a community of owls, flying about at night, killed every crow that they encountered until the crows' roost in a great banyan tree was surrounded by corpses (PT 174.13–15). The crows regarded the owls as an insuperable enemy who, being nocturnal, could slaughter them with impunity (PT 174.18–19). The only way to deal with such an adversary was to employ the expedient of duplicity (PT 179.4). The crow-minister Sthirajīvin sought to infiltrate the owls' stronghold in the guise of a defector. When the owls first found the crow, there was much debate among them. Only one owl-minister, Raktākṣa, counseled his immediate execution: "Lord, what is there to be considered in this case? He should be killed without hesitation" (PT 198.3–4). This response was couched in terms of the appropriate treatment of enemies, that is, he was responding to the traditional enmity between their two *jātis*. As it transpired, Raktākṣa's instincts were correct.

The crow's first act among the owls casts an interesting light on the relationship between "traditional enmity," *svabhāva* and *jāti.* He requested the owls to throw him into a fire: "For the purpose of requiting enmity towards them [i.e., the crows], I desire the state of being an owl" (PT 212.22–23). This was of course part of his subterfuge. The apparent logic is that if he were reborn as an owl, he would avenge himself for the alleged wrongs he had suffered. That is, the hostility that he claimed to feel for his own kind could only reach its fullest expression if he were able to achieve *ulūkatvam,* "the state of being an owl." He sought to change his *svabhāva* by seeking rebirth in another *jāti.*

The owl-minister Raktākṣa argued that, on the contrary, the crow would maintain his crow identity even if he were reborn as an owl, as "one's own *jāti* is hard to overcome" (*svajātir duratikramā* || PT 212.27). To make his point, he told Story 3-13 "Mouse-maiden will wed a mouse." A mouse, which had been changed into girl by a *siddha,* although offered various highly desirable husbands, was still "instinctively" attracted to another mouse because she had retained her mouse *svabhāva,* even though she had acquired a human form.

There seem to be two conflicting views of the relationship between *svabhāva* and *jāti* here. The crow's view was birth in a given *jāti* naturally endows one with the *svabhāva* of that *jāti.* The owl's view is that *svabhāva* will remain unchanged even if one is born into a different *jāti.* This view runs counter to the general thrust of the *jāti* discourse in the *Pañcatantra.* In fact this is a nonargument. The owl's story of the mouse-maiden has nothing to do with rebirth in a different *jāti*—she was turned into a human by the *siddha*'s magical powers and maintained her mouse *svabhāva* in the process. I suspect that this whole narrative sequence from the moment the crow sought immolation and the owl's argument about *jāti* was a literary device employed by the creators of the *Pañcatantra* to provide a context for the embedded Story 3-13. I think that the *Pañcatantra*'s dominant discourse on the relationship between *svabhāva* and *jāti* stands.

To return to the story, the other owl-ministers, for various reasons, advised clemency toward the crow. One said, "Lord, he should certainly not be killed, for, being protected by you, you will perhaps spend time pleasantly with him in mutual affection" (PT 208.6–7). The owl-king, swayed by the majority, spared the crow.

Throughout the subterfuge, the crow remained bent on the owls' destruction. Under the pretext of building a nest, he accumulated a large pile of sticks at the entrance of the owls' cave, and instructed the crows to drop firebrands on it. When they did so, "all the day-blind ones, recalling the words of Raktākṣa, suffered in the manner of Kumbhīpāka" (PT 220.2–3).[11] Despite the traditional enmity that divided them, having embraced, nourished, and nurtured their "natural enemy," all the owls, with their king Arimardana at their head, were roasted alive.

Story 1-12 "Goose and Owl"

This, the final nonpredatory relationship that we will consider, is found in Story 1-12 "Goose and owl." I have already discussed some of the negative associations that attend the owl in Sanskritic culture, I will therefore begin with a brief summary of the cultural associations enjoyed by the goose. As Vogel (1962) has gathered a great number of references to the goose in Indic literature, I will do no more than summaries his findings. In sharp contrast to the owl,

> For the Indians the *haṃsa* is the noble bird *par excellence* worthy of being sung by poets like Kālidāsa and figured on religious monuments. The goose is the vehicle of Brahmā the Creator. In ancient fables he is the embodiment of the highest virtues. . . . (Vogel 1962: 2)

Vogel traces the veneration of geese back to the *Vedas,* in which they were associated with the Aśvins (Vogel 1962: 12). Geese were thought to migrate to Lake Mānasa, the famous *tīrtha* near Mt. Kailāsa, abode of Śiva and Pārvatī. This migration acquired the religious significance of a pilgrimage (Vogel 1962: 3), thereby adding to the goose's reputation. Of specific relevance to this story, as we shall see, is the fact that Indian poets attribute to the goose a "charming voice" (Vogel 1962: 7).

The surface texture of this tale is indicated by the premise, which warns against keeping bad company (PT 72.2) and consorting with dubious friends (PT 72.3). Beneath this lies a relationship between members of fundamentally incompatible *jātis.*

A goose lived by a lake where he passed the time amusing himself. One day, "Death, who would bring about [the goose's] end, arrived in the form of an owl" (*tasyāntakaro mṛtyur ulūkarūpeṇāyātaḥ* | PT 72.10–11). The goose, however, was easily won over by the owl's flattery, invited him to stay, and the two disported themselves together at leisure. The owl spoke of their mutual affection (PT 72.25), and before returning to his own abode, invited the goose to join him. After the owl departed, the goose grew tired of his familiar surroundings and resolved to visit his new friend. On arriving at the owl's home, the goose failed to find him:

> When he looked, searching very carefully, having seen the day-blind one [i.e., the owl], who had resorted to an unpleasant hole, he said, "Good sir, come, come! I, your dear friend, the goose, have arrived." Having heard thus, [the owl] said, "I am inactive during the day. When the sun has gone to its resting place we will meet." (PT 73.8–11)

In spite of this lukewarm welcome and a long wait thereafter, the goose stayed on, and later shared his news with his friend, until, fatigued by the journey, he fell asleep (PT 73.12–13). At dawn, the owl was startled by the blare of a conch shell at reveille in a nearby encampment of traveling merchants, and uttered a "loud, discordant cry" (PT 73.16). Fearing this evil omen, the leader of the caravan ordered an archer to shoot in the direction of the call. The owl had already flown to safety, but the arrow struck and killed the goose.

Every aspect of the owl's character seems negative: his association with death, the perversity of his "day-blindness," his nocturnal nature, his "unpleasant hole," and his "discordant," ill-omened call. The surface text stresses the dangers of bad company and poor choice in friends, but it is only possible to avoid bad company if, unlike the goose, one is able to distinguish bad company from good. The goose consistently failed to recognize the owl's true nature. His failure to assess correctly the fundamental incompatibility between their *jātis* led to his demise.

Enmity/Amity and the Indigo Jackal

In this section, I have attempted to show how natural enmity may be regarded as a given state that exists between certain *jātis.* Taking the Story 1-00 "Lion and bull" as a paradigm, I explored the natural enmity between meat-eaters and grass-eaters. We saw that such relationships were a subset of a broader body of tensions between predators and prey in general. Enmity is also expressed as nonpredatory hostility between members of incompatible *jātis.*

The "natural" enmity that exists among the animal *jātis* is representative of fundamental incompatibilities that are said to exist among different social groups. Olivelle (2002) saw the tension between meat-eaters and grass-eaters as a reflection of a Vedic concept that the upper strata of society "feed off" the lower ones. I found no convincing way of tying the "meat-eaters" of the narrative to the brahmanical society, and therefore proposed a more generalized interpretation. The enmity between meat-eaters and grass-eaters, and between predators and prey in general, is symptomatic of *difference* and *division* rather than status and hierarchy. When discussing enmity, neither party is necessarily privileged above the other. The distinction between these animal *jātis* is illustrative of the differences between groups in general. It speaks of their fundamental incompatibility, their divided nature, rather than their relative status, and of the existence in society of those who are inimical to one's interest by birth.

What are the implications for the indigo jackal of this aspect of the discourse of division? The virtual society inhabited by the jackal was one in which the basic unit of division was the *jāti,* and in which deep and unbridgeable enmity between *jātis* was the norm. It is worth repeating the verse with which the story of the indigo jackal began:

> One who abandons insiders and treats outsiders as insiders meets death, just like the fool Caṇḍarava. (PT 68.10–11)

The jackal's undoing lay in the fact that he failed to recognize that society was divided into *abhyantara,* literally "those who are within"—insiders who can be trusted—and *bāhya,* or "outsiders," that is, those who are outside one's own circle. As we have seen, the *jāti* forms the boundary between "inside" and "outside." Those inside the indigo jackal's own *jāti* were his natural peers and allies. Having abandoned them—he had them seized by the throat and cast out in order to protect his position—he consorted with the "outsiders," that is, the lions, tigers, leopards, and so on, who were not of his own *jāti.* His attempt to shun his natural allies backfired when he heard their howls, and his attempt to embrace the "outsiders" ended when they sprang on him and killed him.

*

To conclude this chapter on the discourse of division in the *Pañcatantra,* we have seen how the *jāti* functions as the basic unit of division in the metasocieties of the narrative, and that certain sets of attributes appear to inhere naturally in each *jāti.* We have seen how, under this discourse, three characteristics are fixed by an individual's station at birth: essential nature, position in the social *maṇḍala* and natural enmities and amities. These constitute the *habitus* of members of each *jāti.* How does the discourse of division manifest in the story of the indigo jackal? Put in the simplest terms, the discourse manifests in three significant ways: first, the jackal possessed an immutable essential nature that it could not counteract; second, it was of inferior social status and was always relegated to the periphery of society; and third, its natural peers were those of its own kind.

Many of the various features of the discourse of division that we have examined in this long chapter appear to be natural and real. The narratives represent the contingent, the constructed, the cultural and the social as if they were all true, real and natural. Discursive statements, like these relating to essential nature, status, and enmity, cannot function in a vacuum. They can only be effective if they appear to be true. They require a certain infrastructure to lend them credibility and authority. The "regime of truth," which enables the discourse of division to function as true, is the subject of the next chapter.

3

The "Regime of Truth" and the *Pañcatantra*

> Each society has its regime of truth, its "general politics" of truth: that is, the types of discourse which it accepts and makes function as true; the mechanisms and instances which enable one to distinguish true and false statements, the means by which each is sanctioned; the techniques and procedures accorded value in the acquisition of truth; the status of those who are charged with saying what counts as true.
>
> —Michel Foucault, *Truth and Power*

The story of the indigo jackal and the other narrative units of the *Pañcatantra* are obviously fictional, but what they seek to convey, both implicitly and explicitly, are normative "truths." We must assume that the creators of the text "believed" in what they were trying to achieve, that the discursive thrust of the narrative embodied some viable, valued social norms. We may say that the levity of *Pañcatantra*'s surface text belies the gravity of the subtext. The discourse of division, which we have described in the preceding chapter and which pervades the *Pañcatantra,* manifests as a discourse of truth. That is, everything these narratives imply about social interactions—both explicitly and implicitly—is presented as practical, well-intentioned advice ("*hitopadeśa*"), a reflection of a social "reality," or perhaps a social "ideality," which is, above all, true. There is no suggestion, for example, that the truths conveyed by the discourse might be socially constructed, contingent or conditioned.

The aim of this chapter is to show how the *Pañcatantra* as a whole and, by implication, the discourse of division that is woven through it, function as "true." I will identify and examine several factors that lend the text and the discourse credibility and authority, and make it possible for the didactic thrust of the narratives to appear and function as a true discourse. This will lead to reflections on a "regime of truth" in brahmanical literary culture.

In this chapter, we will address five topics, beginning with the authoritative voice in which the *Pañcatantra* is enunciated. Under this rubric, I will examine the status of written texts in Indic literary culture, the implications of Sanskrit as the language-of-choice, and the truth-effects exerted by authorship and anonymity. I will also suggest textual strategies that induce certain effects of truth, including the tactical use of particular words and phrases.

Second, we will consider the effects of the spatial and temporal setting of the narratives, and their intended audience, with a view to the truth-effects exerted on the discourse by the apparent "placelessness," timelessness and universal applicability of the stories.

Third, having described the śāstric paradigm (Pollock 1985) and outlined its basic operations, I will explore the ways in which the *Pañcatantra* functions within this paradigm, with particular emphasis on its claims to be a *nītiśāstra.*

Fourth, I will discuss the intertextual nature of the *Pañcatantra,* which exists as "a node in a network" of other texts, some written, some visual, and others oral. I will discuss the cumulative discursive impact of intertextuality.

Finally, I will describe the "naturalization" of the discourse (Smith 1994), showing how the social system of division and its assumptions are projected on to the natural world, and how this image is then recruited to valorize and to legitimize the discourse of division in human society.

I will conclude this chapter by drawing these five elements together, showing how they cause the discourse to function as "true" and suggesting how together they constitute a "regime of truth."

THE AUTHORITATIVE VOICE

In this section I will begin with the function of the "authoritative voice" in which the text is enunciated, including the role of the written word, language choice, anonymity, authorship, and some specific textual strategies. The theoretical background to understanding the authoritative voice has been provided by Bourdieu in *Language and Symbolic Power* (1991). The basic idea is that text itself has no transformative power. Its power is derived from the socially sanctioned authority invested in the author. The power of words is merely a reflection of the power and authority that the dominant culture has delegated to the author (Bourdieu 1991: 107). In the case of the *Pañcatantra,* we have a "collective author," being the long line of creators, compilers, and redactors of the text. The authority instilled in the narrative—and in the case of this study, the transformative power of the discourse embedded in it—is not ultimately to be found in the words themselves, but in the authority of the "speaker."

> By trying to understand the power of linguistic manifestations linguistically, by looking in language for the principle underlying the logic and effectiveness of the language of institution, one forgets that authority comes to language from outside, a fact concretely exemplified by the *skeptron* that, in Homer, is passed to the orator who is about to speak. Language at most *represents* this authority, manifests and symbolizes it. There is a rhetoric which characterizes all discourses of institution, that is to say, the official speech of the authorized spokesperson expressing himself in a solemn situation, with an authority whose limits are identical with the extent of delegation by the institution. The stylistic features which characterize the language of priests, teachers and, more generally, all institutions, like routinization, stereotyping and neutralization, all stem from the position occupied in a competitive field by these persons entrusted with delegated authority. (Bourdieu 1991: 109)

The authority of the *Pañcatantra* is not inherent in the text itself; it does not exist "linguistically," as Bourdieu puts it. For the social power of the text to be received and experienced by its audience and for that power to exert itself, the audience must first be aware of the author's authority. The utterances of the authorized spokesperson embody "the accumulated symbolic capital of the group which has delegated him and of which he is the *authorized representative*" (Bourdieu 1991: 111).

> The symbolic efficacy of words is exercised only in so far as the person subjected to it recognizes the person who exercises it as authorized to do so, or, what amounts to the same thing, only in so far as he fails to realize that, in submitting to it, he himself has

> contributed, through his recognition, to its establishment. (Bourdieu 1991: 116)

The authority of the collective speaker is made manifest in "stylistic features." In this section, I will attempt to describe some of the features by which the collective authors make manifest the social authority invested in them. What factors in and around the text and what "institutional conditions" provide legitimization for the discourse? What is the nature of the *skeptron* held by Pūrṇabhadra and the long anonymous lineage of his predecessors? In the following pages, we will explore the factors that enable the discourse of the *Pañcatantra* to be recognized as authoritative, the "stereotyped symbols" that empower it, and the "stylistic features" by which a recipient of the *Pañcatantra* would recognize the authority of the text and its creators, and thereby know it, and the discourse of division embedded in it, to be "true."

The Written Word

Some classical cultures have yielded masses of secular textual material: cuneiform inscriptions of grain transactions, Roman shopping lists, and oracle-bone inquiries about the weather. In Sanskritic civilization, on the other hand, it seems that little writing of a frivolous nature was preserved. What was the status of the written text in this literary culture?

> The literary in southern Asia comes increasingly in the middle period [1000–1500 CE] to be distinguished not just from the documentary but from the oral, and to be ever more intimately linked to writing, with respect to the authority conferred by it, the textuality associated with it, and the history produced through it. The authorization to write is not, like the ability to speak, a natural entitlement. It is typically related to social and political privileges, which mark literature in the restricted sense as a different mode of cultural production and communication from so-called oral literature. (Pollock 1998: 8)

Everyone in the society to which Pollock refers knew how to speak, but not everyone knew how to write. Literacy implied certain social and political privileges, because society only authorized and empowered a select few to exercise that power. The power and privilege invested by society in the author is manifest in the author's written production. Written literary production reflected privilege, and therefore conferred authority on the written discourse.

Pollock sees written texts as reflections of social power, but they are also repositories of spiritual power. While the purest Vedic tradition was a strongly oral one, written texts have played a key role in all post-Vedic developments, with the result that there is a close relationship between the textual and the scriptural. Scriptural documents speak with divine authority. Sanskritic literary culture was well accustomed to the exercise of spiritual authority through the textual medium. We may speculate on the possibility that the vast bulk of the written corpus being scriptural in nature may have colored the reception of all written documents. It seems possible therefore that in addition to the inherent authority of the written text, the scriptural content of the archive may have indirectly conferred, by association, authority on the nonscriptural part.

Irrespective of this, the written text in Sanskritic civilization has a certain inherent authority derived from the social power and privilege invested and manifest in it. The very apex of the scriptural pyramid is occupied by the *Vedas,* which, as mentioned above, constituted a body of oral texts in their original and ideal form. While we can say nothing with certainty about "a typical reader" or the "readership as a whole" of the *Pañcatantra,* it seems safe to suggest that individuals who function within that Sanskritic civilization paradigm may bring a set of cultural perceptions and sensitivities to their reading. One such sensitivity is an awareness of the preeminence of the written text. As the manifestation of social power, and as the medium of scriptural and spiritual authority, an inherent authority, dignity and "truthfulness" inhere in written texts. As writing was the medium of the elite, it was also the elite medium. Just as power and "truth" created writing, so too writing created "truth" and power in a reciprocal relationship.

Sanskrit as Language of Choice

If written texts are inherently authoritative, what significance, if any, lies in the author's choice of language for a given text? Is there an inherent "truth-effect" in the choice of Sanskrit for their work on the part of the creators of the *Pañcatantra?* Does a narrative written in Sanskrit enjoy some inherent authority, in comparison with one written in another language? Pollock has observed that a "language-for-literature is chosen from among alternatives, not naturally given" (Pollock 1998: 7). During the period of the development of the *Pañcatantra,* from at least the sixth to the twelfth century CE, literary production was undertaken in three known languages in north India, Sanskrit, Prakrit, and Apabhraṃśa, and possibly a fourth, the shadowy Paiśāca. What was the status of Sanskrit vis-à-vis the competing languages of the period? What significance may we attach to the fact that, at some unknown time, an individual author made the conscious decision to write a text in Sanskrit? This question is answered by what Pollock calls "an allegorical account of the origin of literature," the story of the Poetry Man or *Kāvyapuruṣa:*

> Brahmā created a son for the Goddess of Speech, his mouth consisting of Sanskrit, his arm of Prakrit, his groin of Apabhraṃśa, his feet of Paiśāca, his chest of mixed language. (Rājaśekhara, *Kāvyamīmāṃsā* 4, cited in Pollock 1998: 17)

This is a recasting of the *Puruṣasūkta* from the *Ṛgveda* to which we will return in chapter 4. The parallel is quite clear: just as the *brāhmaṇa,* as the mouth of the "Cosmic Man," is first, highest and preeminent, so too is Sanskrit, being the mouth of the "Poetry Man." Sanskrit is placed at the apex of the hierarchy of languages. It is superior to all other contenders, just as the *brāhmaṇa,* according to tradition, transcends members of the other *varṇas.*

Pollock asked what Sanskrit authors were choosing when they chose to write in Sanskrit, as opposed to Prakrit or Apabhraṃśa, the other two approved languages for literature. In answer, he quotes Bhoja's suggestion that Sanskrit alone is the appropriate language for *kāvya,* science and *śāstra.* Sanskrit "represented the expression of the culturally dominant" (Pollock 2003: 42). Sanskrit had "long preserved associations from the sacred domain of Vedic liturgical practices: Sanskrit is also that which is 'rendered fit' for these practices because, like other instruments or objects used in ritual acts, it has been made ritually pure" (Pollock 2003: 62). Even when it carried over into the mundane world of coinage, deeds, inscriptions and indeed literary production, it retained, perhaps, a whiff of power and sanctity. The first answer to the question, then, is that the genre determines the choice of language. Because the *Pañcatantra* was at least nominally a *nītiśāstra,* Sanskrit was the appropriate literary language. The second answer is that the desired social register, which Pollock describes as the degree of rusticity or sophistication, determines the selection of language, with Sanskrit being reserved for the highest register. The third answer is that an author would choose to write in Sanskrit because to do so "was to choose a cosmopolitan readership of truly vast proportions" (Pollock 2003: 74).

Yet the inherent authority of the written word and the power effects of Sanskrit as language-of-choice would be in vain were it not for a degree of "complicity." Bourdieu has identified the necessary collaboration between the producers and consumers of text when the power of language is exerted:

> the language of authority never governs without the collaboration of those it governs, without the help of the social mechanisms capable of producing this complicity, based on misrecognition, which is the basis of all authority. (Bourdieu 1991: 113)

Bourdieu would suggest, therefore, that for the discursive effect of texts like the *Pañcatantra* to come into play, the audience of the text must hold similar, complimentary assumptions to those of its creators. They would have recognized, for example, that the texts they received "had something cosmopolitan, something global, to say," based on the very fact that they were written in Sanskrit.

The use of a particular language presupposes a set of beliefs of which the individual user may not be consciously aware. Thus, readers of texts in particular languages find themselves responsive to certain kinds of arguments (MacIntyre 1988: 394). The brahmanical Sanskrit archive constitutes what MacIntyre would call a "particular tradition of rational enquiry." The very use of Sanskrit as the language of choice, one could argue, may predispose an audience toward the acceptance of dominant discourses of the archive. The choice of Sanskrit therefore may suggest some fidelity to the brahmanical tradition in a world where Buddhist texts were generally associated with Pali and Jaina ones with Prakrit.

Sanskrit also plays a special role in the traditional brahmanical worldview as the language of the *Vedas*. Because the *Vedas* are regarded as uncreated and eternal, so too is Sanskrit. All material entities may have different appellations in different languages, but what they "really" are is preserved in their Sanskrit names, given to them at creation. Sanskrit is regarded as the source of all other languages, but more than this: "It is also the language which is closest to reality. The words and sentences of the Sanskrit language are believed to have some kind of inherent connection with the world we live in" (Bronkhorst 1996: 109).

Having seen how the written text in the Sanskritic cultural universe is invested with power and privilege, and having suggested how the choice of Sanskrit as "language-for-literature" may exert a truth-effect on the discourse, we will now turn to the question of authorship and anonymity.

"Truth-Effects" of Anonymity and Authorship

Several layers of authorship, both fictional and real, are perceptible in the creation of the *Pañcatantra*. At the most basic level, certain anonymous authors created the primary building blocks from which the *Pañcatantra* was assembled. These include the narrative units and the thousand-odd verses, many of which are also found in the *Jātakas*, *dharmaśāstras*, and in the pool of oral tradition on which the *Pañcatantra* may have drawn. The historical individuals who actually composed or wrote this primary material are virtually invisible to us and are therefore usually overlooked.

At the second level, various authors, also anonymous, throughout the history of the *Pañcatantra*, assembled these preexisting units into a narrative whole, while possibly adding their own new content or imposing their own structure on the corpus. It is they who created the various versions of the *Pañcatantra*, from the earliest precursors of the Pahlavi *Pañcatantra* to the *Tantrākhyāyika* and the *textus simplicior*.

At the third level of authorship is Pūrṇabhadra himself. We know from the *praśasti* and from text-critical analysis that he compared, corrected, and combined preexisting versions of the *Pañcatantra*. To this he added a certain amount of new material, either of his own creation or drawn from other written or oral sources unknown to us.

At the fourth level, the *Pañcatantra* as a whole ascribes itself to the hand of the *brāhmaṇa* Viṣṇuśarman at the court of King Amaraśakti (or in the case of the Southern *Pañcatantra*, King Sudarśana of Pāṭaliputra). Viṣṇuśarman is said to have "created" (*cakāra*, PT 1.3) the *Pañcatantra*, and also to have prepared, arranged or composed (*racayitvā*, PT 2.14) the five individual *tantras*. There is nothing, however, to suggest that Viṣṇuśarman himself was anything other than the literary creation of some other authorial hand. Stoler Miller insightfully identified a process by which Indic texts "create" their own authors. The idea of an author existing as a character within a text attributed to him is frequently encountered in Sanskrit literature (Stoler Miller 1994: 6–7). Just as Vyāsa "pops in and out of [the *Mahābhārata*] like Alfred Hitchcock" (Hiltebeitel 2001: 47), so too does Viṣṇuśarman play an active role in the narrative he "wrote."

There are two aspects of authorship that I will explore in this section: the effects exerted by the general anonymity of the text, and the role of the character of Viṣṇuśarman.

Anonymity

It seems at first ironic that a text with two "authors," Viṣṇuśarman and Pūrṇabhadra, might still be regarded as anonymous. I maintain that the text is largely the product of anonymous authors because, as mentioned above, Viṣṇuśarman is a literary creation, and Pūrṇabhadra was primarily an editor of the text, and only secondarily a creator of it.

Irrespective of who first crafted the individual narrative units and the plethora of verses, and irrespective of who undertook the task of drawing the disparate units together into a literary whole, the text enjoys a certain homogeneity, a uniformity and a unanimity. Individual authors created and arranged the text, but like most authors in Sanskrit literary culture, they left behind few perceptible traces of themselves. It is virtually impossible to discern personal, individual motivations in the choice of material, or in a particular turn of phrase. Pūrṇabhadra was the most recent administrator of our text, but the majority of the work was undertaken by a succession of unknown, anonymous creators.

In this section I will examine the impersonal, magisterial and anonymous tone of the text, and I will explore the effects that this exerts on the discourse. Sanskrit literature is in general impersonal, and *kathā* literature is especially so. What we admire is an author's facility with a standard set of moods and *rasas,* not the expression of his personality or the individuality of his text, or the psychological depth of the characters he created. Only rarely does a Sanskrit author refer to himself in the first person, or tell us anything about himself, his likes and dislikes, his opinions and feelings. It is rare indeed, particularly in *kathā* literature, for a Sanskrit author to write the words, 'I think that . . .' or 'In my opinion . . .' The impersonal tone of Sanskritic texts may also arise in part from the fact that their creators were not necessarily their writers. If a scribe were employed to take down his master's words, his transcription would become reportage. His text would then acquire the remote and dictatorial tone of the *Kāmasūtra,* for example, peppered with the phrase "Vātsāyana says . . . ," in place of the authorial "I."

One result of the impersonal tone of Sanskrit literature is that we know little about even the greatest authors—rarely more than their names and the titles of the texts they wrote. With rare exceptions, neither they, nor their successors, wrote as individuals.

Just as Sanskrit literature as a whole is impersonal, so too is the *Pañcatantra.* We are barely conscious of the presence of Pūrṇabhadra or his predecessors as authors or editors. There is no individual, personal voice articulating the narrative. They are, however, silent redactors collating, correcting and expanding the manuscripts before them. As the texts passed through their hands, they left their personal marks in the form of additions and subtractions, but the imprint of their personal identities is difficult to locate.

Pūrṇabhadra's *Pañcatantra* is not presented as the product of a living flesh-and-blood author writing in the first person. His is the invisible hand that transcribed and collated the varied sources. Even his name is barely discernable in the text, appearing only on the 289th page of a 290-page document. He is hardly writing in his own name; on the contrary, he is virtually anonymous, writing as a spokesperson, a delegate of the authority of the hegemonic culture.

I feel that the invisibility of the author functions to heighten his authority and the authority of his narrative. It lends the text a weight that transcends time and place. A potentially fallible human author is barely discernible in the text. A narrative without an 'author' becomes universalized. It exudes an impression of being uncreated and unoriginated. Ironically, in the absence of an author, the text's authority seems to be enhanced. The "authorless" text may indeed appear to be more authoritative than an authored one. When reading an anonymous text we are not, it seems, confronting the mere opinions and prejudices of an individual, but we encounter "truths" that transcend the individual and reflect some deeper communal verities. The impersonality of the text heightens the authority of the discourse. In the absence of a human agent, contingent truths assume the hue of incontestable social essences.

The "Truth-Effect" of the Character of Viṣṇuśarman

The second aspect of authorship that I intend to explore is the effect exerted on the narrative by the character of Viṣṇuśarman. As mentioned above, the *kathāmukha* of the *Pañcatantra* states that it was Viṣṇuśarman who composed the five *tantras* for the edification of the young princes in his charge. As a result, Viṣṇuśarman is regarded by most traditional and modern authorities as the "author" of the *Pañcatantra.* While there is no evidence to indicate that Viṣṇuśarman was a historical figure, I suggest that even his fictional presence exerts a real effect on the narrative and on its reception. The purpose of this section is to explore this effect.

We will begin with an examination of Viṣṇuśarman's character. First, he created the *Pañcatantra* "having studied the cream of all the *arthaśāstras* in the world" (PT 1.2). He was recommended to King Amaraśakti as being a person who had "achieved renown for complete mastery over many *śāstras*" (PT 1.24). He had a reputation worth staking on the enterprize—if he failed in his attempt to educate the princes, he vowed to forsake his own name (PT 2.5). His word was a "lion's roar," and he was an octogenarian who had turned away from the objects of the senses, and who had renounced wealth (PT 2.6–7).

Thus the text ascribes to the character of Viṣṇuśarman the following qualities: he was said to possess wisdom, depth of learning, reputation, advanced years and renunciation, not to mention the fact that be was a *brāhmaṇa* and a male. In brahmanical culture, all these are high-value, high-status attributes. What effect is exerted on the narrative by the fact that its supposed creator was a wise, venerable, renunciant *brāhmaṇa?* Each element contributes to an overall impression that what Viṣṇuśarman was to teach the princes would be "true." That the wise speak the truth is almost axiomatic and need delay us no further. We may pause, however, to examine briefly the truth-effects of age and brahmanhood.

With the exception of the elderly cuckold, who is usually an old man with a young, frisky wife, it is rare to meet an "old fool" in Sanskrit literature: for to be old is to be wise. The *Pañcatantra* itself abounds in characters who are both aged and astute. The old goose (*vṛddhahaṃso*, PT 92.10) in Story 1-15 "Strand-bird and sea" suggested that the birds enlist Garuḍa to punish the ocean. The counsel of another old goose saved the whole community from the fowler's net (Story 1-19 "Goose and fowler"):

> The words of the elders are to be attended to. Those who are old have much knowledge. The flock of geese trapped in the forest was freed by the cleverness of the elder. (PT 92.12–13)

Sthirajīvin, the elderly ancestral minister (*ciraṃtanaṃ pitṛsacivaṃ*, PT 178.33) in Story 3-00 "War of crows and owls," was also the savior of his community. He too drew on his store of wisdom; in this case, the art of deception. The wise old monkey (*vṛddhavānareṇa*, PT 279.19) in Story 5-08 "Ape's revenge" was the only member of his community to escape the holocaust. In the epics, the nexus between age and wisdom is perhaps best illustrated in the *Mahābhārata* in the person of Bhīṣma, font of wisdom and most venerable and ancient of the Kurus. Finally, we may add one piece of linguistic evidence: the word for "young" (*bāla*) also means "foolish." Just as the old are by implication wise, the young are, by the same logic, ignorant.

If Viṣṇuśarman's age has a truth-effect on the discourse, what impact is exerted by his social status of a *brāhmaṇa?* It comes as little surprise that the brahmanical archive abounds in references to the excellence of that *varṇa.* For example:

> Of beings, those that breathe are thought to be the best; of those that breathe, those which live by intelligence; of the intelligent, men; and of men, the *brāhmaṇa*; of *brāhmaṇas,* the learned. . . . A *brāhmaṇa,* being born, is born as the highest on earth, lord of all beings, for the protection of the treasury of *dharma.* Whatever exists in the world is the *brāhmaṇa*'s own; on account of the excellence of his origin, the *brāhmaṇa* is indeed entitled to all. (MS 1.96–99)

The condition of being a *brāhmaṇa* lends credibility: in *kathā* literature, we occasionally meet a *brāhmaṇa* who is a naive fool (e.g., Story 3-04 "*Brāhmaṇa,* goat and three rogues," Story 5-03 "Lion-makers"), but never, as far as I am aware, one who is a rogue or a liar. In the broader context of Sanskrit literature, or at least that portion which constitutes the brahmanical archive, *brāhmaṇas* are the custodians and the repositories of truth and wisdom, as they constitute the *varṇa* with access to the *Vedas* and scriptural orthodoxy. In the archive in general, the *brāhmaṇa* is the incorruptible paragon of virtue. Because of the caustic, satirical slant of much *kathā* literature, and because we do meet the occasional foolish *brāhmaṇa,* it may be more accurate to say that when paragons of orthodox brahmanical virtue are required, they are most frequently recruited from among the *brāhmaṇas,* just as paragons of velour are usually *kṣatriyas.* When we meet a foolish *brāhmaṇa,* it is his foolishness that is at issue, not his brahmanhood. There are plenty of fools in the *Pañcatantra: brāhmaṇas, kṣatriyas, vaiśyas,* and *śūdras* in almost equal measure. The moral preeminence which *brāhmaṇas* accorded themselves in Sanskrit literature should hardly come as a surprise, as the archive functions as an ideological weapon in the brahmanical class-war against all comers.[1]

We can test the truth-effect of Viṣṇuśarman's brahmanhood on the narrative by conducting a simple mental experiment. Imagine for a moment that the *skeptron* is taken from the hand of the *brāhmaṇa* and given to a laundryman, for example, or a *caṇḍāla* or hunter. The scene is no longer the palace, but the riverbank, the cremation ground or the forest. The audience consists of ragged urchins, not elegant, lazy princes. The language of choice is no longer Sanskrit, but is perhaps a vernacular. Suddenly, it is more difficult to conceive of these stories as being "hegemonic," as being as highly valued or effective, or that they would profoundly influence the sons of a king. In this experiment, the stories are now enunciated at and from the periphery of the *maṇḍala.* By shifting the social locus of the narrator to the periphery, the narrative is also deprived of its centrality, its apical cultural status. The peripheral status of the enunciator appears to colonize the narrative and to detract from the truth-value of the discourse.

As a member of the *varṇa* that claimed for itself a corporate monopoly on the production and distribution of truth, Viṣṇuśarman's brahmanical status exerts a significant truth-effect on the discourse. Being placed in the mouth of a *brāhmaṇa,* the narratives—and by implication, the discourse embedded in them—become party to the power, credibility, and authority of his *varṇa.* Viṣṇuśarman's centrality and power become the centrality and power of the discourse.

Textual Strategies and Authority

Bourdieu observed that "authority comes to language from outside." Authority manifests in the text in the "stylistic features which characterize the language of priests, teachers and, more generally, all institutions." These stylistic features, which make manifest the social authority invested in their creators, are the subject of this section.

Pūrṇabhadra's Pañcatantra opens with the Jaina *mūlamantra,* "*arham.*" This is followed by homage to Sarasvatī and a verse describing briefly how Viṣṇuśarman came to compose the *Pañcatantra.* The text proper begins with the words: "This, as follows, is heard" (*tad yathānuśrūyate* | PT 1.4). A similar construction is repeated at the opening of the first *tantra* (PT 3.4).

The verb *anuśrūyate* "it is heard" is in the passive voice. This voice is, of course, very common in Sanskrit, and here as elsewhere it emphasizes the reception by the audience, rather than the production of the narrative. The expression "It is heard" suggests that the text must have a preexisting receptor—it must be "heard" by someone—and yet this construction draws a veil over the text's creator. The text is already self-existent in the ether, it is not contingent or created, but is unoriginated and above authorial agency. Just as we observed in relation to anonymity, the relegation to the background of the agent of textual production removes the text from the realm of fallible human endeavor. It is no longer the mere reflection of personal predilections. This process of obscuring the creative agency lends an air of distance, impersonality, transcendence and, I suggest, authority to the discourse.[2]

Just as the narratives of the *Pañcatantra* are introduced by the authoritative voice exerting its delegated authority and demanding to be heard, so too a "call to order" is frequently issued before a didactic verse is introduced into the narrative. Common introductions to verses include, "It is heard that . . ." (*śrūyate,* e.g., PT 36.14) and variations such as "Has it not been heard by you in this regard . . ." (*kim iha na śrutaṃ bhavatā* | PT 37.18–19). Expressions like "It is said . . ." (*uktaṃ ca*) are very common, as are "It is well said . . ." (*sādhv idam ucyate* | PT 1.10) and its variations (e.g., *suṣṭhu khalv idam ucyate* | PT 59.12–13).

As with *anuśrūyate,* these introductory phrases create the impression that there is a preexisting, primordial quantum of wisdom in existence in society in the form of countless, timeless, placeless verses. The fact that they were all once the production of a human hand is nowhere apparent; it is gracefully elided. Although many have been traced (e.g., by Sternbach) to one or other of the "hegemonic" texts—typically the *dharmaśāstras* and *arthaśāstras,* no provenance or attribution is ever given in the *Pañcatantra.* Even in the case of quotations from well-known authoritative texts, the verses preserve an air of anonymity. Even in those cases where the supposed source of a verse has been identified, these sources themselves are ascribed to remote, saintly, sagely figures of near-mythic power and authority: Manu and Kauṭilya, for example, are certainly not "normal" human authors.

The emphasis is never on the production and origin of the narrative units or the verses, but on their reception. The potentially fallible human authors are effectively rendered invisible by the use of these textual devices. The displacement of social agency and contingency, the act of divorcing the text from its conditioned origins, lends them an air of ubiquity and infallibility, both of which help to ensure that the authority of the text remains unassailable.

The Authoritative Voice and the *Pañcatantra*

To summarize what we have found, Pūrṇabhadra's *Pañcatantra* and its embedded discourse of division are enunciated in an authoritative voice. The social authority invested in its creators is made manifest in the fact that it is a written text, and that it was written in Sanskrit, the power-language of the brahmanical archive. Despite being the creation of generations of individual human agents, the text maintains a pretence of anonymity. Paradoxically, it is attributed to the fictional authorial character of Viṣṇuśarman, whose brahmanhood and general status place the narrative at the centre of the social *maṇḍala*. Certain textual features, such as the use of the impersonal passive voice, which privileges reception over production, serve to intensify the apparent truthfulness of the discourse. The net effect of the authoritative voice is to lend the narrative and the discourse unassailability and unimpeachability. It renders both unchallengeable; they can be neither brooked nor gainsaid. The authoritative voice in which the *Pañcatantra* is enunciated serves to make the discourse function as "true."

Universalizing the Discourse: Space, Time, and Audience

Like most Sanskrit texts, Pūrṇabhadra's *Pañcatantra* appears to transcend time and place, and surrounds itself with an aura of universal applicability. In this section I will describe these aspects of the text and I will explore the effect they exert on the discourse.

"Placelessness": Literary Space and Truth

We will now examine the ways in which the physical settings of the narrative units of the *Pañcatantra* affect the discourse. Jahn, who uses the expression "literary space," has formulated a useful approach to the theory of narrative settings. He defines literary space as "the spatial environment and the inventory of objects created in the reader's imagination."

> Literary space is more than just "place" or "setting"—it includes landscapes as well as climatic conditions, cities as well as gardens and rooms, and all spatially located objects and things. (Jahn 1999: N6.1)

For this discussion, it will be useful to think of Pūrṇabhadra's *Pañcatantra* as consisting of six major narrative sections: the overall framing device in which Viṣṇuśarman educates the sons of King Amaraśakti, and the five *tantras,* which he narrated to the princes and which are embedded within this frame. Each of these six units is ascribed to a particular geographical location that determines its literary space. The overall frame-story opens with the words "In the southern land, there was a city named Mahilāropya" (PT 1.4).

What can we say about Mahilāropya? Monier-Williams, citing the *Pañcatantra* as his only reference, simply records the fact that Mahilāropya is a "city in the south of India" and offers the parallel form "Mihilāropya." Macdonell, somewhat unconvincingly, glosses Mahilāropya as "N[ame] of a town in the South near Madras," but gives no further reference for this assertion (Macdonell 1924: 222). H. H. Wilson, cited by Rajan, suggested that Mahilāropya might be Mayilāpura, "now part of the capital of Tamil Nadu" (Rajan 1993: xi). I have found no other references to Mahilāropya, and I suspect that it is unique to the *Pañcatantra,* and as such, is probably fictional. In short, the literary space for the story of Viṣṇuśarman and the princes is Mahilāropya, and hence the space in which the five *tantras* are narrated is somewhere in "the south."

Confusingly, Viṣṇuśarman also begins his first *tantra,* Story 1-00 "Lion and bull," with the words, "In the southern lands, there was a city named Mahilāropya" (PT 3.4–8). From a narrative point of view, it makes no sense that Viṣṇuśarman, who was already said to be in Mahilāropya, should tell the princes a story set in "a city named Mahilāropya in the southern lands." Surely Viṣṇuśarman and the princes already knew where they were. Either Viṣṇuśarman was a poor judge of an exotic location for his story, or the princes were even dimmer than the text implies. A third and more likely explanation is that an editorial blunder has resulted in the duplication of the name Mahilāropya and the reference to the "southern lands" in both the *kathāmukha* and the first *tantra.*

What can be said about the literary space of the other four *tantras?* The frame-story of the second *tantra,* Story 2-00 "Dove, mouse, crow, tortoise and deer," is set near a city named Pramadāropya—which may also mean "to be ascended by women"—and is also said to be in the south (PT 126.6). The action of the third *tantra,* Story 3-00 "War of crows and owls," takes place near Pṛthvīpratiṣṭhānam, another city in the south (PT 174.9). The frame-story of the fifth *tantra,* Story 5-00 "Barber who killed the monks," is set in a southern location in a city called Pāṭaliputra (PT 257.6).[3] There is some confusion here as Pāṭaliputra is the name of a city on the Ganges in northern India. Either the author is mistaken, or perhaps he imagined another city of the same name in the south. Only the frame-story of the fourth *tantra,* Story 4-00 "Ape and crocodile," is not specifically located in the south, but its literary space is nevertheless exotic, "other" and indeed "southerly": the shores of an ocean (PT 228.5).[4]

In addition to these major narrative units of the *Pañcatantra* which are explicitly set in southern lands, the embedded Story 2-02 "Mouse and two monks," like the frame-story of the second *tantra,* is set in Pramadāropya (PT 134.25).

There are at least three other mentions of the south in the text: in Story 1-08 "Weaver as Viṣṇu," the remote and hostile king Śrīvikramasena resided in the south (PT 53.3). In Story 4-08 "Adulteress tricked by paramour," a ploughman's wife, bored with her aged husband, ran away with her new lover in a southerly direction (PT 249.15). Also in the frame-story of the second *tantra,* the crow proposed a visit to his friend, and said, "In the south, in the middle of a forest thicket is a great lake. There is a tortoise by the name of Mantharaka. . . ." (PT 133.18–19).

By contrast, I have found only two mentions of the north in the whole text. Both are associated with mountains and treasure: in Story 1-09 "Grateful beasts and thankless man," the tiger invited the *brāhmaṇa* to his treasure-filled cave, which was on the northern side of a many-peaked mountain (PT 62.10). In Story 5.02 "Four-treasure seekers" a yogin advised the four adventurers to go to "the northern face of the Himācala" to look for treasure (PT 264.19).[5] The few mentions of east and west are, with a single exception, made in connection with the rising and setting of the sun, and are of no interest to this discussion.

What significance can we attribute to the apparent preoccupation with the south as a literary setting? Most studies of the *Pañcatantra* (with the exception of Edgerton's) regard the fact that the court of Amaraśakti was set in the south as evidence of the collection's northern origins (see, e.g., Olivelle 1997: xiii). This seems reasonable, but there are other implications to be drawn from this. Here the richness of the term "literary space" comes into play, as it incorporates more than just physical setting. It also indicates the importance of the images created by the setting in the reader's imagination. For a northern audience, the south is exotic, unknown, "other." Goldman suggests that, for the poet of the *Rāmāyaṇa,* for example, anything south of the Ganges, and particularly peninsular India, was "a dimly known realm that he could safely represent to an originally provincial audience as inhabited by ogres, magicians, and talking beasts." South India was "known to him only as a distant and wild land ideally suited to his purposes in pitting his fearless hero against the terrifying dark forces" (Goldman 1984: 27–28). This attitude to the south may also have inspired, or have been inspired by, scriptural references such as this one from the *Padmapurāṇa:* "A twice-born should not live in any other country than the auspicious one between the Himālaya and the Vindhya and the eastern and western seas" (PP 3.48.21–22). A similar passage in Manu and the *dharmasūtras* refers to this region as Āryāvarta, the "Land of the *Āryas*" (MS 2.22, BD 1.2.9–10, VD 1.8–12). The north is privileged over all other areas: "The practices in that land are authoritative" (BD 1.2.9).

The south appears to function as the narrative equivalent of a "land far away" or a "distant kingdom" in Western literature. The embedded stories examined above further suggest that the south is the direction of wonder, promise, new opportunities and new beginnings.

The act of locating a story in a remote geographical location has the effect of creating a literary space that is novel, exciting and fictional. The authors have weakened the factuality of their narrative by situating it in a fictional or imaginary setting, and are effectively informing their readers of the fictional nature of the content of the narrative. In the Western literary tradition, as soon as the audience hears the words, "Once upon a time . . . ," the narrative is firmly located in the specific genre of fairy story or tale. We are primed to receive the narrative that follows in a certain way, with a certain set of expectations and preconditions. We are conscious of the narrative's fictional nature, but are unconsciously prepared for the reception of the moral or truth for which the narrative is the vector. Perhaps the same may be said of the *Pañcatantra.* The fictionality of the narrative is highlighted when the narrative is located in an exotic literary space. At the same time, the narrative's membership in the genre of didactic tale is effectively brought to the fore. Is it possible that the audience is being primed to receive a "true" discourse by situating the narrative in a fictional setting?

An audience knows what is "true" in its own specific sphere of experience. If one sees a truth played out in a "land faraway," that truth appears to be generalized beyond one's own sphere. By selecting a location for the narrative in the audiences' "other," the creators of the narrative induce the effect of universalizing the discourse. How would we receive the *Pañcatantra* if it were set in the next village or in the next city? I suggest that the use of such a mundane location would exert a diminished truth-effect on the discourse.

Not all the stories in Pūrṇabhadra's *Pañcatantra* are set in the south or in locations that are strictly fictional: individual narratives are also located in Vardhamāna (Story 1-03 "Merchant and king's sweep," PT 17.2), Puṇḍhravardhana "in the lands of the Gauḍas" (Story 1-08 "Weaver as Viṣṇu," PT 46.2), Ayodhyā in the lands of the Kośalas (Story 1-22 "King, minister and false monk," PT 102.28) and Rājagṛha (Story 1-23 "Maid weds a serpent," PT 104.18). Story 5-10 "Blind man, hunchback and the three-breasted princess' is set a city "in the north" called Madhupura (PT 285.5). At this temporal and cultural distance from the creators of these texts and their audiences, it is impossible to discern what cultural associations these five cities may have held. We can, however, assume that no authors would actively seek to make their narratives more pedestrian or less novel. We can only suppose, therefore, that the selection of these locations effectively heightened the appeal of the narrative in some way: they must at least have been regarded as interesting.

Let us turn now from the question of literary space of the major narrative units to the shorter, embedded stories. Like the frame-stories above, most of the embedded stories begin with a statement giving the location. A typical story might begin with the words, "There was in a certain place . . ." (*asti kasmiṃścit pradeśe* . . . e.g., PT 5.17, PT 35.2). The text provides such locations for sixty-eight embedded stories. Of these, sixty-four are set in unnamed, indefinite and generalized locations, as follows:

a certain place (*kasmiṃścid adhiṣṭhāne, pradeśe, deśe, sthāne*)	30
a certain forest (*kasmiṃścid vanoddeśe, araṇye*)	15
a certain city (*kasmiṃścid nagare, pure*)	7
a certain lake (*kasmiṃścit sarasi, hrade, jalaśaye*)	5
other (ocean, palace, mountain, tree, anthill, well, etc.)	7

What impact does the indefinite nature of a setting such as "a certain place" or "a certain forest" have on the reception of the narrative and the discourse? Paradoxically, a "certain place" is an uncertain place. The phenomenon of generalizing the location of folktales, didactic tales and fables seems to be common to many cultures. This is the spatial equivalent of the temporal generalization, "once upon a time." I suggest that by divorcing the narrative from a specific identifiable location, both narrative and discourse become universalized. A "certain place" is effectively anywhere and everywhere. The radius in which the discourse is applicable is extended beyond the local and the specific, to incorporate all places and situations. Lacking a specific location, the narrative, and by implication the discourse, can never be verified, and hence never falsified.

The formulaic opening line "There was in a certain place . . . ," like "Once upon a time," serves to "unlocate" the narrative geographically, but it also locates the narrative discursively within the *kathā* genre. The audience is immediately alerted to the fact that the narrative that follows will be fictional. As I argued above, by highlighting the fictional nature of the narrative itself, the "true" aspect of the discourse in the didactic tradition is brought to the foreground. We know parables, folktales, fairy tales, etc., to be fictional, yet we expect them to say something valid, that is, "true," about some human condition. I suggest that the same may be the case here. The formulaic device "There was in a certain place . . ." clearly indicates the fictional nature of the narrative, but at the same time, it identifies a didactic discourse which, for the reasons outlined in this chapter, functions as "true."

In this section I have argued that the fabulous settings of the major narrative units, particularly those in the "south," and the nonspecific settings of the embedded narrative units, exert a truth-effect, primarily by serving to generalize the discourse, and secondarily, I speculate, by locating the text within the *kathā* genre, the audience is sensitized to receive some social truism via a patently fictional narrative.

Timelessness: Temporal Universalization

As we have seen, the spatial settings of the various narrative units of the *Pañcatantra* are either remote or generalized. I will first describe the temporal settings of the *Pañcatantra,* and I will then suggest the possible effects that this temporal framing may have on the reception of the narrative.

In what timeframe are the narratives of the *Pañcatantra* situated? We can derive some sense of this by examining the way in which the stories are introduced. The overall framing story, as we saw above, opens with the words, "In the southern land, there was a city named Mahilāropya" (*asti dākṣiṇātye janapade mahilāropyaṃ nāma nagaram* | PT 1.3). The verb *asti* is in the present tense and might indeed have the usual present sense inherent in that form. Perhaps the creators of this narrative wished to convey the impression that the city of Mahilāropya was contemporaneous with their act of narration. But is the verb *asti* really a present tense, or is it better understood as the "historical present" (Macdonell 1955 [1927]: 205), that is, a present verb with a past sense?

The same verb *asti* is used in many of the narratives in the *Pañcatantra* in senses that are indeed the "historical present." For example, the opening lines of Story 1-01 "Ape and wedge" reads, "There was a city in a certain place" (*asti kasmiṃścit pradeśe nagaram* | PT 5.17). The next line tells us that a place of worship was "caused to be built" there (*kāryate sma* |

PT 5.18). It is also possible in this context that the present sense was intended, but the historical present sits more comfortably with the past tense of the second sentence.

Returning to the main frame-story set in Mahilāropya, having introduced the location, the text then introduces the protagonist, the king Amaraśakti (*tatra . . . [a]maraśaktir nāma rājā babhūva* | PT 1.4–6). The verb *babhūva* is in the perfect tense, which is "properly restricted to the statement of facts of the remote past, not coming within the experience of the speaker" (Macdonell 1955 [1927]: 206). As the combination of a historical present and other past tenses is common in the great majority of stories in the *Pañcatantra,* we may safely assume that the *asti* of the overall frame-story is also a historical present, and in combination with the perfect *babhūva,* establishes a temporal setting for the entire *Pañcatantra* at an indefinite time in the remote past.

At the level below the overall frame, each of the five *tantras* is also set in a particular time frame. In the first *tantra,* we read that the merchant Vardhamāna, owner of the bull Saṃjīvaka, lived in Mahilāropya. In this case the verb is *prativasati sma* (PT 3.09), which also establishes the narrative at some time in the indefinite past. Similar phrasing is used to introduce the protagonists of the fourth and fifth *tantras:* in both cases a historical present is used with a past tense (*asti* and *prativasati sma* PT 228.6, 7; PT 257.6, 7). The time frame for the second and third *tantras* is indicated by the use of the historical present alone (*asti,* PT 126.6, 7; and *asti, tiṣṭhati,* PT 174.9,10, respectively).

At the third narrative level, that of the individual embedded stories, the temporal framing provided by the *tantras* is repeated with variations: the time frames of some stories are suggested by the use of the historical present, some are formed with past tenses using *sma* and others with past passive participles.

We can say in general, then, that the narratives of the *Pañcatantra,* at all three levels of framing—the overall frame, the five individual *tantras* and the embedded stories—are all set in the indefinite and remote past. What Lévi-Strauss said about the time frame of the myth, its timelessness and its explanatory powers, applies equally well to the *Pañcatantra:*

> On the one hand, a myth always refers to events alleged to have taken place long ago. But what gives the myth an operational value is that the specific pattern described is timeless; it explains the present and the past as well as the future. (Lévi-Strauss 1963: 209)

Max Lüthi made a similar remark with reference to the phrase "Once upon a time" and its German equivalent:

> the phrase "*Es war einmal*" by no means is intended to stress the fact that events in the tale took place in the past. The intent is to suggest the very opposite: what once occurred, has the tendency continually to recur. (Lüthi 1970: 47)

What effects might this distant temporal setting exert on the discourse? The effects, like those suggested for the spatial settings, are twofold. First, the effect of setting the narratives in the indefinite and remote past is to generalize the discourse in a temporal dimension. By reaching back in time, the narrative effectively stretches the temporal radius of the discourse. That which functions as true now also functioned as true in the past. This truth transcends time. By illustrating the functioning of true discourses in a remote or historical time frame, the narrative provides an additional temporal dimension to the truthfulness of the discourse, which compliments the spatial dimension described above. Pollock has suggested that what he terms "the lack of historicality in Sanskrit intellectual discourse" marks a conscious choice on the part of *brāhmaṇa* intellectuals "to remove every spatiotemporal constraint from discussions of problems viewed as transcending space and time" (Pollock 2002: 438). Although the context under consideration here is different, the principle remains the same. The text gives no inkling of the fact that this discourse applies only to a particular time or place. The opposite is in fact the case: the narrative shows the discourse to be both spatially and temporally transcendent.

Applicability: Universalizing the Audience

What does the text tell us about its intended audience? To whom do these narratives apply? To whom is it relevant? We may consider this question at two levels. Firstly, at the level of the text itself, we have described the fiction that Viṣṇuśarman composed the *tantras* for the princes. For this reason, and perhaps because of the relatively unsophisticated nature of the narratives, the *Pañcatantra* has almost universally been regarded as a text for children. The *Pañcatantra* itself states that it exists "for the edification of the young" (*bālāvabodhanārthaṃ*, PT 2.15). At another level, that of discourse, there is no suggestion that the applicability is confined to the young. What the *Pañcatantra* has to say, the truth of its discourse, is presented as if it were equally applicable to people of all ages, times and places. As the *kathāmukha* boasted, "one who reads or hears this *nītiśāstra* will never be overcome, even by Indra" (*yo 'traitat paṭhati prāyo ' nītiśāstraṃ śṛṇoti vā* | *na parābhavam āpnoti ' sa śakrād api karhicit* || PT 2.17–18). This relative–correlative construction is open-ended, inclusive and all-embracing. Further, we are told that the *Pañcatantra* "has spread forth across the surface of the Earth" (PT 2.16). This primary evidence from the text itself suggests that it perceived its audience to include anyone, anywhere. This may be supplemented with secondary evidence suggested by Pollock, who, as we saw above, argued that:

> Accordingly, when poets chose to write in the Sanskrit language, they were choosing, along with a certain aesthetic, a certain readership—in this case a cosmopolitan, virtually global readership. And they did this, we may accordingly infer, because they had something cosmopolitan, something global, to say. (Pollock 2003: 75)

This gives an indication of the breadth and inclusiveness, of the universality, of the *Pañcatantra*'s audience. This is how the creators of the *Pañcatantra* regarded their text and its embodied discourse: they saw it spreading across the surface of the whole world. In addition, there is a confidence in the enunciation, typified by the authoritative voice. This accentuates the impression that while narratives may have been created for children, the creators regarded the discursive truths, for which the stories are vectors, as having a universal audience.

To conclude this section on the universalization of the discourse, we have seen how the ideas expressed in the *Pañcatantra* are not just supposed to be relevant to a particular time, place, or audience. On the contrary, the text conveys the confident impression that it is universally applicable. The discourse does not simply hold true for a given audience fenced off by a set of temporal, spatial, or demographic boundaries. By appearing to hold true for all times, places, and audiences, the truthfulness of the discourse is effectively universalized.

The Śāstric Paradigm

We will now turn to the relationship between the *Pañcatantra* and the class of texts known as *śāstras.* I will investigate the ways in which the *Pañcatantra* gains authority and credibility by being aligned with two classes of *śāstras*, the *nītiśāstras* (treatises on kingly conduct) and *arthaśāstras* (practical treatises on statecraft and governance). These two subgenres have strong and clear associations with the court, the ruling elite, and power. I will begin with a description of the genre of *śāstra,* and the nature of its inherent authority.

In Sanskritic culture, the *śāstras* are a class of texts that contain sets of rules. According to a traditional definition, a *śāstra* "teaches people what they should and should not do" (Pollock 1985: 501). On the function of this genre, the *Pañcatantra* says, "In the *śāstra,* the wise advocate good conduct" (PT 125.1). There are *śāstras* for a wide range of human endeavors, from the veterinary care of elephants (see Winternitz 1967 [1889]: 608) to the arts of sexual intercourse: śāstric "codification of behavior was represented across the entire cultural spectrum." *Śāstras* have been "invested with massive authority" and possess "a nearly unchallengeable claim to normative control of cultural practices" (Pollock 1985: 499, 500). They have an interest:

> in bringing to consciousness or making explicit behavior that is largely tacit or pre-conscious. But more than this, such texts at the same time *constitute* an activity as a "science," and thus as a target of intervention by the dominant culture. (Pollock 1985: 507–508)

Their status in the world of practice is analogous to the position of scripture in the world of ideas. *Śāstras,* as the ultimate source of all knowledge, provide a direct guide to practice. The learned, therefore, do not "creatively reason" from the *śāstras,* they simply behave in accordance with them. The *śāstras* are presented as primordial, divinely inspired or divinely revealed. Their knowledge is static and finite. It does not change or grow. They permit no concept of progress other than better or closer application of an existing *śāstra.* While there was in fact some innovation, it was disguised to resemble renovation and recovery (Pollock 1985: 515). Pollock perceived the origins of the paradigm in the traditional attitude to the *Vedas,* which were seen as eternal, infinite, self-existent and infallible. The *śāstra* came to share in the *Vedas'* "transcendent attributes" (Pollock 1985: 519). The śāstric paradigm is summarized below:

> We may in fact characterize the ideological effects of the shastric paradigm more broadly as follows: First, all contradiction between the model of cultural knowledge and actual cultural change is thereby at once transmuted and denied; creation is really re-

> creation, as the future is, in a sense, the past. Second, the living, social, historical, contingent tradition is naturalized, becoming as much a part of the order of things as the laws of nature themselves: Just as the social, historical phenomenon of language is viewed by Mīmāṃsā as natural and eternal, so the social dimension and historicality of all cultural practices are eliminated in the shastric paradigm. And finally, through such denial of contradiction and reification of tradition, the sectional interests of premodern India are universalized and valorized. The theoretical discourse of *śāstra* becomes in essence a practical discourse of power. (Pollock 1985: 516)

How do *śāstras* naturalize and dehistoricize? They naturalize—that is, make cultural practices appear natural and hence normal—by claiming for themselves a divine, or predivine, primordial origin. *Śāstras* have gathered unto themselves all authority and made it their own. They preclude argument, experimentation or innovation. Cultural practices under the śāstric paradigm are "as much a part of the order of things as the laws of nature themselves." Because such practices are viewed as natural and eternal, "the social dimension and historicality of all cultural practices are eliminated" (Pollock 1985: 516).

Pollock speaks of the *śāstra* as part of a normative discourse formulated by the Mīmāṃsā tradition, "the most orthodox and in many respects most representative of Indian traditions, and the one that most effectively formulated many of the fundamental cultural orientations of Sanskritic culture." They became in time a "rigorously normative code" (Pollock 1985: 503–504). The *śāstras,* as part of a "larger power discourse," are one of the media through which the dominant tradition exerted its social power. Significantly for this study, "True knowledge as such belongs, axiomatically, to the domain of *śāstra*" (Pollock 2001: 198).

The *Pañcatantra*'s Claim to Be a *Śāstra*

The creators of the *Pañcatantra* consciously and conspicuously aligned their work with this genre. At many prominent junctures in the text, they remind us that the *Pañcatantra* is itself a *śāstra,* and in doing so they effectively invoke śāstric authority. The work becomes enmeshed within, or subject to, the śāstric paradigm and all that it entails. In its very opening lines the *Pañcatantra* at once acknowledges its supposed lineal descent from the *arthaśāstras* and self-consciously seeks to place itself within the body of śāstric literature. After the homage to Sarasvatī, the first words of the *Pañcatantra* are as follows:

> Having consulted the cream of all the *arthaśāstras* in the world, Viṣṇuśarman composed this highly pleasing *śāstra* with five *tantras.* (PT 1.2–3)

Again, at the conclusion of the *kathāmukha* the work is identified as a "*nītiśāstra* by the name of *Pañcatantraka*" (PT 2.15), and in its concluding verse, the *kathāmukha* recounts the benefits to all who "read or listen to this *nītiśāstra*" (PT 2.17).

Just as the *kathāmukha* of the *Pañcatantra* opens with references to the *śāstras,* we also find references to the fact that the *Pañcatantra* is a *śāstra* in the *praśasti* which concludes the text. Here the work is described as "the *nītiśāstra Pañcākhyānaka,* also known as the *Pañcatantra*" (PT 289.15). In the following line the *Pañcatantra* is said to be a "*śāstra* on the conduct of kings" (*nṛpanītiśāstram* | PT 289.16). Again, Pūrṇabhadra's own text is referred to as "this *śāstra*" (*śāstram idam* || PT 289.23).

The fact that the text both opens and closes with explicit references to its supposed śāstric nature and affiliations seems to set the timbre for the whole work. The opening and closing references provide the ultimate śāstric frame for the entire narrative and serve to remind the reader where the text stands.

As an element in a normative, didactic tradition, and as a self-proclaimed *śāstra,* the functions and goals of the *Pañcatantra* become congruent with those of the *śāstras* as a whole: "to teach people what they should and should not do." For this reason, much of what may be said about *śāstras* as a genre, and about the śāstric paradigm, is, I believe, also highly relevant to the *Pañcatantra.*

Arthaśāstra and *Nītiśāstra*

We have seen that the *Pañcatantra* sought to associate itself with the class of *śāstras* in general, and more specifically, with the *artha-* and *nītiśāstras.* What are these two subclasses? The word *artha* has a broad range of meanings, but the most useful ones in this context are "advantage, use, utility" (MMW). The concept of *artha* in the sense of material gain is often juxtaposed with spiritual endeavor (*dharma*) and sensual pleasure (*kāma*), and later, with liberation (*mokṣa*). Together these constitute the basic goals of the ideal brahmanical life, as defined in the *dharmaśāstras* and *-sūtras*. As we shall see, *artha* in this context also has distinctly royal connotations, encompassing the day-to-day, practical business of government. *Nīti*, too, has many shades of meaning: the most relevant for us are "conduct," but especially "right, moral or wise conduct," but also "policy and political wisdom or science" (MMW). On this basis, the *arthaśāstras* and *nītiśāstras* are, respectively, specialized treatises on conduct and treatises on the attainment of practical goals, specifically in the sphere of kingship, statecraft and governance. There is, in fact, much overlap between the two genres:

> The Indians understand by the term Arthaśāstra all the theories and manuals taken together that deal with practical life—Technique, Domestic Economy, Administration and in particular Politics. The most important branch of Arthaśāstra is Politics that is mentioned also as the independent science of Nītiśāstra, the science of "guidance" or of "government" In particular knowledge is necessary for the king for the purpose of domestic affairs and for administration. It constitutes a section of "Politics," so much so that sometimes the term Arthaśāstra and Nītiśāstra are used as synonyms. Since the Indians could not conceive of any form of administration, other than monarchial, this science is called also Rājanīti, "King's Politics"; and since the most important instrument of administration was the power of punishment, it was also called Daṇḍanīti, "Punishment Politics." (Winternitz 1967 [1889]: 570)

Keith seems to follow Winternitz:

> The fable, indeed, is essentially connected with the two branches of science known by Indians as the *Nītiçāstra* and the *Arthaçāstra*, which have this in common as opposed to the *Dharmaçāstra* that they are not codes of morals, but deal with man's action in practical politics and conduct of the ordinary affairs of every-day life and intercourse. We must not, however, exaggerate the contrast between these Çāstras, for in the *Arthaçāstra* and the *Nītiçāstra* alike there is much common sense, and that is often in accord with practical morality. . . . (Keith 1920: 243)

Keith proceeds to qualify this distinction by saying that both subclasses contain some moral instruction and that there is a lingering influence of the *dharmaśāstras,* as one would expect for a book intended for the instruction of the young by *brāhmaṇas.* Keith, like Winternitz, tends to use the two terms *nītiśāstra* and *arthaśāstra* more or less interchangeably (Keith 1920: 450). One indigenous view, as presented in Kamandaki's *Nītisāra,* holds that the *nītiśāstras* are a subset of the *arthaśāstras,* or more poetically, that the former is the nectar churned from the great ocean of the latter (NS 1.6).

The meaning, in a practical sense, of *nītiśāstra* can be gauged from the way the term is used in the *Pañcatantra.* In Story 1-05 "Crows and serpent," the crow husband soothed his wife by assuring her that he had "wise friends skilled in the *nītiśāstras*" (PT 36.3). Sthirajīvin, the aged crow strategist who engineered the victory over the owls, is described as "having reached the further shore of all the *nītiśāstras*" (PT 178.33).[6] Without exaggerating the difference between these two subclasses, in the following section I will briefly survey the most important texts in each. I will then compare these with the *Pañcatantra.*

As mentioned above, *artha* in this context is best understood as the practical goals of everyday life, especially in the administration of a state. Hence a specialist treatise on the subject of *artha,* an *arthaśāstra,* deals with these matters in the context of the court and kingship, and is a handbook for the practical aspects of governance and policy. The most prominent extant work of this genre is the *Kauṭilīya Arthaśāstra.* I have consulted the text edited by Kangle and published by Motilal Banarsidass (English translation: Shamasastry 1951, usefully summarized by Keith 1920: 452–458). In fact, while the *Arthaśāstra* had a certain number of predecessors, it was so comprehensive and successful that, like Pāṇini's *Aṣṭādhyāyī,* it appears to have superceded all its competitors, and is almost the only contender left in the field.

The *Arthaśāstra* consists of fifteen sections on such topics as the upbringing and education of princes, duties of functionaries and officials, laws and punishments pertaining to the trades and professions, taxes and wages, the arts of kingship and the conduct of politics, the arts of war and deception, and drugs and magic. This is all highly practical information for the hands-on day-to-day administration of a state. It is the kind of text that an administrator might keep at his elbow as a ready reference. It does not speak in allegories or allusions; it is direct and factual. The *Arthaśāstra* would be a handy reference for anyone who needs to know how much to fine a laundryman who does not wash clothes properly (6 *paṇas,* Shamasastry 1951: 228), or how to evade watchdogs with a *mantra* (Shamasastry 1951: 451). Its tone is amoral, ruthless and pragmatic.[7]

Let us now proceed to the *nītiśāstras,* emphasizing what the main exemplars have in common. Theoretically, a *nītiśāstra,* according to the definition above, is a specialist treatise on *nīti,* that is, right, moral, or wise conduct, but especially in the context of policy and political wisdom. The following verse from the *Pañcatantra* stresses the practical and pragmatic nature of the *nītiśāstras,* and their preoccupation with metaphors of victory and success.

> One who knows the true sense of the *nītiśāstras,* one who knows how to identify the right place and time—wherever he seeks victory, there he will find unexcelled accomplishment. (PT 184.14–15)

The genre of *nītiśāstras* is well known and frequently mentioned, but surprisingly, like the *arthaśāstras,* there are relatively few works in the genre as a whole. Another interesting point is that the main *nītiśāstras,* such as Kāmandaki's *Nītisāra* and Somadeva's *Nītivākyāmṛta,* are little more than reworkings of the *Kauṭilīya Arthaśāstra,* or are at least works that draw heavily on it or its predecessors. Keith describes the *Nītivākyāmṛta* as "a treatise on royal duties," in which the author exhorts kings to behave well and prudently (Keith 1920: 463). This sounds like a nitty-gritty handbook for those who are running kingdoms: perhaps these really were for kings and ministers, like Hemacandra's lost *Bṛhadarhannītiśāstra,* which he wrote at the behest of a king, Kumārapāla (Winternitz 1967 [1889]: 604).

On the other hand, Kāmandaki's *Nītisāra* (700–750 CE?), "The essence of policy," also appears to be a reworking of the *Arthaśāstra,* omitting some sections while amplifying others (Keith 1920: 462). It is "intermediate between a textbook and a work of didactical poetry" (Winternitz 1967 [1889]: 596). Somadeva's *Nītivākyāmṛta* (tenth century CE) is "strongly dependent upon Kauṭilya," but;

> It is not like the Arthaśāstra of Kauṭilya, a practical hand-book of politics and economics, but it is rather a pedagaugical [*sic*] work that contains fine counsels for the king. With Somadeva the concept of Nīti includes perhaps "political wisdom" as well as "moral conduct of life." Hence the work begins quite as a handbook of morals and here in several chapters the moralic tone is throughout dominant. (Winternitz 1967 [1889]: 600)

Similarly, Bhartṛhari's *Nītiśataka,* "Hundred verses on conduct," is a loose collection of verses of a generally dharmic tone. There is no sense in which they could be regarded as political or to be specifically for royal consumption.

From this brief survey, we can see that the main *nītiśāstras* fall into two broad and overlapping classes: practical textbooks on governance that resemble the *Arthaśāstra,* and collections of gnomic verses.

Pañcatantra, Arthaśāstra and *Nītiśāstra*

How does the *Pañcatantra* compare with the *arthaśāstras* and *nītiśāstras?* A certain amount of the material found in the *Arthaśāstra* is also used in the *Pañcatantra.* For example, the *Arthaśāstra*'s sixfold policy of peace, war, neutrality, marching, and so on, has a clear parallel in the third *tantra,* which describes the war of the crows and owls. The pragmatic tone of the two works is comparable in places; for example, both authorize deceit as a legitimate means to an end in certain circumstances. The *artha-* and *nītiśāstras* do not exclude all narrative: Somadeva Sūri's *Nītivākyāmṛta* includes a version of Story 1-09 "Grateful beasts and thankless man."

Despite these minor areas of similarity, even the briefest glance will show that the *Pañcatantra* and the *śāstras* are of two entirely different types. The *Pañcatantra* differs from the main *arthaśāstras* and *nītiśāstras* in both style and content, and to a large degree in disposition. The latter are mostly in either *sūtra* or verse form, and deliver their points directly, with little elaboration or prolongation. Most versions of the *Pañcatantra,* on the other hand, are narrative prose in *kathā* form, with embedded verses. They make their point through the narrative. The tone of the two *śāstra* genres and the *Pañcatantra* are also very different. One can easily imagine an administrator consulting the *Arthaśāstra* on a point of law. The *arthaśāstras* and *nītiśāstras* are dry, practical and filled with the realia of existence. The *Pañcatantra* is humorous and irreverent, and was read primarily for pleasure first and enlightenment second. Viṣṇuśarman himself stated that the work was "entertainment based on eloquence" (*sarasvatīvinodaṃ,* PT 2.7–8). It is easy to imagine real princes reading or listening to the *Pañcatantra:*

> [A prince] should spend the forenoon in training in the arts concerning elephants, horses, chariots and weapons, and the afternoon in hearing the *itihāsas.* The *itihāsas* include the *purāṇas,* histories, tales, stories, *dharmaśāstras* and *arthaśāstras.* (AŚ 1.5.12–14)

Stories (*ākhyāyika,* remembering that one version of the *Pañcatantra* is called "*Tantrākhyāyika,*" i.e., "*tantra*-stories") and illustrative examples (*udāharaṇa*) were indeed part of the curriculum of a prince's education. But this does not prove that these tales were created primarily or exclusively for a princely audience. Certainly, the *Pañcatantra*'s audience was spread far and wide beyond the palace walls.

Deep down within the *Pañcatantra* one may discern some of the themes of the *arthaśāstra/nītiśāstra* tradition: the conduct of kings, fortifications, strategy, armies, and so forth. But this does not necessarily make it a *nītiśāstra.* These examples form only a small part of the whole: the *Pañcatantra* is a broad collection of generally didactic stories, some of which may, almost incidentally, pertain to the arts of government. The *Pañcatantra*'s resemblance to the *Arthaśāstra* is wafer-thin, and if we take the mainstream members of the *nītiśāstra* genre as a guide, it can at best be considered a distant outlier of the nītiśāstric archipelago.

Ultimately, whether the *Pañcatantra* is properly an *arthaśāstra,* a *nītiśāstra* or neither is a matter of opinion. It certainly differs markedly in many important aspects from other works of both genres. It is easier to argue that these categories and their delimitations are not ultimately very important or useful. We may, however, say this with certainty: the *Pañcatantra* claims to be a *śāstra* in general, and a *nītiśāstra* in particular. For our purposes, whether the *Pañcatantra* is "really" an *arthaśāstra,* a *nītiśāstra,* or both, or neither, is of secondary significance. The important points are that firstly the text claims such a lofty pedigree, and that secondly, such claims are widely assumed to be true. The *Pañcatantra* derives status, credibility and truthfulness by claiming an association with the *arthaśāstras* and *nītiśāstras,* even if such associations are tenuous. The important fact is that it functions as a *śāstra.* The text's own claim to be a *nītiśāstra* exerts a truth-effect on the discourse, with the result that it appears to be kingly, courtly and, above all, śāstric, as we shall see below.

Truth-Effects of Śāstric Pretensions

Keith observed that the opening verses of many of the related collections of gnomic verses, *Rājanītisamuccaya, Cāṇakyanīti, Cānakyarājanīti, Vṛddha-Cāṇakya* and *Laghu-Cāṇakya,* promise a treatise on the conduct of kings (*rājanīti*), but the actual number of verses that can be assigned to that topic is in fact negligible (Keith 1920: 228). There is a clear parallel between these collections of didactic verses disingenuously claiming to be about kingship on the one hand, and the *Pañcatantra,* which makes similar claims on the other. In both cases, I perceive a truth-effect deriving from royal pretensions. In English we would call this snob-value. It is not unlike the supposed added prestige that is provided by a monarchical coat of arms on a tin of biscuits. The *Pañcatantra* can hardly be said to be an *arthaśāstra* or a *nītiśāstra* in the senses described above, and yet in the Sanskrit literary imagination it is continually and inseparably associated with both. Viṣṇuśarman, we are told, "having consulted the cream of all the *arthaśāstras* composed this *nītiśāstra* in five *tantras*" (PT 1.2–3). By claiming to be a *nītiśāstra* and by identifying itself as a direct descendant of the *arthaśāstras*, the *Pañcatantra* gains credibility and authority through its association with those hoary, respected genres—it becomes "true." When I read this quotation from Nietzsche, I thought of the *Pañcatantra:*

> This has given me the greatest trouble and still does: to realize that what things *are called* is incomparably more important than what they are. The reputation, name, and appearance, the usual measure and weight of a thing, what it counts for—originally almost always wrong and arbitrary, thrown over things like a dress and altogether foreign to their nature and even to their skin—all this grows from generation unto generation, merely because people believe in it, until it gradually grows to be part of the thing and turns into its very body. What at first was appearance becomes in the end, almost invariably, the essence and is effective as such. (Nietzsche 1974 [1887]: II.58, 121–122)

The *Pañcatantra* is called a *nītiśāstra,* and whether this claim is true or not is less important than the fact that it is *effective* as one.

The "Fürstenspiegel Effect"

If, as I suggest, the *Pañcatantra* benefits from a truth-effect by virtue of its assumed position within the śāstric genre, yet another truth-effect is exerted by the narrative itself. The fiction that Viṣṇuśarman composed the five *tantras* for the three dull princes is presented as if it were a fact. The illusion is that the five *tantras* we read today are the very same ones that he prepared for his young charges:

> Having composed the five *tantras*, "Splitting of friends," "Acquisition of friends," "The crows and owls," "Loss of one's gains' and "Rash deeds," the king's sons were caused to study them. (PT 2.13–14)

All the *tantras*, with the exception of the first, open with Viṣṇuśarman intoning a verse that encapsulates the "moral" of the framing narrative that follows. In response to the verse, the princes asked "How was that?" (*katham etat*), and the *brāhmaṇa* then proceeded to narrate the frame-story for that *tantra*. In this way, at the beginning of four of the five major narrative units, we are reminded of the claim that the stories were composed for and imparted to princes. This is a text, if we choose to believe its own claims, which was written in the first place for royal consumption.

Everyone from Ibn al-Muqaffaʿ to Olivelle and Rajan seems to have accepted at face value the twin claims that the *Pañcatantra* was written for a royal audience and that it is about governance and kingly conduct. Few have ever doubted that the *Pañcatantra* is just what it claims to be: it is "unquestionably a text-book for the instruction of kings in politics and the practical conduct of every-day life" (Keith 1920: 248). Olivelle cites government policy and political strategy as two of the *Pañcatantra*'s goals (Olivelle 1997: x). Edgerton alone expresses some skepticism when he says that the *Pañcatantra* was "supposed to be a kind of *Fürstenspiegel* or *Mirror for Magistrates*" (Edgerton 1924: 4). The irony is that few scholars have accepted at face value the story of Viṣṇuśarman and the princes, but few seem to doubt that the *Pañcatantra* was written for a princely audience.

It is probably neither possible nor necessary to prove or to disprove the *Pañcatantra*'s own claim that it was written for princes. There is nothing to suggest that Viṣṇuśarman and the princes were historical personages, and it is barely conceivable that it were true. It is also very common for Sanskritic literary works to include fictional accounts of their own creations. Yet Pūrṇabhadra compiled this recension at the behest of a minister, one Śrīsoma (PT 289.18), and, as we saw above, Hemacandra wrote *Bṛhadarhannītiśāstra* for King Kumārapāla. It is, of course, not impossible that an author at a royal court somewhere drew together existing stories, mixed perhaps with his own material, in a form that became one of the earlier *Pañcatantras*, such as the *Tantrākhyāyika* or Southern recension. There is simply no way of knowing whether or not the text was originally written for a princely audience.

Clearer than the historicity of the *Pañcatantra*'s origins, however, are the truth-effects of such a claim. Whether or not the stories really were written for princes, the *idea* that they were created for a princely audience endows them with a certain added value. The lofty associations of the culture, power and prestige of the court are transferred by implication to the narrative and to the discourse. The narrative is elevated and ennobled by its supposed association with courtly culture. Imagine, again, for a moment that this was a collection of stories told by a potter to his son, or by a weaver or a laundryman. What has become of the authority, the dignity and the prestige of the narrative?

It is possible to test the impact of the courtly setting on the reception of Pūrṇabhadra's *Pañcatantra* in other ways. There are at least three versions of the *Pañcatantra* that lack the overall framing device involving Viṣṇuśarman and the princes. These are the two "*Bṛhatkathā*" versions, which launch directly into the first *tantra,* and one of the Southern *Pañcatantras,* the *Tantropākhyāna.* The Southeast Asian offshoots of the latter all have a "thousand-and-one nights"-type introduction in which a story was told each evening by a servant-girl in order to save her friend, a minister's daughter, from the king's clutches (Huilgol 1987: 22). Artola concludes that the original *Tantropākhyāna* probably also had such a *kathāmukha.* What effect is brought to bear on the discourse by stripping from the *Pañcatantra* the courtly *kathāmukha,* with its fictional setting of the *brāhmaṇa* and the princes? Does the narrative of *kathāmukha* cause the discourse to function in a certain way?

We have discussed the contents of the "*Bṛhatkathā*" versions above, and found that they both contained most of the core stories, as does the *Tantropākhyāna.* We can say, therefore, that the "*Bṛhatkathā*" versions, the *Tantropākhyāna* and Pūrṇabhadra's *Pañcatantra* share a common narrative core, and the discourse of division embedded in them is similar. Without the courtly *kathāmukha,* however, and although they and the *Pañcatantra* share similar contents, neither the "*Bṛhatkathā*" versions nor the *Tantropākhyāna* have śāstric pretensions. Without the *kathāmukha,* the *Pañcatantra* stories in the "*Bṛhatkathā*" versions sit comfortably with the other tales of foolishness and cleverness with which they are surrounded and interspersed. There is nothing especially "*nītic,*" and even less, śāstric, about them. While I disagree with Artola's conception of the *Pañcatantra* in the following passage for the reasons outlined above, it is interesting to note what he says about the *Tantropākhyāna:*

> The *Pañcatantra* of Viṣṇuśarmā is primarily a textbook of *nīti* and in it the technical and non-technical precepts of *nīti* predominate. The unique feature of the *Tantropākhyāna* is its apparent neglect of such precepts. The impression is conveyed that the stories have been told for their own sake, almost exclusively in order to entertain. (Artola 1957: 222)

Huilgol agrees that the absence of what he calls Viṣṇuśarman's *kathāmukha* changes the way in which the stories of the *Tantropākhyāna* are received. Significantly, these stories "are meant for entertainment" (Huilgol 1987: 23).[8]

I do not propose to attach too much weight to results of these observations, but it is my impression that these three versions of the *Pañcatantra* which lack the *kathāmukha* function less definitively as *nītiśāstras.* Without the courtly setting, they are treated as run-of-the-mill "fool stories" and "entertainment." The *Pañcatantra,* on the other hand, functions as a *nītiśāstra* because the *kathāmukha* clearly aligns the text with that genre. Conversely, when no such claim is made, the text ceases to function as such. There is, I suspect, little that is inherently *nītiśāstric* in the text itself, other than the fact that it is regarded as one. The claim that it is a member of the genre activates certain preconditions and expectations for the way in which it is received. "*Nītiśāstra*" is perhaps more usefully understood as a functional category than as a formal one.

How might we summarize the effects of the śāstric paradigm on the discourse of the *Pañcatantra*? As we have seen, the creators of the *Pañcatantra* presented the wisdom they passed on as timeless, ahistorical, and nonnegotiable. There is no sense in which some wisdom may be understood as old and some new. Scope for negotiation only exists in choosing which snippet of several contending pieces of wisdom to apply to a specific situation.

Not every facet of the śāstric paradigm applies to the *Pañcatantra.* For example, our text claims to be the creation of a human agent—Viṣṇuśarman—and therefore lacks the primordial or divine origins typically claimed by other *śāstras.* This does not diminish the overall śāstric truth claims of the text itself. It still derives its authority as much from its association with the śāstric corpus as from its own internal workings.

We have seen how the five *tantras* are ascribed to the lips of the fictional Viṣṇuśarman, and we know that the stories and verses were obviously the creation of various real human authors at various times. But not one of the explicit virtues promoted by the text, nor any of the more profound verities that give shape to the subtext, are attributed to human agency. As a śāstric text, there is no suggestion that the truths, either implicit or explicit, in either the *śāstras* or the *Pañcatantra,* were ever produced by people. The social origins of contingent, cultural practices are invisible. The truths are no longer the product of human agency, but like all śāstric truths, appear to be transcendental, immanent, and primordial. Like the *śāstras* in general, the *Pañcatantra* legitimizes social practices by borrowing the eternal, transcendent authority of the *śāstras.* This, in summary, is the result of the text's claims to be a handbook for kings, or what we might call the "Fürstenspiegel effect."

INTERTEXTUALITY

We have observed how the authoritative voice, universalization, and the śāstric paradigm allow the discourse of division to function as true. We will now explore the ways in which the intertextual nature of the *Pañcatantra*—the fact that it is "a node in a network" of texts—exerts an effect on the discourse. I will first summarize the theoretical background to intertextuality, and I will then describe briefly the wide and complex net of intertextual links in which Pūrṇabhadra's *Pañcatantra* is situated. Drawing mainly on Sternbach's *Kāvya portions* (1971), I will show how the narrative units and verses found in Pūrṇabhadra's *Pañcatantra* fit into a network of other normative texts. I will then suggest how this intertextual network of references augments the apparent truthfulness of the discourse.

Theoretical Background

The theory of intertextuality, as developed by Kristeva, Barthes, and Foucault, emphasizes the fact that texts are pastiches of quotations and discursive influences from earlier sources. This approach has immediate and obvious appeal for the investigation of "collective" works like the *Pañcatantra,* which are composed of units derived from multiple sources. As Kristeva wrote in one formulation of intertextuality, "[A]ny text is constructed as a mosaic of quotations; any text is the absorption and transformation of another" (Kristeva 1980: 66). Both Foucault and Barthes could almost be describing the *Pañcatantra* genre when they wrote:

> The frontiers of a book are never clear-cut: beyond the title, the first lines, and the last full stop, beyond its internal configuration and its autonomous form, it is caught up in a system of references to other books, other texts, other sentences: it is a node within a network. . . . The book is not simply the object that one holds in one's hands . . . , its unity is variable and relative. (Foucault 1972: 23)

> Any text is a new tissue of past citations. Bits of code, formulae, rhythmic models, fragments of social languages, etc. pass into the text and are redistributed within it, for there is always language before and around the text. (Barthes 1981: 39).

Intertextuality is not just concerned with sources and influences—this is what Sternbach has done—but as originally conceived by Kristeva, involves "the components of a *textual system* . . . , the transportation of one or more *systems* of signs into another, accompanied by a new articulation of the enunciative and denotative position" (Roudiez 1980: 15). With intertextuality, we are looking at something deeper, more subtle and more pervasive than sources: "the intertext is a general field of anonymous formulae whose origin can scarcely ever be located; of unconscious or automatic quotations, given without quotation marks" (Barthes 1981: 39). We are less concerned with a particular verse that may or may not appear in the *Manusmṛti* or the *Arthaśāstra,* but with the "anonymous formulae" and the "unconscious or automatic quotations." Intertextuality embraces the "anonymous discursive practices, codes whose origins are lost, that make possible the signifying practices of later texts" (Culler 1981: 103).

With reference to the *Pañcatantra,* these "anonymous discursive practices," these "codes," are encompassed within the discourse of division. We are concerned then to discover how the intertextuality of the *Pañcatantra* enhances its discursive function. In the following section I will describe the intertextual network in which the *Pañcatantra* is enmeshed, beginning with the narrative units in textual and other media, before proceeding to an examination of the verses in the *Pañcatantra.* Our ultimate concern is the net effect on the *Pañcatantra* arising from its position in an intertext.

Narrative Units

Sternbach carried out an exhaustive study of the sources of narrative units and verses found in many branches of *kathā* literature. He says of the main collections of stories that he studied:

> Although the main topic of the five collections of tales is different, they are interrelated. Not only a number of stories were borrowed from the Pañcatantra by Nārāyaṇa for his Hitopadeśa, but we find several Pañcatantra stories in the Śukasaptati and the Vikramacarita

> and the Vetālapañcaviṃśatikā; and the Vetālapañcaviṃśatikā stories in the Vikramacarita. Some Pañcatantra and Hitopadeśa stories are found in summarised form in the Kathāsaritsāgara and the Bṛhatkathāmañjarī and all the Vetālapañcaviṃśatikā stories in the two latter works. . . . Also some stories of the Mahābhārata are found in some *kathā* works. (Sternbach 1971: 4)

The relationship between the *Pañcatantra, Hitopadeśa, Kathāsaritsāgara,* and *Bṛhatkathāmañjarī* has been described above. The details of stories found in the *Pañcatantra* and the other works mentioned by Sternbach are as follows:

Śukasaptati: Five *Pañcatantra* stories are found in the *Śukasaptati:*
Story 1-07 "Lion and hare" (ŚS 146–148)
Story 1-19 "Goose and fowler" (ŚS 260–262)
Story 1-26 "Good-heart and Bad-heart" (ŚS 204–206)
Story 1-28 "How mice ate iron" (ŚS 165–168)
Story 4-00 "Ape and crocodile" (ŚS 262–268)
(see also Haksar 2000)

Vikramacarita: Story 1-08 "Weaver as Viṣṇu" appears in the so-called Metrical Recension (Edgerton 1926: 1.xxviii, xxxiv).

Vetālapañcaviṃśati: Story 5-03 "Lion-makers" appears as "How four brahmans resurrected a tiger" (VPV 104–106).

Mahābhārata: Story 3-08 "Self-sacrificing dove" (Mbh 12.141–145)
Story 4-10 "Jackal's four foes" also occurs in some versions of the *Mahābhārata,* but not apparently in the Pune critical edition. See Ganguli 1993 (1883–1896), vol. 1 ("*Adi Parva*"): 297–299 (Section 142).
"King Śibi." Note that this story is not found in Pūrṇabhadra's *Pañcatantra,* but is in *Tantrākhyāyika* III.7 (Hertel 1909: vol. 2, 122–123). It is not in the Pune critical edition, but see Ganguli 1993 (1883–1896), vol. 3 ("*Vana Parva*"): 401–403 (Section 196).

In addition to these occurrences of *Pañcatantra* stories in other works of *kathā* literature, many *Pañcatantra* stories are also found as *Jātaka* tales. I will omit this fact from the present consideration, because I am unsure of the status of *Jātaka* stories in mainstream Sanskrit literary culture. I am assuming that readers of the *Pañcatantra* may have had ready access to other works in the *kathā* genre, such as the *Śukasaptati,* for example. The same may not necessarily be said of the Buddhist collections, even those translated into Sanskrit, which are not strictly part of the brahmanical archive.

Apart from other works of *kathā* literature in Sanskrit, stories from the *Pañcatantra* may also be found in vernacular versions of the *Pañcatantra,* which exist in most major Indian languages (Olivelle 1997: ix).

Most writers have restricted their enquiries into intertextuality to written texts. It is instructive in the case of the *Pañcatantra* to broaden the definition of "text" to include visual-arts resources and vernacular "texts" from the oral tradition. We know too that some of these stories are widespread in oral and semi-oral traditions (Brown 1919: 13–16) and in the visual arts (Patil 1997). We will briefly consider the classes of oral and visual "texts" in the following paragraphs. *Pañcatantra* narratives have provided the subject for sculptural art in monuments in many parts of India. Some examples are given below.

Story 1-00 "Lion and bull" is depicted at two sites: Navalinga temple, Kukanur and Somesvara temple, Abbalur in Karnataka (Patil 1997: 48). These show a lion attacking a bull in a forest.

Story 1-16 "Two geese and tortoise." Klokke has identified seven depictions from Mallar, Nagunūr, Mathura, Bodh Gaya, Nalanda, Alampur, and Bellagame. These show various combinations of the three "moments" of the story: the geese and tortoise on the ground, the geese carrying the tortoise through the air, and the tortoise being killed on the ground (Klokke 1991: 182). This story is also found at Muktesvara Temple, Bhubaneshwar, Orissa (Sivaramamurti 1977: 497).

Story 1-26 "Good-heart and Bad-heart." This is depicted in sculpture at Sirival, Karnataka (Patil 1997: 59).

Story 2-04 "Too greedy jackal." One example from Andhra Pradesh and five from Karnataka. All depict the jackal with a bow piercing his skull (Patil 1997: 54).

Story 4-00 "Ape and crocodile." According to Patil, this story is "very popular in Indian sculptures" (Patil 1997: 50). He lists eleven examples from Karnataka and one from Orissa. This story is also illustrated at Muktesvara Temple, Bhubaneshwar, Orissa (Sivaramamurti 1977: 497).

Story 5-01 "*Brāhmaṇī* and mongoose." Patil lists four examples from Karnataka and one from Andhra Pradesh. They chiefly depict the child asleep in a cradle, the dead snake and the woman killing the mongoose with a pestle (Patil 1997: 51–52).

In addition to these visual "texts," narratives from the *Pañcatantra* are also found in the oral vernacular tradition, and as such comprise oral "texts." Nearly one hundred years ago, Brown surveyed three thousand published versions of Indian oral stories and identified numerous examples of seventeen stories also found in the *Pañcatantra.* Of these, twelve were only recorded in one or two collections, but others appeared many times. Story 1-07, "Lion and hare," for example, was found in eight collections of oral folktales from India proper (Brown 1919: 24). Despite the many methodological problems that beset Brown's data, it is at least indicative of the fact that *Pañcatantra* narratives were also found—and were perhaps commonly or widely found—in the oral tradition.[9]

Such is the nature of the textual, plastic and oral intertextual network in which the *Pañcatantra* is located. What is the discursive impact of the *Pañcatantra*'s position in the intertext? What happens to the discourse when a story appears in multiple collections, and in multiple media. A story has been deemed worthy of preservation and repetition by so many creators in so many media only if they perceived some intrinsic value in it. If a narrative were of no value, if it were not "true," why would it have been preserved and perpetuated? Any story that has been preserved and perpetuated in multiple contexts and media must have been perceived to embody some inherent truth value, and the more widespread or frequently encountered, the higher the truth value. When a narrative unit is encountered over and over again, when it becomes particularly well known, it acquires a patina of credibility. The existence of the *Pañcatantra* and its constituent narrative units in a web of intertextuality functions to accentuate the impact of the narrative. The intertextual nature of the narrative exerts a truth-effect on the discourse. The more widespread and frequently encountered a narrative unit, the "truer" it appears to be. Seeing or hearing the story of the indigo jackal on one occasion will leave a certain impression on the receiver; how much greater is this impression when the same story is encountered repeatedly in multiple texts, in oral tales, in art and on the temple wall?

Verses

Verses (*subhāṣitas*) exude authority and seem to proclaim explicitly their own inherent truthfulness. Perhaps their perspicacity is already implied in the word verse itself. The meaning of *su* is very broad: MMW gives among others "good," "excellent," "right," "virtuous," "beautiful," "easy," "well," and "rightly." As *bhāṣita* means "spoken," "that which is truly spoken" is a reasonable translation of the term. The very point of a verse is that it must be "true." The use of verses embedded in narrative prose to convey little kernels of truth was by no means an innovation of the *Pañcatantra:* verses as sources of truth in texts are found as early as the *Aitareya Brāhmaṇa* (Keith 1920: 244).

The great majority of verses in the *Pañcatantra* are in *śloka* form. Olivelle makes the interesting observation that versified text has an inherent "aura of authority" of its own, and that texts were composed in verse form to give them authority (Olivelle 2004a: xxiv). These verses are also, I believe, inherently authoritative on account of their form alone.

In the *Pañcatantra,* truths and discourses are elaborated implicitly in the stories, but are made explicit in the verses. To reuse the Indic metaphor we saw above, the verses are the nectar churned from the ocean of the narrative, or to use an alchemical one, they are the distillation, the quintessence, of the discursive truth of the stories. Many narrative units in the *Pañcatantra* are introduced with a standard formulaic device incorporating a verse. Like Viṣṇuśarman in the frame-stories, other characters recite a verse, whereupon their interlocutors inquire "How is that?" (*katham etat*). The first character then responds by narrating a story to expand on or illustrate the point made in the verse. In this context the verse contains the basic thrust of the story that follows. It contains the heart of the narrative and "moral" that is to be demonstrated. As such the introductory verses are distillations of the "truth" of the narrative.

In the epilogue, the *Pañcatantra* describes itself as being "provided with the verses of the true poets" (*satkavisūktayuktaṃ* ׀ PT 289.16). A *satkavi* is a "good or true poet" (MMW), one whose words are "true." A *sūkta* is that which is "well or properly said or recited," and by extension, "good recitation or speech, wise saying, song of praise" (MMW). This term generally refers to verses of the *Ṛgveda,* and therefore has resonances that are particularly authoritative and normative. The creators of the *Pañcatantra* seem aware of the fact that verses are inherently veracious and seek to remind their audience of that fact. In addition to their inherent truthfulness, the verses exert a further truth-effect on the discourse that arises from their intertextuality, similar to that we saw in the case of the narrative units.

Pūrṇabhadra's *Pañcatantra* includes just over one thousand verses, which Sternbach calls "stanzas" or "sententious verses." Like the narratives, the verses also exist in a web of intertextuality. Their provenance is rarely if ever explicitly acknowledged in the *Pañcatantra,* but as Sternbach has shown, many may be traced to various hegemonic texts, or are at least shared with them. Many hundreds of verses in the *Pañcatantra* also occur in other works of Sanskrit literature, the most important being the *Arthaśāstra, Mahābhārata, Rāmāyaṇa, Manusmṛti,* various *purāṇas,* Bhartṛhari's *Śātakas,* Kāmandaki's *Nītisāra, Hitopadeśa, Vikramacarita, Śukasaptati, Vetālapañcaviṃśatikā,* and numerous others (Sternbach 1971: 49).

The verses in the *Pañcatantra* exist in an intertextual network: a particular verse may appear in multiple locations within the brahmanical archive. We have suggested how verses appear to be inherently true by their very nature. As was the case with the narrative units examined above, I suggest that the intertextual nature of the verses also exerts a truth-effect on the discourse as a whole, for similar reasons. A verse that reappears in many different works has been deemed veridical and therefore worthy of repetition by many compilers. If a verse lacked intrinsic value within the culture that created it, why would it be preserved and repeated? That countless generations of compilers and copyists have regarded the text as true and worthy of preservation endows the verse with an additional air of credibility.

We have seen how both the narrative units and the verses occur in multiple contexts and, in the case of the stories, in multiple media. Before concluding this examination of the intertextual nature of the *Pañcatantra,* I will briefly explore the role of the invocation verses.

Invocation and Intertextuality

Like most works of Sanskrit literature, the various *Pañcatantras* open with an invocation. The following dedicatory verse is found in the *Tantrākhyāyika,* the Southern *Pañcatantra,* the Nepalese recension and in one version of the *textus simplicior.* Pūrṇabhadra's *Pañcatantra,* as mentioned above, begins with the Jaina *mūlamantra, arham,* followed by a simple homage to Sarasvatī, the deity usually associated with eloquence, writing, and music. Obviously what I say below in relation to this invocation will not apply directly to our recension, but by examining its discursive effects in these closely allied versions we may learn something about the functioning of the discourse in a general sense in Pūrṇabhadra's recension. This is the dedicatory opening verse of the *Tantrākhyāyika:*

> Homage to the authors of the *śāstras* on kingship: Manu, Vācaspati, Śukra, Parāśara and his son, and to the great Cāṇakya. (TA 1.6–7)

This invocation explicitly ties the discourse to some very powerful figures. Manu, the brahmanical lawgiver par excellence, was the reputed author of the *Manusmṛti* or *Mānavadharmaśāstra,* the great legal text that bears his name. By invoking Manu and his authority, the authors of this verse seek to establish a relationship between their texts and Manu, and, in doing so, effectively position their text within the śāstric paradigm. The name of Manu brings to bear on the discourse the considerable hegemonic authority inherent in that figure and in the *Manusmṛti.*

The same could be said about the other figures named in the invocation. Vācaspati, the "lord of speech," is an epithet of Bṛhaspati, preceptor of the gods. Śukra was preceptor of the Asuras, while Parāśara was the father of Vyāsa, the reputed compiler of the *Vedas* and author of the *Mahābhārata.* By invoking Vyāsa, and Cāṇakya, to whom the *Arthaśāstra* is ascribed, some quantum of the authority of these great hegemonic, normative works is brought to bear on the *Pañcatantra.*

I repeat that this invocation is not found in Pūrṇabhadra's recension, yet I have chosen to remark on it because it explicates what is implicit in our recension. The use of the invocation in these other recensions illustrates the sorts of cultural sensitivities and social assumptions that might be activated on approaching a text like Pūrṇabhadra's. Not only does the invocation bring to bear the discursive power of the hegemonic texts mentioned above. The creators of this verse effectively weave their own text into the web of intertextuality formed by those works. They make it apparent that the *Pañcatantra* is indeed a "node within a network" which includes these hegemonic texts. At the same time, their texts become subject to the discursive forces that form and inform the entire "intertext."

To summarize our findings on intertextuality, the literary, visual, and oral "texts" of the *Pañcatantra* do not exist independently of one another, but are indeed all nodes in an intertextual network. All these sources form a single intertext, the various manifestations of which reinforce and sustain one another. The discursive authority of a literary text, for example, is heightened and accentuated, I suggest, by the existence of an analogous visual or oral text within the intertext, or by the existence of many versions in multiple collections. Their existence within an intertextual network strengthens the effect of the individual nodes, and of the intertext as a whole. In short, the existence of units of the *Pañcatantra* in multiple "texts" adds to the apparent truthfulness of each individually, and exerts a truth-effect on the intertext as a whole. Discursive power flows though the network of intertextuality in which Pūrṇabhadra's *Pañcatantra* is situated.

THE "NATURALIZATION" OF DISCOURSE

We will now turn to the final topic for this chapter, the "naturalization" of the discourse. We will explore the ways in which cultural phenomena, which are the products of human society, are projected in the *Pañcatantra* on to the natural world, specifically the realm of animals. The effect of this process is to provide validation for contingent social practices by making them appear natural, normal, and "true." I will begin this section by introducing the theoretical background to "naturalization" of discourse, drawing on Pollock's work on Sanskritic epistemology (Pollock 1985) and on Smith's *Classifying the Universe* (Smith 1994). I will then describe in detail the ways in which the various social constructs embodied by the discourse of division are naturalized in the *Pañcatantra.* I will conclude this section with a discussion of the truth-effect exerted by the process of naturalization on the discourse.

What Is Naturalization?

We have already touched on the concept of naturalization in the preceding discussion of the śāstric paradigm. Pollock observed that in the *śāstras,* "the living, social, historical, contingent tradition is naturalized, becoming as much a part of the order of things as the laws of nature themselves" (Pollock 1985: 516). The idea that contingent social phenomena are "naturalized" when projected on to the natural world is taken further by Smith. He describes how the *varṇa* system of ancient Indian society was "integrated into—and therefore ratified and legitimated by—a categorical system with universal scope and persuasive power" (Smith 1994: 3).

> Brahmin priests (who composed these texts, and not without an eye to their own advantage) and the Kshatriya rulers and warriors (who also materially benefited from these classificatory schemes) displaced their superior social statuses, or aspirations for them, onto the natural, supernatural, religious, and ritual worlds—*and did so surreptitiously.* (Smith 1994: 7)

As a result, arbitrary social status or status claims could be presented as natural and sacred; "that is, social hierarchy was presented as inexorably part of the immutable and divinely given order of things" (Smith 1994: 7). The world of the gods, the divisions of time and space, the natural world of flora and fauna, and the revelatory world of scripture were all shown to be divided into *varṇas.* Not just humans, but the gods, seasons, texts, and plants were also classified into the four *varṇas* of *brāhmaṇa, kṣatriya, vaiśya,* and *śūdra.* Smith's contention is that by "revealing" the *varṇas* into which every aspect of the universe was classified, those who had "seized the enunciative function," the hegemonic *brāhmaṇa* class, sought to legitimize the division of human society into *varṇas,* and thereby secure their own superior social position and privilege.

The key concept for the present enquiry is the projection of contingent social phenomena on to the natural world, which has the effect of providing those very social contingencies with legitimation. In the narratives of the *Pañcatantra,* the social system of division and its attendant assumptions are projected on to the fictional realm of animals. This image of a divided natural world, itself the product of the discourse of division, then has the effect of validating and reinforcing the discourse of division in human society. The effect of the discourse seems to be this: just as animals in the natural world are ordered and characterized by discourses of division, so too is it "natural" that human society is ordered and characterized in a similar way. There is indeed no concept of a clear dichotomy between the human and animal realms, between nature and culture, in this regard. People and animals alike, living within the one *"varṇic"* universe, are all "naturally" and equally subject to a single, unified discourse of division.

Naturalization of Discourse in the *Pañcatantra*

In chapter 2, we identified three facets of the discourse of division in the *Pañcatantra:* essential nature, status and enmity. Here I will describe how each of these has been naturalized in the text, that is, the ways in which these phenomena have been projected into the world of nature.

Essential Nature

We know from our own experience that individuals of a given species share certain sets of behaviors. We may observe a cat's behavior and the behavior of other cats, and draw from our observations a certain set of inferences. As a result, we formulate a picture of typical cat behavior. Some of this behavior is learned; some we may call "instinct." Sanskrit authors perceived a driver behind this observable behavior, a force that determined and shaped the actions. They called this force *svabhāva,* the essential nature shared by all members of a kind.

In Story 5-05 "Ass as singer," for example, endurance was described as an aspect of the essential nature of donkeys. In Story 3-03 "Cat as judge between partridge and hare," the cat was responding to its essential nature when it caught and killed the two litigants. The understanding is that every donkey and every cat will respond in similar ways to a given situation: donkeys will all display resilience and cats will always chase birds.

According to the contemporary way of thinking, there is in fact no such thing as an animal's *svabhāva*—all we can observe is behavior. We cannot say whether the idea of *svabhāva* was first formulated in reference to animals or to people. But we can state with certainty that the idea of essential nature is a social construction, and that is has been projected in this case on to the realm of animals.

There is a clear parallel between the ways in which essential nature is attributed to groups of animals in the natural world, and to groups of individuals in human society. Each of the four *varṇas* in the idealized society of Sanskrit literature has its own essential nature, which gives rise to the sorts of action and characteristics—the *svadharma*—to which each *varṇa* is destined. I will return to the relationship between *svabhāva* and *svadharma* in the brahmanical archive in chapter 4.

The discourse of division maintains that in both the natural world and in human society the sum of all characteristics and the trajectory of all individuals of a given kind are determined by their birth.[10] The *jāti* of animals and the *varṇa* of humans determine their *svabhāva,* and their *svabhāva* determines their relative position in social space and their "natural" friends and enemies. Just as the forest realm is divided into jackals, lions, and the rest, each with their own *svabhāva,* the idealized human realm as depicted in the normative texts is divided into *varṇas,* each with an analogous set of characteristics, *svadharma,* and all that it entails. The "discovery" of *svabhāva* in different species of animals in the forest has the effect of making the divisions in human society appear just as "natural." The *śūdra* and the *kṣatriya* are as different from one another as, for example, the jackal and the lion. Just as animals of different kinds naturally behave in certain ways, members of the various *varṇas* must also follow their allotted paths. Indeed, they can do nothing else. The authors of these stories did not necessarily set out to enforce conformity to *varṇa* practices among their audiences. They simply believed that it was natural and normal for each *varṇa* to follow its *svadharma,* just as it was for cats to behave like cats. The natural world and the human world both fall under the same single overarching discourse of division. The same discursive rules apply equally in all situations.

The apparent process of creation of the narratives appears to be this: first, *svabhāva* is observed in animals. These observations are then incorporated into the narratives for didactic purposes. The instinctive howl of the indigo jackal serves as "proof" that individuals cannot change their natures, and that low-status individuals can never rise to a higher position. In fact, the starting point is a set of social constructs: that *varṇas* and *svabhāva* exist, that social stability is desirable, that individual humans cannot change their social standing, that some are born low, and others are born to rule, and so on. These constructs are unconsciously projected on to the natural world in the minds of the creators of the narratives. The creators then incorporate their conditioned observations of nature into the narratives, where they provide "natural" analogues and justification for those very social constructs with which they began.

Status

We will continue this investigation by observing how the concept of inherent social status is projected into the natural world, starting with the perceived inferiority of the indigo jackal in Story 1-11. This story reached a climax when the jackal was at the apogee of power, replete with retinue and regalia. All the externals of kingship were in place. He sported the indigo color of his "consecration" with pride; he was attended by the lion-minister, tiger-chamberlain, and the rest; and he had banished his fellow jackals from his presence.

As we have seen elsewhere, the jackal occupies a specific locus in Sanskritic literary culture—on the periphery of society—as the result of an anthropomorphic interpretation of its natural, observable behavior. The jackal is a scavenger, and is therefore seen on the fringes of human habitation, or in association with larger predators. That the jackal is "naturally" base, lowly, inferior, peripheral, inauspicious and inherently unsuited to kingship, are all social constructs. They are human interpretations and translations of natural phenomena. In Sanskrit literature a puny jackal could never be expected to lord it over a lion, being, as we have seen, an inferior fringe-dwelling scavenger.

The jackal in this story was imbued with an essentially inferior "jackalness" that remained, in spite of his external transformation, impervious to change. He enjoyed for a time the external trappings of superiority, the exercise of sovereignty, the appointments, the accoutrements and the *rājadharma* that he exercised. But his kingliness, like his indigo exterior, was only skin deep. Beneath the surface lay an immutable jackal *svabhāva*, one aspect of which was an inherently peripheral status. The jackal's essential nature reasserted itself as a natural, spontaneous and overwhelming response to the howls of his fellow jackals in the distance. The sense of the narrative is that the jackal was powerless to resist the fatal impulse of his "jackalness"; he was powerless in the face of his own *svabhāva*. Not only was he unable to resist the force of his own nature, but his *svabhāva* drew him inexorably to a horrible death. Nor is this story about an individual jackal that was uniquely unsuited to kingship. The discourse is generalized to embrace all jackals, which as a kind share a common "jackalness." All jackals would have howled in response to the exiles, and all would have come undone.

The idea that particular kinds of animals or classes of individuals are naturally inferior and are innately unsuited to kingship is also the key theme of 3-01 "Birds elect a king." As we observed in chapter 2, the consecration of an owl as king of all birds was interrupted by a crow. The crow's objections were based on the owl's essential nature, which was clearly reflected in his physical appearance. The reasons for the crow's stated aversion to the owl are twofold: firstly the owl's "terrible appearance," namely its hideous hooked bill, squinting eyes, and cruel visage. Second is the owl's "essential nature," which is described as fierce, very terrifying and cruel (PT 182.9–20). Pollock speaks of physical deformity being an index of moral deformity in the case of *rākṣasas* (Pollock 1991: 72). Here, too, the external appearance seems to be the outward manifestation of the owl's inner nature. The text suggests that owls are "naturally" unsuited to kingship because they are cruel, fierce, and ugly. They are excluded by their very natures from positions at the center of the social *maṇḍala*.

Consider the following description of a hunter approaching a flock of pigeons in the second *tantra:*

> He was of terrifying appearance, with splayed hands and feet, bulging muscles, a very coarse complexion, red-rimmed eyes, being followed by dogs, his hair tied up, nets and sticks in his hands—why say more? He was like a second Death with snares in his hands, the *avatāra* of evil, like the heart of *adharma*, the teacher of all wickedness, like the friend of Death. (PT 126.13–17)

There are several parallels between the descriptions of the owl and the hunter: both are terrifying, ugly and physically deformed. The hunter, like the owl, is the "other" located on the fringes of society, often not even in the village or the city, but sometimes living in the forest, barely elevated above the wild animals (Story 1-29 "Good makes good, bad makes bad"). As a killer of living things, he is relegated to the ranks of the outcastes, along with the *caṇḍālas,* who are sometimes represented as butchers. Here the hunter is the manifestation of death. As we have seen, the owl is also associated with death: in Story 1-12 "Goose and owl" we read that "Death arrived in the form of an owl" (*mṛtyur ulūkarūpeṇāyātaḥ* | PT 72.10–11).

No doubt the anthropomorphic assessment that owls are cruel is based on the observation that, like the hunter, they catch and kill live prey. Yet the idea that owls are "cruel" is clearly the projection of a human value. It is true that some animals kill others, but the notion of cruelty—the wanton or intentional infliction of suffering—belongs not to animals but to humans. Cruelty is a social quality, not a biological one.

Cruelty, and its surface manifestation as ugliness, are inherent characteristics of owlish *svabhāva.* As we saw with the jackal above, the problem is not that this particular owl was peculiarly unfit for consecration. Nor was it a question of seeking out some better-suited candidate from among that *jāti.* Owls are excluded generically from centrality on the basis of the essential nature that is shared by all members of their kind.

In the idealized world of Sanskritic literary culture, only a certain type of person is really suited to kingship—a *kṣatriya.* Just as the society of birds in these narratives is divided into many kinds, each of which is supposed to have an essential nature, "natural" allies and enemies, and a "natural" place in the *maṇḍala,* human society is also divided in a similar way. The various divisions of human society also have their specific characteristics. Just as the divisions in the world of birds are "natural" and immutable, so too are the divisions in the human world. The owl is naturally unsuited to kingship, just as the hunter or any of his kind is "naturally" unsuited to an analogous position in human society. The court of birds is an allegory for human society, and the fact that the owl is unsuited to centrality "proves" that the hunter, or any other individual of "inferior" birth in human society, are also naturally unsuited to authority.

This, at any rate, is how the discourse appears to function: first, the natural divisions among animals are incorporated into the narrative. From the narrative follow certain inferences with regard to human society. As we saw in the case of essential nature above, the discourse functions by reversing the logical order of these two statements: the actual starting point is the social contingencies—the divisions within human society and the relative status of each. These are projected on to the natural world, and this "natural" process of division is then "revealed" in the narrative. This has the effect of legitimizing those very social contingencies. The discourse functions to present the contingent as natural. Just as human society is divided and characterized, corresponding image of social values and a social system is also projected on to the natural world. The presence of such socially contingent values and a system of hierarchical categorization in the natural world is then "surreptitiously" (to use Smith's term) drawn into the discourse as documentary evidence in support of the "naturalness" of those same values and that same system in human society, in this case, inherent status.

A similar observation may be made in the case of the indigo jackal. The fact that a jackal cannot be king appears to "prove" that certain sections of human society cannot occupy the analogous central positions in the *maṇḍala.* The apparent sequence of the logic is this: the starting point is an observation of the natural world, and the end result is a social inference. I suggest that the actual sequence is the reverse. First, the discourse of division imputed an inherent status to individuals of different *varṇas,* and that certain sections of human society cannot occupy central loci in the *maṇḍala.* Second, in creating the narrative, the social constructs of king, court, inauspiciousness, baseness, and so forth were projected on to animals. In doing so, a discursively charged image of the natural world was also brought into existence. These constructs were then used in the narrative, and now appear as innocent analogues from nature, but they effectively provide legitimacy for that social inference on which they were premised.

Let us return briefly to the twinned stories 4-03 "Potter as warrior" and "Jackal nursed by lioness." The significance of station at birth as the determinant of status in a human social setting in the first story is mirrored in a natural setting in the second story. Here we see a conscious attempt by the creators of the narratives to juxtapose the social manifestation of the discourse in the potter's tale with the naturalized discourse in the story about the jackal. A clear parallel is drawn between the socially constructed inferiority of the potter and the "natural" inferiority of the jackal. The subtext suggests that the inferiority of the man is just as "natural" as that of the animal. The inferiority of the two is of the same nature, as jackal and potter, animal and human, are all bound within the one classified universe.

In these three examples—the indigo jackal, the owl-king, and the adopted jackal—we saw that each of the individuals was a member of a group which was "naturally" unsuited to positions of power and centrality. The suggestion is that just as some groups in the fictive realm of the forest are unsuited to centrality, so too are certain sections of human society "naturally" inferior to others. We have seen how the socially constructed concept of inherent status was projected on the natural world. This manifested in the narratives as the inherent inferiority of, for example, the indigo jackal. This story then has the effect of providing "evidence" from the natural world for the inherent inferiority of certain sections of human society and the superiority of others.

Enmity/Amity

In chapter 2, we saw how the *jāti* functioned as the natural boundary between one character and another in the fictional society of the forest: those "inside" one's own *jāti* were one's natural allies, while one's natural enemies were "outsiders." We saw many examples from the natural world: Story 1-27 "Heron, serpent and mongoose," Story 3-03 "Cat as judge" and Story 4-01 "Frog's revenge overleaps itself."

Herons eat crabs, cats eat birds, and snakes eat frogs: these are all observable phenomena. The idea that enmity exists between these dyads, however, is not natural, but is a social projection, an anthropomorphic interpretation of a value-free biological interaction. Animals do not naturally have "friends" or "enemies." The heron and the crab are not enemies: it is simply a case of one eating the other.

In these stories, the creators of the *Pañcatantra* repeatedly show how associations with individuals, or classes of individuals, whose interests are ultimately inimical to one's own, lead to disaster. The enmity that exists between an individual in human society and those who are potentially hostile to that person is as deep, wide and "natural" as that which exists, for example, in the biologically determined predatory relationship of the heron and the crab.

According to the discourse, such an enmity in either the natural or the human worlds may never be averted, assuaged or sidestepped. The *Pañcatantra* is indeed littered with the bones of those who ignored this self-evident "truth." While enmities do of course exist in human society, they are not natural, but are conditioned, contingent, social or cultural constructs. By "finding" in the natural world parallels to the enmities and divisions of the social world, the social enmities themselves are made to appear "natural." As we saw in the cases of essential nature and status, the social divisions are validated and legitimized by the "discovery" of their natural analogues.

In the frame-story of the second *tantra,* we found the following examples of "natural" enmity: the mongoose and the snake, grass-eaters and those with claws, water and fire, the *devas* and the *daityas,* dogs and cats, mutual rivals, lions and elephants, hunters and deer, crows and owls, the wise and the foolish, faithful and unchaste women, and good and bad people (PT 131.8–11). This passage draws an explicit parallel between pairs of perceived enmities in the natural world involving animals and pairs of social enmities involving humans. In doing so, the social enmities are placed on the same footing as their natural counterparts. By implication, all these enmities share a single nature. The social enmities are as "natural," normal, unpreventable, and irreversible as those that exist between the pairs of rival animals. By seeking parallels in the natural world, the creators of this passage, either consciously or unconsciously, succeeded in elevating socially contingent enmities to the level of "nature."[11]

The discourse of division implies that just as the natural world is fraught with irrevocable enmities, and rent by unbridgeable differences, so too is the social world. The divisions in human society, which are the conscious or subconscious models for the narratives, are to be seen as no less irrevocable or unbridgeable than those between lion and bull.

The Truth-Effects of Naturalization

It may, of course, be true that a single jackal will howl in response to others in the distance, and that a mongoose will kill a snake. What the *Pañcatantra* says about animal behavior, or the other phenomena discussed above, is not necessarily inaccurate. These are not, however, disinterested observations of nature. There is a social agenda, or at least a set of socially determined preconceptions, behind the selection and presentation of these examples.

According to the discourse of division as we perceive it in the text, different individuals or, more important, different groups of individuals, are born with inherent sets of characteristics and dispositions, and "naturally" occupy a given space in the social *maṇḍala.* According to the discourse, an individual's inherent characteristics—which include "natural" inferiority or superiority—are all innate and immutable in humans, just as "jackalness," for example, and all that it entails, is the essential, innate nature of the jackal. The common assumption that underpins this is that individuals of a given kind share a common, fixed essential nature. The discourse suggests that humans' social natures and stations are similarly determined. The two phenomena, that both animals and humans are subject to their *svabhāvas,* are really one, and are governed by the same set of precepts. That is, all beings—jackals and humans included—are constrained by their birth. That we can witness such "truths" in action in the natural world provides validation for the same "truths" as they apply to human society. The jackal failed to change its *varṇa,* remembering the Sanskrit pun here: *varṇa* means both "caste" and "color." He failed in his attempt to move to a more central social position. Within the parameters of the discourse of division, it is similarly impossible for individuals in human society to leave their social locus. The discourse shows how the jackal in the natural world cannot change its nature and its social standing. This covertly "proves" that humans, too, are unable to do likewise.

The perceptions of the creators of the *Pañcatantra* were colored by the discourse of division in such a way that they projected socially constructed phenomena including essential nature, status and enmity on to animals in the natural world. These phenomena in the natural world were incorporated into the narratives "to teach good conduct" as part of a conscious program to propagate social norms.

I am not suggesting that there was a conscious conspiracy on the part of the authors to present a false image of the natural world in these narratives to somehow dupe their audience. They too believed in what they were saying about essential nature, a natural place in the order of things, and so on. They believed that society, like the world of the forest, was naturally divided, and that these divisions were useful and beneficial. Their projection of these social constructs into nature was I believe unconscious, but had the real effect of perpetuating a particular view of the world. By making social divisions appear "natural," they also made them appear to be "true."

A "Regime of Truth" for the *Pañcatantra*

In the quotation at the beginning of this chapter, Foucault suggests that each society has its own "regime of truth," its "general politics of truth" which determines the types of discourse that are accepted and "made to function as true." A "regime of truth" also embodies the mechanisms for distinguishing true and false statements, the means by which each is sanctioned and the status of those who are charged with saying what counts as true (Foucault 1977: 131). In this chapter, we have examined various phenomena that serve to elevate the apparent truthfulness of the *Pañcatantra*, that is, those factors that enable it and its embedded discourse to function as "true." First, we saw how the *Pañcatantra* is enunciated in an authoritative voice, and observed the ways in which this conferred truthfulness on the discourse. The fact that it was a written text, as opposed to an oral one; that it was written in Sanskrit, the "power-language" of the brahmanical archive; that it possessed a paradoxical anonymity and at the same time brahmanical "authorship"; that it was subject to a variety of authoritative textual strategies: all these contributed to its veracity.

We then discussed the ways in which the narrative and its embedded discourse are universalized in terms of spatial, temporal, and receptive radius. The frame narratives and embedded units are all located in fantasized or generalized settings; the narratives at all levels are ascribed to some remote, indefinite, historical time; and the text implicitly claims for itself a universal audience. The apparent "placelessness," "timelessness," and universality effectively generalize the discourse beyond time and place, and thereby make it appear to be applicable to all situations.

As a self-described *nītiśāstra*, the *Pañcatantra* is party to the śāstric paradigm and enjoys the considerable truth-effect that the paradigm confers on all its constituents. As a *nītiśāstra*, the *Pañcatantra* positions itself among a genre of texts which enjoy unimpeachable authority and are regarded as inherently and axiomatically "true." The courtly associations which adhere to the *Pañcatantra* as a "handbook for princes" also confer a quantum of power and prestige on the text.

The *Pañcatantra* exists as an "intertext," and as a "node in a network" of texts, in various modes and media. I have argued that the intertextual nature of the work exerts a cumulative discursive effect. The multiple occurrences of textual units in different media and contexts exert a truth-effect on the narrative as a whole and on the embedded discourse.

Finally, we examined the naturalization of the discourse—the process by which contingent social phenomena are projected into the natural world. Analogues to social phenomena (essential nature, status, and enmity) are "discovered" in the natural world, and are then recruited to legitimize those same phenomena. The process of naturalization, I argued, also confers a certain veracity on the discourse.

These five phenomena exert collectively a truth-effect on the narrative and on the threefold discourse. As such, they constitute key elements in the regime of truth under which the *Pañcatantra* operates. To express these findings in terms of our paradigmatic narrative, all that the *Pañcatantra* says and implies about the rise and fall of the indigo jackal—about its essential nature, its inherent status and its natural enmities and amities—all this appears to be true and functions as true because it is enunciated under the auspices of a regime of truth.

4

The Discourse of Division and the Brahmanical Archive

> When they divided the Puruṣa, into how many parts did they apportion him? What was his mouth? What were his two arms? What do they call his thighs and feet? The *brāhmaṇa* was his mouth. The two arms were made into the *rājanya.* Those that were his two thighs were the *vaiśya.* From his two feet the *śūdra* was born.
>
> —*Ṛgveda*

We have now described the discourse of division as it relates to the story of the indigo jackal and to the *Pañcatantra* as a whole, and we have seen how the discourse functions as "true." Where did the ideas of division, essential nature, status, and enmity originate? How do they relate to the broader cultural context of the brahmanical archive? The *Pañcatantra* is an orthodox work and the indigo jackal is an orthodox story. For this reason, I have "cherry-picked" those passages from the archive that support or illuminate the themes we identified in the narratives, while leaving aside the critiques of *varṇa* found in the Jaina, Buddhist, Bhakti, and Tantric traditions.

In compiling this overview, I scanned the indexes of the following works: the *Vedas,* the *Brāhmaṇas,* the *Dharmasūtras,* and *Dharmaśāstras,* the *Purāṇas* and the epics. While this survey is by no means comprehensive, as the number of references continued to grow, the rate at which fresh material emerged began to decline. Even in this small sample a saturation point was reached. We might still double the breadth of references to *varṇa* without gaining more depth.

During the two millennia from the earliest *Vedas* until the latest *Purāṇas*, the concept of *varṇa* underwent a certain amount of development, but in the last millennium—from the date of the latest *mahāpurāṇa* until the present—the brahmanical archive has formed a single, stable, discursive entity. Furthermore, this last millennium is of chief concern to us, because it is also, roughly speaking, the period during which Pūrṇabhadra's *Pañcatantra* has been in existence. As far as readers of these stories are concerned, the archive has been a static, unchanging entity. The fact that an account of the *varṇa* system in *Vedas* may be older than one from the *Manusmṛti* may be significant for an Indologist, but it was almost certainly irrelevant to readers of the *Pañcatantra.* It is not my intention, therefore, to offer a diachronic perspective on the discourse of division. Rather, I have chosen an unfashionable but, I hope, defensible synchronic approach, treating the archive as a more-or-less unitary block during the period under consideration.

How normative was the brahmanical archive? Rocher argued, for example, that Orientalism has exaggerated the importance of Manu in relation to other non-Sanskritic and nontextual normative texts (Rocher 1993: 229). It is true that the British administrators were looking for an indigenous legal code on which to run the judicial system. In doing so, it has been suggested that they were strongly influenced by their local advisers, the *brāhmaṇa* pandits, and by their own Western, Protestant tendencies, to privilege textual sources, particularly "ancient" ones, over other potential sources (e.g., Persian, vernacular or oral sources). They were looking for a normative legal discourse in a field of potential candidates in Indian society as a whole. On the other hand, I am interested in worldviews as they manifest in Sanskrit literature. In this much narrower field, the *Dharmaśāstras, Dharmasūtras,* and the rest are indeed the legitimating, normative texts. The British judges were perhaps mistaken in assuming that these were the best or indeed the only source of law in Indian society, but I maintain that the brahmanical archive is the best and indeed the only authority when it comes to hegemonic ideology in orthodox brahmanical culture.

I will begin this survey with an outline of the origin of the *varṇa* system. I will then discuss the discourse of division in the brahmanical archive under subheadings analogous to those that were introduced in chapter 2: *svadharma,* status and enmity/amity. I will conclude each section by comparing the discourse in the archive with that which we described for the *Pañcatantra.*

The Origins of *Varṇa*

It would be difficult to overstate the importance of the concept of *varṇa* in the brahmanical archive and the prominence accorded to it. From the time of the *Vedas,* as we shall see, through all the major branches of orthodox literature, in many and varied contexts, Sanskrit authors declared again and again the centrality of the *varṇa* system. It was indeed the fundamental organizing principle of human society.

The *Manusmṛti,* for example, opens with the lawgiver Manu, sitting in meditation. The great sages approached him, saying, "*Bhagavan,* it befits you to describe to us the *dharmas* of all the *varṇas* properly and in order, and of those born between the *varṇas*" (MS 1.2). It is significant that the *Manusmṛti,* usually regarded as the most important of the hegemonic law texts, opens with the very question that concerns us. All twelve chapters that follow might be construed as Manu's response to this one question. The *Manusmṛti* is thereby couched as a discourse on *varṇa* and the respective duties of each. It is of course much more than this, and yet this is the impression created by the *ṛṣis'* question.

Another great *śāstra,* the *Arthaśāstra,* gives a similar degree of prominence to *varṇa,* as it opens its description of society with a recital of the duties, the *svadharmas,* of each of the four *varṇa* (AŚ 1.3.5–8). The question of *varṇa* is also naturally of primary concern in the *Dharmasūtras.* The opening *sūtras* of the *Āpastambadharmasūtra* describe the *varṇas* and the duties assigned to each (ĀŚ 1.1.4–8). Indeed, the bald, magisterial statement that "There are four *varṇas: brāhmaṇa, kṣatriya, vaiśya* and *śūdra*" (e.g., ĀD 1.1.4; BD 1.16.1; VD 2.1) reverberates with great discursive power back and forth throughout these hegemonic texts.

In the brahmanical archive, most descriptions of the creation of the world in general, and human society in particular, include a reference to the origin of the *varṇa* system and the sacred duties that it prescribes. As we shall see, despite great variety in their detail, the same fundamental themes are restated repeatedly: the *varṇa* system is primordial, divine, and cosmogonic; it confers *svadharma* on its members; it is ordered hierarchically; and it determines one's relationships within society. Already we can perceive the outlines of the three-fold discourse as it applies to our paradigmatic narrative.

In the following pages I will survey the various accounts of the origin of the *varṇa* system that are found in the brahmanical archive. Many of these accounts attribute the origin of the *varṇas* to the division of a deity's body, but there are in addition many other explanations. In spite of the heterogeneity and the apparently contradictory nature of these accounts, they share several important features that we shall draw out.

The Division of the Deity

The brahmanical archive abounds in stories that attribute the creation of the *varṇa* system to the fourfold ritual or sacrificial division of the body of a divine being or god. As we shall see, this concept, which has very ancient roots, is found in a variety of guises throughout the archive.

The logical place to begin a discussion of the origins of *varṇa* is the *Puruṣasūkta,* or "Hymn of the Cosmic Man," from the *Ṛgveda* (ṚV 10.90). This may be regarded as the *locus classicus* for the discourse of division in the brahmanical archive. As the hegemonic reference for social division par excellence, it is repeated throughout the length and breadth of the archive, and has occupied the minds of many Indologists.[1] The central figure of this song is the Puruṣa, literally "Man," but in this context, it represents a "cosmic giant" (Doniger O'Flaherty 1981: 29) or "Primeval Being" (Sharma 1978: 294). The *Puruṣasūkta* reads as follows:[2]

> The Puruṣa has a thousand heads, a thousand eyes and a thousand feet. Having pervaded the earth in all directions, he stood above it [at a height of] ten fingers. (1)
>
> The Puruṣa is all this, that which has been and that which will be. He is the ruler of immortality as he grows up with food. (2)
>
> Such is his greatness, but the Puruṣa is more than this. All beings are a quarter of him. Three quarters are what is immortal in heaven. (3)
>
> Three quarters of the Puruṣa rose up. One quarter of him still remained here. From there he spread over everything, into that which eats and that which does not eat. (4)
>
> From him Virāj was born; from Virāj, the Puruṣa. When he was born, he spread beyond the world, behind and in front. (5)
>
> When the gods spread the sacrifice with the Puruṣa as the offering, spring was the clarified butter, summer was the kindling, and autumn was the oblation. (6)

> It was the Puruṣa, born at the beginning, which they sprinkled on the sacred grass as the sacrifice. With him, the *devas, sādhyas,* and *ṛṣis* sacrificed. (7)
>
> From that sacrifice in which everything was offered, the *pṛṣadājya* was collected. It made the creatures of the air, the forest and the village. (8)
>
> From that sacrifice in which everything was offered, the verses (*ṛcaḥ*) and chants (*sāmāni*) were born. The meters (*chandāṃsi*) were born from it. The formulae (*yajuḥ*) were born from it. (9)
>
> From it horses were born, and all animals with two rows of teeth. Cows were born from it. From it were born goats and sheep. (10)
>
> When they divided the Puruṣa, into how many parts did they apportion him? What is his mouth? What are his two arms? What do they call his thighs and feet? (11)
>
> The *brāhmaṇa* was his mouth. The two arms were made into the *rājanya.* Those that were his two thighs were the *vaiśya.* From his two feet the *śūdra* was born. (12)
>
> The moon was born from his mind. From his eye the sun was born. From his mouth, Indra and Agni. From his breath Vāyu was born. (13)
>
> From his navel there was the air. From his head the sky arose, from his two feet arose the earth, and the cardinal directions arose from his ear. Thus they fashioned the worlds. (14)
>
> There were seven enclosing sticks for him, and three times seven bundles of kindling, when the *devas,* spreading the sacrifice, bound the Puruṣa as the sacrificial animal. (15)
>
> With the sacrifice the *devas* sacrificed to the sacrifice. These were the first sacrificial rites. These powers reached the sky where the ancient *sādhyas* and *devas* are. (16)

As this song, like many Vedic texts, abounds in obscurity, ambiguity, and circularity, it is impossible to interpret every passage with certainty. The first challenge is to determine the sequence of the events described. Is there a natural temporal flow from beginning to end? If so, why does the Puruṣa appear as the bound sacrifice at the end of the song, after the sacrifice has taken place? If there is no temporal sequence, how are the various elements related to one another? The song seems to describe four generative events, but because the temporal sequence is uncertain, we cannot determine whether these are four distinct occurrences, or four descriptions of the one event, or some other permutation. As this conundrum is probably insoluble, we can only describe the four acts individually.

The first two creative events in the song may be passed over briefly, as they are not of central concern to us. In the first, three quarters of the Puruṣa rose to heaven to become the immortal gods, while one quarter remained on earth to become "all beings" (verses 3–4). The second event is described in verse 5: the Puruṣa—who is, as we saw, the essential male—gives rise to Virāj, the "active female creative principle" (Doniger O'Flaherty 1981: 31). In this process we encounter a typical Vedic reflexive cycle, in which the Puruṣa gives rise to Virāj, who in turn gives rise to the Puruṣa.

Verses 6–10 contain the central sacrifice, which constitutes the third creative episode. The Puruṣa seems to be the offering, perhaps the bound sacrificial animal mentioned in verse 14, which is to be burned on a fire. From this act a substance called *pṛṣadājya* is collected. According to Monier-Williams, *pṛṣadājya* is "curdled or clotted butter, [or] ghee mixed with coagulated milk." Doniger describes it as "Literally, a mixture of butter and sour milk used in the sacrifice; figuratively, the fat that drained from the sacrificial victim" (Doniger O'Flaherty 1981: 32). This substance is the basis of the third generative act of the song: from the *pṛṣadājya* are created all birds and animals, both domestic and wild. The verses, chants, and formulae (*ṛcaḥ, sāmāni,* and *yajuḥ,* i.e., the *Ṛg-, Sāma-,* and *Yajurvedas*) and the meters in which these were composed also arose from this cosmogonic gravy.

In verses 11–14 we witness the fourth, and for our discussion, the most significant creative event: the "dividing" of the Puruṣa. It is not clear whether this is the dismembering of a "cooked" sacrificial offering, or a separate event unrelated to the preceding sacrifice. In either case, "they," presumably the *devas* who presided over the sacrifice, divided the body of the Puruṣa into four: his mouth (*mukhaṃ*) became the *brāhmaṇa.*[3] His two arms were made into the *rājanya,* a "kingly, princely or royal person," but in this context it is universally assumed to be equivalent to the *kṣatriya,* a member of the second *varṇa,* that is, a warrior. From the thighs and feet of the Puruṣa arose the two remaining *varṇas,* the *vaiśya* and the *śūdra* respectively. In this same cosmogonic episode, the sun and moon, the deities Indra, Agni and Vāyu, and heaven and earth were also created. There are two further reflexive cycles here: first, the deities sacrificed the Puruṣa, who in turn gave rise to the deities; second, the Puruṣa, who was described as "all this" in verse 2, becomes "these worlds."

Being in the tenth *maṇḍala,* this is regarded as one of the more recent songs of the *Ṛgveda* (Renou 1957: 6). The older portions of the *Vedas* mention three *varṇas:* the *brahma,* the *kṣatra,* and the *viś.* The *Puruṣasūkta* is the first and only place in the *Ṛgveda* where the words *rājanya, vaiśya,* and *śūdra* are used (Sharma 1978: 295), but more significantly, it constitutes the earliest formulation of the *cāturvarṇya* system, that is, the division of society into four *varṇas.* As we shall see, the simple statement that the *brāhmaṇa,* the *kṣatriya,* the *vaiśya,* and the *śudra* arose from the mouth, arms, thighs, and feet of a primal creative being went on to exert enormous discursive influence in the brahmanical archive as a whole. In order to illustrate just how far and wide this concept spread, I shall present some examples from various hegemonic texts in the following pages.

There are many references in the archive to the creation of the *varṇas* from the body of a deity, but the identity of that deity and the manner of creation varies from context to context, for example, the later creator deity Brahmā appears in the place of the original Vedic Puruṣa. Let us begin with an example of the creation myth in the *Karṇaparvan* of the *Mahābhārata.* Duryodhana had asked Śalya to act as Karṇa's chariot-driver, and in the process of formulating his objection, Śalya said:

> According to the *śrutis,* Brahmā created the *brāhmaṇas* from his mouth, and the *kṣatriya* from his arms. He created the *vaiśyas* from his two thighs and the *śūdras* from his feet. (Mbh 8.23.32)

Śalya argued with great indignation that it would therefore not befit a *kṣatriya* like himself to serve as a driver—a low-status profession—for Karṇa, whom at that stage was still thought to be a driver's son. In the following example from the *Manusmṛti* Brahmā is again the agent of creation:

> And for the sake of the increase of the worlds, he [i.e., Brahmā] caused the *brāhmaṇa,* the *kṣatriya,* the *vaiśya,* and the *śūdra* to proceed from his mouth, his arms, his thighs and his feet. (MS 1.31)

This is the standard condensed account of the creation of the *varṇas* by Brahmā, which is found, variously expressed, in countless locations in the archive.[4]

In all these examples, the Vedic Puruṣa, the "cosmic man," has been superseded by a more "modern" monotheistic entity, Brahmā or Prajāpati. Further, the ritual "division" of the Puruṣa, with its overtones of sacrificial dismemberment, has been toned down, morphing into "emission" or "creation," a concept conveyed by the root *sṛj.* The Puruṣa is no longer dismembered to become the *varṇas;* Brahmā now "emits" them from his body.

According to the Sāṃkhya system of philosophy, the three *guṇas—sattva, rajas,* and *tamas*—are the dominating principles or "qualities" of the world. They are analogous to the four elements of classical European thought: earth, air, fire, and water. The three *guṇas* are difficult to translate: Doniger and Smith (1991: 281) use "lucidity," "energy," and "darkness"; but I have chosen to leave them in Sanskrit. Many passages in the brahmanical archive posit a relationship between the *guṇas* and the division of the various primal beings into the *varṇas.* The nexus between *guṇa* and *varṇa* is clearly illustrated in this passage from the *Viṣṇupurāṇa:*

> In former times when Brahmā, meditating on truth, desired to create the world, those in whom *sattva* was dominant arose from his mouth, O best of the twice-born. Similarly, those in whom *rajas* was dominant come into being from the breast of Brahmā. Similarly, those in whom *rajas* and *tamas* were dominant, [arose] from the thigh. Brahmā created other beings, those in whom *tamas* was dominant, from his feet. From that [arose] the system of the four *varṇas.* (VP 1.6.3–5)[5]

In this context the *brāhmaṇas* are associated with *sattva,* the noblest quality. *Kṣatriyas* are dominated by *rajas,* which ties in with their energetic, martial *dharma. Vaiśyas* are dominated by both *rajas* and *tamas,* and *śūdras,* always at the bottom of the heap, are, by their very nature, dominated by *tamas,* the basest element, which associated with darkness, ignorance, and so on.

In the *Vāyupurāṇa,* we find an interesting elaboration of this idea: not only do we encounter the system of *guṇas* in the generation of *varṇas,* but we also find a solution to this problem: How did society evolve, if only one member of each *varṇa* was created?

> Then, creation being suspended, when Brahmā, desiring to create, was contemplating living creatures and meditating on truth, he emitted a thousand couples from his mouth. These people

> abounded in *sattva* and were high-minded. He emitted another thousand couples from his breast. All these, some valiant and some not, abounded in *rajas*. Having further emitted a thousand pairs from his thigh, they were thought to abound in *rajas* and *tamas*, and to be the common people in this world. And the thousand couples he emitted from his feet all abounded in *tamas*, were destitute of glory, and had little *tejas*. (VāyP 1.8.35–39)

In the *Bhāgavatapurāṇa*, we see the now-familiar association of the four *varṇas* with the respective parts of the deity's body, but with a further twist. It is no longer explicitly stated that the *varṇas* are emitted from the body of the "Great Being" (*Mahātman*, i.e., Brahmā). Here the four *varṇas* have come to characterize him: "The Great Being is *brāhmaṇa*-mouthed, *kṣatriya*-armed, *vaiśya*-thighed and has the black *varṇa* at his feet (BP 2.1.37, see also BP 2.5.34–38). The commentary elaborates the point that the four *varṇas* now describe the deity. I have placed the commentator's explanations in braces:

> Whose two arms are *kṣatra* {the *kṣatriya*}, whose two thighs are the *viś* {the *vaiśya*}, at whose feet are the black *varṇa* {the *śūdra*}, his face {mouth}, is *brahman* {the *brāhmaṇa*}. (BP 2.1.37 commentary)

In this example, the four *varṇas* do not arise from the deity, but they *are* the deity, or he, perhaps, *is* them: the *brāhmaṇas* are his mouth, the *kṣatriyas* his arms, and so forth.

In all these post-Vedic accounts, the generative being has been Brahmā or Prajāpati. In contrast to these, the *Skandapurāṇa* superimposes Viṣṇu at the apex of the creative chain of command. Brahmā bowed down at the foot of Viṣṇu's throne and stood before him with hands joined in salutation. Viṣṇu granted to Brahmā the boon of creative power, and said:

> Having meditated on your identity with me as Vairāja, create beings with your *samādhi*. If a task cannot be accomplished by you alone, think of me, the granter of desires. (SkP 2.9.24.31)

With this boon from Viṣṇu, Brahmā then proceeded to create the entire universe by emitting a hundred *brāhmaṇas* from his mouth, a hundred *kṣatriyas* from this arms, and so on, as per the preceding accounts (SkP 2.9.24.41–42).

One of the functions of the *Skandapurāṇa* was to glorify Viṣṇu, and to illuminate that deity in the best possible light. To these ends, the creator Brahmā—who in the other accounts appears as an autonomous agent and supreme being—is depicted in loyal supplication to Viṣṇu as his obedient subordinate. As a king grants a boon to a subject, so Viṣṇu granted Brahmā the power to create the universe.

One account of the creation in the *Bhāgavatapurāṇa* begins with a more-or-less standard version of the division of the Puruṣa, but then states that:

> These *varṇas* worship their own preceptor Hari, from whom they were born along with their livelihoods, by [pursuing] their *svadharmas* with faith, for the purpose of purifying themselves. (BP 3.6.34)

The phrase, "from whom they were born" (*yajjātāḥ*) offers an interesting insight. Although the author accepted that the *varṇas* were created by the Puruṣa in accordance with the Vedic account, one suspects that he was merely paying lip-service to it. The *varṇas* and their *svadharmas*, and presumably the rest of the universe, were "actually," it seems, created again and again from or by Hari/Viṣṇu.

A similar ambiguity about who actually created the *varṇas* is found in the *Brahmāṇḍapurāṇa.* At one point, Brahmā upbraided Rāma for vowing to destroy the world "which was created by me, O beloved, with difficulty, at his [i.e., Viṣṇu's] behest" (BAP 2.3.31.30). This tallies with the account in the *Skandapurāṇa* above, in which Viṣṇu oversaw Brahmā's creation of the universe. Then we encounter the following statement:

> This eternal creation, along with the *brāhmaṇas, kṣatriyas, vaiśyas* and *śūdras,* appears from Hari and vanishes again and again. (BAP 2.3.31.32)

This gives Hari/Viṣṇu a much more active role in the creation of the *varṇas.* All these passages in which Viṣṇu is featured represent an attempt to reconcile the earlier Vedic Puruṣa creation story with the later Vaiṣṇava tradition, in which Viṣṇu is the supreme creator.

By the time of the *Bhagavadgītā,* we find Kṛṣṇa fulfilling the role of creator of the *varṇa* system and the disposer of the *svadharmas:*

> The system of four *varṇas* was created by me, and the apportioning of their qualities and actions. Although I am their creator, know me as the imperishable non-creator. (Mbh 6.26.13)

Other Accounts of the Origins of *Varṇa*

All the above accounts of the *varṇa* system, which involve the division of the primal Vedic Puruṣa or the emission of the *varṇas* from a later divine entity, are in reality variations on the one basic idea that the *varṇas* arose from the body of a deity. In addition to these, there are other explanations in the archive of how the *varṇas* began, which form the subject of the following section.

The *Śatapathabrāhmaṇa* is a prose exegesis of Vedic practice associated with the *White Yajurveda.* This text may be older than the *Puruṣasūkta,* because, like the earlier Vedic material, it lists only three *varṇas* and uses the earlier forms *brahma, kṣatra* and *viś.* The *Śatapathabrāhmaṇa* contains an account of the creation of the *varṇas* quite different from the ones discussed above:

> Uttering *bhūr,* Prajāpati generated this [earth]; uttering *bhuvaḥ,* the atmosphere; and uttering *svaḥ,* the sky. All this [universe] is so much as these worlds. Uttering *bhūr,* Prajāpati generated the *brahma;* uttering *bhuvaḥ,* the *kṣatra;* and uttering *svaḥ,* the *viś.* All this [universe] is so much as the *brahma,* the *kṣatra* and the *viś.* (ŚPB 2.1.4.11–12)

The significant point in this passage is that Prajāpati, the "lord of creation," created the *varṇas* by uttering the three syllables, which are well known from the *Gāyatrī mantra, bhūr, bhuvaḥ,* and *svaḥ.*

This version never achieved the discursive influence of the division-type accounts, nor has it been repeated as widely or as often in the archive. Even though it differs from the former accounts in terms of content, it contributes to the overall discourse of division in a similar way: it shows that the division of society is primordial, cosmogonic and divinely sanctioned. Each *varṇa* was created as a unique and distinct entity, and occupies a definite position in a hierarchy.

The next passage, originally a quotation from some other unidentified source, is found in the *Vasiṣṭhadharmasūtra.* In this account, Prajāpati gives rise to each of the *varṇas,* not with syllables, but with a different Vedic meter. Here, too, the relative superiority of the various *varṇas* is linked to the perceived hierarchy of the meters (Smith 1994: 293–304, Olivelle 2000: 646).

> He created the *brāhmaṇa* with the *gāyatrī* metre, the *kṣatriya* with the *triṣṭubh* and the *vaiśya* with the *jagatī,* but he created the *śūdra* without any metre. (VD 4.3)

The *Taittirīyabrāhmaṇa,* a text associated with the *Black Yajurveda,* contains yet another account. Like the *Śatapathabrāhmaṇa,* it refers to only three *varṇas,* suggesting that it also belongs to an earlier tradition.

> All this [world] was created by Brahmā. From the *Ṛg[veda]* was born the *vaiśya varṇa.* The *Yajurveda* was the origin of the *kṣatriya,* they say. The *Sāmaveda* was the procreator of the *brāhmaṇas.* (TB 3.12.50)

First, the unique aspect of this passage is that the three *varṇas* arise from the *Vedas* themselves, highlighting, perhaps, their inherent creative power. Second, the order in which the *varṇas* are attributed to the texts appears at first to be surprising, as Indology has come to regard the *Ṛgveda* as the preeminent *Veda.* At first glance, one might expect the *Ṛg* to give rise to the most prestigious *varṇa,* the *brāhmaṇa.* And yet, in the *Bhagavadgītā,* Kṛṣṇa also privileged the *Sāmaveda* when he said to Arjuna, "Of the *Vedas,* I am the *Sāmaveda*" (Mbh 6.32.22). We also find the "triple *Veda*" listed with the *Sāmaveda* first in the *Arthaśāstra* (AŚ 1.3.1). Despite our preconceptions, there is indeed some consistency in the way in which the texts and *varṇas* are related: they are arranged according to a permissible indigenous scheme in order of increasing prestige.

There is an interesting alternative account for the origin of the *varṇas* in the *Vāmanapurāṇa.* Here, everything began with a "cosmic egg" lying in an ocean. In this egg, Brahmā lay asleep. It was broken open by the "Lord" (*bhagavān,* but I cannot determine whether this refers to Brahmā or Viṣṇu), and the four syllables *om, bhūr, bhuvaḥ,* and *svaḥ* arose. From these syllables *tejas* was produced. This *tejas* escaped from the egg and caused the surrounding ocean to evaporate. When Brahmā emerged from the egg, there was at his navel a great lake:

> In the middle was a great banyan tree in the form of a pillar. From it emerged the *varṇas: brāhmaṇas, kṣatriyas, vaiśyas* and *śūdras* who arose from it to serve the twice-born ones. (VāmP 22.38–39)[6]

This account of the *varṇas* arising from the banyan-tree differs markedly from all the accounts discussed above, and yet exhibits the same significant discursive traits to which I have alluded above.

In the *Mahābhārata,* we find a dialogue between the sages Bhṛgu and Bharadvāja, in which the former attributed a color to each *varṇa*: "White is the color of the *brāhmaṇas,* red of the *kṣatriyas,* yellow is the color of the *vaiśyas,* and similarly, black of the *śūdras*" (Mbh 12.181.5). Bharadhvāja challenged this observation, and suggested that humans were essentially all the same, as all are subject to desire, anger, and fear, and all produce sweat, urine, feces, and phlegm. This being the case, he asked Bhṛgu on what basis the *varṇas* were apportioned. Bhṛgu replied that there was no difference between the *varṇas.* I assume that, by this, the sage meant that there was *originally* no difference between the *varṇas,* that is, no fundamental, biological difference. Bhṛgu said, "Everything in the world was of Brahmā; it was created by Brahmā, but became divided into *varṇas* because of actions." According to this account, all humans were originally *brāhmaṇas,* but those who were attached to pleasure, violence, etc., who had abandoned *brāhmaṇa svadharma,* and "whose limbs were red" became *kṣatriyas.* Those *brāhmaṇas* who bred cattle, took part in agriculture and were "yellow" became *vaiśyas,* and those who suffered from multiple shortcomings, did all sorts of odd-jobs, and were "black" became *śūdras* (Mbh 12.181.8–13).[7]

This differs substantially from the division-type accounts in which the four *varṇas* were divinely created as different entities. In this Lamarckian model, all were created first as *brāhmaṇas,* but "evolved" into the other *varṇas* as a result of their individual actions. No deities are actively involved in this process, but it enjoys a mythic unassailability, and possesses a similar discursive thrust to the other accounts.

Early in the *Mahābhārata,* Vaiśaṃpāyana was telling Janamejaya the history of his clan, the Kurus, beginning with the origin of humankind. According to this account, Pracetas, an ancient seer and lawgiver, had ten virtuous sons, one of whom was Dakṣa. Described as the grandsire of the world (*lokapitāmahaḥ* Mbh 1.70.4), Dakṣa had a thousand sons and fifty daughters. One of his daughters gave birth to many deities, including Vivasvat. Vivasvat had a son called Yama, who had a son called Mārtaṇḍa;

Mārtaṇḍa in turn had a son called Manu. "This lineage of Manu became famous as [the lineage] of men, because men—the *brāhmaṇas,* the *kṣatriyas* and the others—were born from that Manu" (*manor vaṃśo mānavānāṃ tato 'yaṃ prathito'bhavat* | *brahmakṣatrādayas tasmān manor jātās tu mānavāḥ* || Mbh 1.70.11). Although it is mythological, primordial, and not without divine agency—gods and sages are active throughout—this is a straightforward genealogy. Like the preceding account in which the *varṇas* arose from individual behavior, this version also seems almost biological.

Varṇa in the Brahmanical Archive

To conclude this survey of the origins of *varṇa* in the brahmanical archive, several important points remain to be made. First, while these accounts are many and varied, they are bound together by several significant themes. We saw the *varṇa* system arise from the dismemberment of the Puruṣa, and we saw it emitted from the body of various deities. We also saw it arise from the *Gāyatrī* syllables, the Vedic metres and from a tree in the middle of the cosmic lake. We saw two "biological" models in which the three lesser *varṇas* "evolved" from the *brāhmaṇas,* or descended from Manu. Such are the differences in content and detail among the various accounts. What are the similarities? All these versions agree that society is "naturally" divided into *varṇas* and that they did not arise through conscious human effort. They were divinely created or arose through a "natural" process that we might call "karmic evolution." Most accounts agree that humans not only exist in four different *varṇas,* but that they were created this way, by divine agency, at the same time as the universe was created or shortly thereafter.

While all these creative acts differ from one another in matters of detail, their thrust is similar. They do not need to be unanimous to be discursively effective. The requirement of internal consistency and unanimity of argument is in this case, I suggest, an Occidental predilection. The discursive effects of a set of propositions—such as these—under the Western paradigm come into play if they function under the particular regime of truth governed largely by logic and reason. To the traditional Western mind, these various versions of the truth cannot all function as true because they are mutually contradictory. Under this particular Sanskritic paradigm, in which a regime of truth of a different kind is in force, these accounts may function as true simultaneously, because they are supported by scripture, and so forth. In these circumstances, the two systems have different criteria for truth. Thus, these various versions, which appear to be mutually contradictory, are discursively in agreement. The identity of the creative deity may vary from one account to another, and yet the *varṇas* are always the same: primordial, cosmogonic, and divinely created. All agree on a natural hierarchy, and all attribute a *svadharma* to each *varṇa*. Deities come and deities go, yet the *varṇas* go on forever.

Did the authors of these texts think of human society as being divided into four portions? There is little evidence for the idea of a single, unitary human society here; "humanity" and "society" are not particularly Sanskritic concepts. The basic unit is not one human species or one human society as we see it, but rather, the *varṇa*. A more Sanskritic idea would be that there are four distinct human societies or four kinds of humans. The forces that divide them into *varṇa* are much stronger than those that unite them into either a species or a society. Just as an animal cannot change its species, it is not possible, desirable or thinkable that a human could move from one *varṇa* to another.

What are the implications of the archive's discourse on *varṇa* for our understanding of the indigo jackal and rest of the *Pañcatantra*? The concept of division as we have distilled it from the brahmanical archive forms part of the background against which the discourse of division may be viewed. All those divisions that we described in chapter 2—between the indigo jackal and the lion (Story 1-11), the owl and the goose (Story 1-12), the frog and the snake (Story 4-01)—were read, heard and understood by people for whom the divisions in society were as deep, wide, and unbridgeable—as "natural"—as those we have observed in the brahmanical archive. An audience familiar with the archive's discourse on *varṇa* would understand that societies are divinely and primordially divided. Such patterns of division date back to the creation of the world. Social divisions, such as *varṇas*, are universally acknowledged to be the handiwork of the gods, not mere contingent social constructs. We have already outlined the importance of the concept of *jāti* in the *Pañcatantra*, and we saw how the fictional metasocieties of the forest were deeply, irrevocably and naturally divided into kinds. Just as the world of humans is divided into *brāhmaṇas*, *kṣatriyas*, and so on, the *jātis* were the basic building blocks of that animal realm. We can see now how the *Pañcatantra*'s use of *jāti* in the animal world meshes neatly with the broader concept of division into *varṇa* as it is expressed in the brahmanical archive.

SVADHARMA—"ESSENTIAL DUTY"

Having witnessed the creation of the four *varṇas* from the division of the Vedic Puruṣa and his successors in the preceding section, we will now turn to the question of the essential occupations or duties allotted to each *varṇa.* As we saw above, the idea of a *dharma* for each *varṇa,* known as its *svadharma* or "own *dharma,*" was not made explicit in the *Puruṣasūkta,* but was introduced, and then greatly elaborated, in later texts.

Throughout the brahmanical archive we see passages relating to *svadharma* repeated in various configurations and contexts. Hardly an account of the creation of the *varṇa* system lacks a complementary description of their *svadharmas.* Most of these accounts agree in principle, but differ in matters of detail. The concept in its simplest form is this: society is naturally divided into *varṇas,* and each *varṇa* is naturally endowed with its own traditional set of characteristics, occupations, and so forth. The origins of both the *varṇa* system and the *svadharmas* are primordial, divine, and cosmogonic. *Svadharma* is indeed an inalienable aspect of *varṇa.* It is difficult to imagine one without the other, as it is ultimately the *svadharma* that gives each *varṇa* its shape, purpose, and function. In many accounts, the *svadharmas* were created immediately after the *varṇas* themselves:

> For the purpose of protecting all of this creation, the being of great splendor [i.e., Brahmā] made separate activities for those born from his mouth, arms, thighs and feet. (MS 1.87)

> Prajāpati formerly created the activities for each of the four *varṇas* and the four *varṇas* [themselves] solely for the purpose of sacrifice. (Mbh 13.48.3)

The *svadharmas* play a central role in the *varṇa* system. The following passage suggests that Manu composed the *Manusmṛti* with the primary purpose of defining the *svadharmas:*

> In order to define the actions of the [*brāhmaṇa*] and of the remaining *varṇas* in order, Manu, scion of the Self-created One [Brahmā], composed this *śāstra.* (MS 1.102)

There are two comprehensive accounts of the duties assigned to the *varṇas* in the *Mahābhārata,* one in the *Śāntiparvan* (Mbh 12.60), and the other in the

Anuśāsanaparvan (Mbh 13.131). The context of the first is straightforward: Yudhiṣṭhira asked Bhīṣma, who was lying on his bed of arrows, "What are the *dharmas* of all the *varṇas*? Which are specific to the four *varṇas* and to the four stages of life (*āśramas*), and which are the *dharmas* of a king?" (Mbh 12.60.2). The fifty-odd verses of Bhīṣma's response comprise one of the most complete descriptions for the four *svadharmas* that I have seen. In brief, the *svadharma* of a *brāhmaṇa* is given as the performance of sacrifice, self-control, study, and teaching, in addition to the gamut of responsibilities that pertain to each of the four *āśramas.* The sacred duties of the *kṣatriya* are that he may perform sacrifices, but he may not officiate at the sacrifices of others. He may study the *Vedas,* but may not teach them to others. His secular responsibilities center on the duties of kingship: protecting his subjects, waging war, supporting the *brāhmaṇas,* and so on. The *vaiśya* is enjoined to make gifts to the *brāhmaṇas,* study the *Vedas,* perform sacrifices, and acquire wealth, primarily through animal husbandry (many other accounts add trade as an acceptable occupation). The duties of the *śūdra* are simple: he must serve the three higher *varṇas* (Mbh 12.60.9–52).

Four hundred chapters later, in what is surely the world's longest death-bed scene, Bhīṣma, still on the arrows, repeated to Yudhiṣṭhira a discourse between Umā and Maheśvara (i.e., Pārvatī and Śiva). Umā asked her consort the same question that Yudhiṣṭhira had asked Bhīṣma in the section above. In reply, Maheśvara described in nearly thirty verses the respective *svadharmas* of each of the four *varṇas.* The duties are similar to those described above, with some notable exceptions. The dietary observance of the *brāhmaṇa,* his duties toward guests and his daily household routine are dealt with in more detail here, but the duties of the other three *varṇas* are much the same (Mbh 13.128.28–59).[8]

In many places in the archive we encounter the same ideas repeated in an abbreviated form. Here is an example from the *Manusmṛti:*

> He [i.e., Brahmā] made teaching and study, sacrificing [for themselves] and sacrificing for others, and giving and receiving for the *brāhmaṇas.* Protecting his subjects, giving, causing sacrifices to be performed, study and freedom from attachment to the objects of the senses are assigned for the *kṣatriya.* Protecting livestock, giving, causing sacrifices to be performed, study, the life of a merchant or moneylender, or farming are for the *vaiśya.* But the Lord assigned a single task to the *śūdra*: serving these [other] *varṇas* without complaint.[9] (MS 1.88–91)

Accounts of *svadharma* are often summarized in just one, two or three verses. Here is a typical short version, also from the *Mahābhārata:*

> The *brāhmaṇa,* on account of his birth alone, was born over the earth, as the lord of all creatures, for the protection of the treasury of *dharma.* Then [Brahmā] made the second *varṇa,* the *kṣatriya,* the protector of the earth, the wielder of the rod, for the protection of the people. And the *vaiśya* should support these three *varṇas* with wealth and grain. And the *śūdra* should serve them. Such were Brahmā's instructions. (Mbh 12.73.6–8)[10]

Svadharma comes, however, with an escape clause.[11] During times of distress (*āpad*), members of a given *varṇa* may pursue the occupations proper to the *varṇas* below them, with certain limitations, which vary from source to source (see, e.g., Mbh 12.79). All texts, however, make it clear that this is the exception to the rule, and that in normal circumstances, one must follow only the *dharma* of one's *varṇa.* As Arjuna learned at Kurukṣetra, following one's *svadharma* is a worthy goal in itself, irrespective of the consequences:

> It is better to perform one's own *dharma* poorly than another's *dharma* well. To die in the performance of one's own *dharma* is better. The *dharma* of another should inspire fear. (Mbh 6.25.35)[12]

> In performing action prescribed by one's own nature, one commits no transgression. One should not abandon the actions into which one is born, Kaunteya, even with their imperfections, for all undertakings are enveloped in fault, just as fire is enveloped in smoke. (Mbh 6.40.47–48)

Such is the discourse relating to *svadharma* in the brahmanical archive. The accounts of the origins of *varṇa* are remarkable for their heterogeneity; in contrast, the discourse relating to *svadharma* is notably consistent. Despite the escape clause and some variation in the amount of detail, all these accounts agree on a certain number of fundamental points: first, that every *varṇa* has a *svadharma;* second, that the *svadharmas* encompass a certain number of specific duties; and third, that *svadharma* was divinely allocated at or shortly after the creation of the *varṇas* themselves, more or less at the beginning of time. Thus every individual in this highly idealized version of orthodox society as it is portrayed in the archive possesses a predetermined trajectory and occupation.

What are the implications of the concept of *svadharma* for our understanding of the discourse of division in the *Pañcatantra*? The discourse of *svadharma* in the archive is so pervasive that it is barely conceivable that the audience of the *Pañcatantra* could have remained untouched by it. Any literate person must have been familiar with the idea that each *varṇa* had its own divinely ordained *svadharma*. I suggest that the readers of the *Pañcatantra*, if they accepted the thrust of the orthodox discourse on *svadharma*, would have readily assimilated the idea that every individual had a natural complement of responsibilities and characteristics determined by birth. I further suggest that a consciousness of the idea of *svadharma* might predispose the audience of the *Pañcatantra* toward the ideas of *svabhāva*. *Svabhāva*, or "essential nature," which we discussed at length in chapter 2, was attributed to individual characters, particularly to animals as members of a particular *jāti*.

The following passage from the *Bhagavadgītā* illustrates the relationship between *svabhāva* and *svadharma* in the archive:

> The actions of *brāhmaṇas, kṣatriyas, vaiśyas,* and *śūdras,* O enemy-scorcher, are distinguished according to the qualities arising from their own *svabhāva*. Calm, restraint, austerity, purity, patience, sincerity, spiritual and worldly knowledge and orthodoxy are the actions of a *brāhmaṇa,* and which are born of his *svabhāva.* Prowess, glory, steadfastness, ability, not fleeing even in battle, generosity and lordliness are the actions of a *kṣatriya,* which are born of his *svabhāva.* Agriculture, tending cattle and trade are the actions of the *vaiśya,* which are born of his *svabhāva.* The actions of the *śūdra,* which are born of his *svabhāva,* consist of service. A person delighting in all his own actions will gain complete accomplishment. (Mbh 6.40.41–45)

The *svabhāva* of members of each *varṇa* determines their propensities, dispositions and occupations. The above passage suggests that *svabhāva* is the underlying nature that drives and shapes *svadharma.* The former is the unseen cause; the latter is the observable surface effect. *Svabhāva* manifests as *svadharma* in social practice.

It is unthinkable that a *brāhmaṇa* might shirk his sacrificial duties or that a *śūdra* might perform any function other than service. Sacrifice and service are the inherent activities of all the members of these two *varṇas.* They are the innate, divinely ordained functions, which are in reality simply manifestations of their very natures. To be born a *brāhmaṇa* is to be born for the sacrifice. The very reason for the existence of this and the other *varṇas* is the performance of their respective *svadharmas.* Similarly, to be born a jackal is to be born with the *svabhāva* of the jackal: he is the heir to inauspiciousness, peripherality and inferiority. Like the member of any *varṇa,* the essential nature, status, and appropriate peers of the members of any *jāti* are determined by their birth. It is impossible for a jackal to turn its back on its jackal nature. The indigo jackal howled back at its fellows because it could not resist the tendencies of its *svabhāva*—because it was following its jackal *dharma.*

STATUS

What does the brahmanical archive say about the relative status of each of the *varṇas*? In every account of the origins of the *varṇa* system, the four *varṇas* are listed in this order: *brāhmaṇa, kṣatriya, vaiśya,* and *śūdra.* Whether the creative deity is the Puruṣa or Brahmā, whether the *varṇas* are the result of a sacrificial division of the body or an emission from a limb, a book or a tree, and even though the order is occasionally reversed, the relative status of each is invariable. The order in which they were created and in which they are listed indicates their position in the hierarchy. In the following exchange between the two sages Bhṛgu and Bharadvāja, we see various entities listed in order of creation. Here, too, the order reflects their precedence:

> Bhṛgu said, "Brahmā Prajāpati first created divine power, produced by his own energy and equal in splendor to the sun or fire. Then the Lord created truth, *dharma,* austerities and the eternal *Veda;* observances and purity for getting to heaven; the *devas, dānavas, gandharvas, daityas, asuras* and the great snakes; *yakṣas, rākṣasas, nāgas* and *piśācas;* and the humans: *brāhmaṇas, kṣatriyas, vaiśyas* and *śūdras,* O best of *brāhmaṇas,* and the other multitudes of teeming beings, he created those also. (Mbh 12.181.1–4)

The four *varṇas* are usually listed in this particular sequence, from *brāhmaṇa* to *śūdra,* indicating their hierarchical precedence from highest to lowest. As mentioned above, on rare occasions, the sequence is reversed: "Work is for the *śūdra,* agriculture for the *vaiśya,* administration of justice for the king, and *brahmacarya,* austerities, *mantras* and truth for the twice-born ones" (Mbh 12.92.4). The hierarchical position of each *varṇa* is invariably the same, the *brāhmaṇa* is always at the top and the *śūdra* is at the bottom.

The part of the body from which they were created also reflects their social position. To illustrate this, we must temporarily raise the Puruṣa from his sacrificial pyre and stand him upright. His head is now his uppermost part, his arms or chest and his thighs are respectively lower, and finally his feet, being on the ground, are his lowest member. In this way, the hierarchical position of each *varṇa* is expressed as a function of its elevation. The head is preeminent, perhaps because it is uppermost. The mouth may also be regarded as sacred because of it is the site of Vedic recitation, and as the inlet for food, it must also be pure. The following quotation illustrates the relationship between parts of the human body and privilege:

> A man is said to be purer above the navel. Therefore, the Self-existent One said that his mouth was the purest part. Because he was born from the highest part of the body, because he is the eldest, and because he possesses the *Vedas,* according to *dharma,* the *brāhmaṇa* is the lord of all this creation. (MS 1.92–93)

The feet, the place of origin of the *śūdras,* are conversely the lowest. They are closest to the ground, and are impure as they come into contact with dust and filth.

Superiority

We have seen how the hierarchy of the *varṇas* is implicit in the order in which they were created, the parts of the deity with which they are associated, and the order in which they are listed. The brahmanical archive also abounds with explicit references to the superiority of the *brāhmaṇas* and the increasing inferiority of the subsequent *varṇas.* This is hardly surprising in view of the archive's role in maintaining brahmanical power and privilege. A few examples below will serve to illustrate this point.

> Of created things, living beings are the best; among living beings, those that live by their intelligence [are best]. Of the intelligent, men are best; among men, *brāhmaṇas* are thought [to be the best]. (MS 1.96)

> The very birth of a *brāhmaṇa* is an incarnation of eternal *dharma,* for he is born for *dharma,* and is suited to become one with *brahman.* A *brāhmaṇa,* being born, is the highest on earth, the lord of all beings, for the protection of the treasury of *dharma.* Whatever

> exists in the world is the property of the *brāhmaṇa*. On account of the excellence of his birth the *brāhmaṇa* is indeed entitled to everything. The *brāhmaṇa* eats only what is his own, wears only what is his own, gives only what is his own. Other people subsist through the benevolence of the *brāhmaṇa*. (MS 1.98–101)

The superiority of the *brāhmaṇas* is often attributed to their birth, or to the fact that they, as a *varṇa,* were "born" first, or, as we have seen, that they were "born" from the mouth of the deity.

> From the mouth of the Puruṣa, O son of Kuru, arose the *Vedas* and the *brāhmaṇa*. Because he came from the same mouth, he became the foremost of the *varṇas* and their preceptor. (BP 3.6.30)

Inferiority

The superiority of the *brāhmaṇa* is complemented by an unrelenting discourse on the natural inferiority of the *śūdra* and other members of lower social strata. The brahmanical archive as a whole, and the *Dharmasūtras* and *-śāstras* in particular, overflow with references to the *śūdras'* natural inferiority in every respect. For example, punishments are generally heavier for them than for twice-born miscreants (GD 12.8–14). Sacrificial offerings are spoiled if a *caṇḍāla* or an outcaste looks at them (GD 15.24). If a *brāhmaṇa* is touched by a person who has himself touched a *caṇḍāla,* then he must undergo ritual purification (GD 14.30). The punishment for killing a *śūdra* is no more than for killing a crow, a frog or a rat (BD 1.19.6).

The whole tone of the *Dharmasūtras* is explicitly set to ensure the superiority of the *brāhmaṇa* in particular, and of the three "twice-born" *varṇas* in general, vis-à-vis the *śūdra.* Great effort was expended, in theory at least, to ensure that *varṇa* distinctions were applied to every situation. For example, if a *kṣatriya* man had sex with a *brāhmaṇa* woman he was to be wrapped in *śara* grass and thrown into a fire. If the man was a *vaiśya, lohita* straw was to be used. If he was *śūdra,* he was wrapped in *vīraṇa* grass (VD 21.1–3). That is to say, an adulterer's *varṇa* determined even the kind of fuel with which he was immolated.

One of the lowest categories into which a person "dominated by darkness (*tamas*)" may be reborn included "elephants, horses, *śūdras,* despicable *mlecchas,* lions, tigers and boars" (MS 12.43). The killer of a *brāhmaṇa* was said to be reborn as a "dog, pig, donkey, camel, cow, goat, sheep, wild animal, bird, *caṇḍāla* or *pulkasa*" (MS 12.55). *Śūdras* and *caṇḍālas* are already well-known to us; *mleccha* is a catchall for non-Āryan barbarians, while a *pulkasa* is a member of a "despised mixed tribe" (MMW). In terms of status and hierarchy, these classes of people are ranked no higher than the animals with which they are listed, and are just one rung above worms, bugs, fish, snakes, and turtles. *Śūdras,* barbarians, and outcastes are barely human. The dominant sentiment in the discourse is that the difference between the twice-born members of the three top *varṇas* on the on hand, and the *śūdras* and outcastes on the other, is almost a biological one. That members of different *varṇas* might interbreed is regarded as an abomination. As we have observed previously, the distinction between the *varṇas* is similar to the one we might draw between different kinds of animals.

The inferiority of the *śūdra* is both total and natural. Being divinely created and divinely decreed, it is also inescapable. This point is well illustrated by the following passage from the *Manusmṛti.*

> But a *śūdra,* whether purchased or not, may be compelled to do servile work, for he was created by the Self-created One to be the slave of a *brāhmaṇa.* A *śūdra,* even though emancipated by his master, is not released from servitude. Since it is innate in him, who can set him free from it? (MS 8.413–414)

We have no way of ascertaining whether the *Dharmasūtra*'s punishments for adultery were ever actually carried out, or whether the killer of a *brāhmaṇa* is reborn as a donkey, a pig, or a *caṇḍāla.* We can say with certainty, however, that the discursive effect of these passages is real. The constant reiteration of the ideas of hierarchy and status enhances the power of the discourse of division. What these quotes show, and what this whole section on status shows, is that there is a basic underlying belief that society is not only "naturally" divided into groups, but that these groups are naturally endowed with differing status and are arranged hierarchically. The inherent hierarchy of the *varṇas* is as fundamental to the system as their divine origins and the concept of *svadharma.* Every aspect of their creation and the duties assigned to each reflects and perpetuates their relative position in social space.

What are the implications of this concept of a natural, immutable hierarchy that is determined by birth? To anyone reading the *Pañcatantra* within the cultural context of the brahmanical archive, the idea that societies are inherently hierarchical appears to be a very natural and forceful one. Some individuals, notably *brāhmaṇas* and *kṣatriyas,* are born to power and privilege at the center of the social *maṇḍala,* while others are born to serve them from their stations at its periphery. The archive provides the cultural context in which the natural superiority of the lion and the natural inferiority of the jackal are to be understood. The superiority of the twice-born *varṇas* is innate and immutable, as is the status attributed to the characters in the forest society of the *Pañcatantra.* According to the archive, a *śūdra* can never be a king because of his innate peripheral status. He is born on the outer and will remain there. Within the Sanskritic cultural paradigm, it is a self-evident truth that all men were created unequal. The discourse of division as it manifests in the archive allocates a natural status to members of human societies based on their *varṇa.* The same discourse is in operation in the *Pañcatantra* where it allocates a natural position in social space to members of a given *jāti.* This is why a lion is the "natural" king, and this is part of the reason why the fall of the indigo jackal was inevitable.

ENMITY/AMITY

We have now reviewed the discourses pertaining to *varṇa, svadharma,* and status in the brahmanical archive and compared these to what we found in the *Pañcatantra.* In each case, we were able to discern parallels between the archive and the text, and we have begun to delineate the cultural context in which the discourse of division in the *Pañcatantra* may have been produced and received. In the above discussion, we were fortunate to have copious material to work with. The situation with enmity/amity is more complicated as there is relatively little in the archive that bears directly on this subject. There are definitions of friends and enemies in the *Arthaśāstra,* but as these are in a military context, they are not particularly useful for this discussion.

When the audience of the *Pañcatantra* reads of a doomed and destructive relationship between a bull and a lion, or between a frog and a snake, what cultural images and stereotypes are summoned to ascribe meaning to the narratives? What cultural stereotypes are activated when the indigo jackal betrayed the other members of his own kind, and struck up his association with "outsiders"? The ill-fated relationships played out in the *Pañcatantra* fly in the face of deep-seated, unbridgeable enmities between "natural" foes, typically predators and their prey, and an equally strong sense of loyalty to members of one's social circle.

The relationship between predator and prey is a very ancient metaphor for the relationship between different social groups, which may be traced back to the *Vedas*. This relationship, in which the higher *varṇas* "feed off" the lower ones, has been explored in detail by Smith (1990 and 1994) and by Olivelle (2002). I will take a different but complementary approach to the relationship of the discourse of enmity/amity in the *Pañcatantra* and the brahmanical archive.

In view of the paucity of material about friendship in the normative literature, we may fruitfully explore another deep and intractable "natural" enmity: the relationship between *brāhmaṇas* and members of peripheral groups, including *śūdras, caṇḍālas,* other outcastes and barbarians. By adopting this approach, we strike a rich vein of resource material.

The archive focuses on the great divide between the twice-born *varṇas* of *brāhmaṇa, kṣatriya* and *vaiśya* on the one hand, and the "once-born" *varṇa* of *śūdra* on the other. I have seen no evidence to suggest that contact with a *vaiśya,* for example, may have been polluting for a *brāhmaṇa.* It seems that twice-born people did not contaminate one another. Further, the archive is almost exclusively preoccupied with keeping *brāhmaṇas* and *śūdras* apart. There is no mention, for example, of the effects that contact with a *śūdra* may have on a *kṣatriya* or a *vaiśya.* Perhaps it was more important to keep the *brāhmaṇas* pure as they were in charge of the sacrifice. Whatever the reason, the archive focuses on quarantining *brāhmaṇas* from *śūdras* and other outsiders.

We will begin our survey of enmity with this arresting observation: "According to some, *śūdras* are a cremation ground" (VD 18.11). When we think of the smoldering corpses, the hair and bones, the discarded clothes, the dogs and kites, this becomes a very powerful image. It encapsulates in a single utterance all the fear and loathing that the brahmanical archive expresses for the *śūdra.* Like the cremation ground, the *śūdra* is the locus of impurity and inauspiciousness. Throughout the archive, there is a deep-seated horror that a *śūdra* might somehow contaminate a *brāhmaṇa,* through direct physical contact including touch or sex. To prevent such contamination, there is a general prohibition on all social interaction between *brāhmaṇas* and outcastes (ĀD 1.21.5). Such is the polluting potential of these low-status individuals that even indirect contact between them and a *brāhmaṇa* through sharing food, seats, carriages and so on is forbidden.

> As it is a transgression to touch a *cāṇḍāla,* so is it to speak or to look at one. For touching, [the expatiation is] submerging completely in

> water; for speaking, speaking to a *brāhmaṇa;* for looking, looking at the heavenly lights. (ĀD 2.2.8–9)[13]

As even the presence of a *śūdra,* let alone direct contact with his person, is polluting and inauspicious: the *Veda* should not be recited within his earshot (VD 18.12). It is a heinous crime for a *brāhmaṇa* to reveal the *Vedas* to a *śūdra,* or to marry a *śūdra* woman. The first degrades the sacred text, the second the *brāhmaṇa* himself. The punishments for these offences are the same as for having sex with the wife of an elder, drinking liquor, or murdering a *brāhmaṇa* (VD 1.19–21). In the case of teaching the *Vedas,* after death, both *brāhmaṇa* and *śūdra* end up in a hell-realm called Asaṃvṛta (MS 4.81).

If a *brāhmaṇa* has direct physical contact with a *śūdra,* outcaste, or *caṇḍāla,* or with a third person who has touched any of these, he must wash himself (GD 14.30). Indirect contact, including traveling in the same vehicle, sitting on the same seat, or eating together, constitute lesser offences. In such cases, the guilty *brāhmaṇa* will become an outcaste within a year (VD 1.22).[14] Terrible punishments were prescribed for a *śūdra* who comes into direct physical contact with a *brāhmaṇa.* One who sat on the same seat was to be branded on the buttock and banished. If he spat at a *brāhmaṇa,* his lips were to be cut off; if he urinated on him, his penis; if he broke wind against him, his anus (MS 8.281–283).

To minimize the chances of all forms of contact, both direct and indirect, *brāhmaṇas* and *śūdras* were directed to live apart. A *brāhmaṇa* was warned against living in a country "swarming with men of the lowest orders" (*nopaṣṛṭe 'ntyajair nṛbhiḥ* || MS 4.61). "He should not stay with outcastes, *cāṇḍālas, pulkasas,* fools, haughty people, *antyas,* or *antyāvasāyins*" (MS 4.79).[15] Low-status individuals should ideally live apart from the rest of society. It is acceptable for them to interact with one another, but contact with other groups must be avoided:

> Living in a common settlement, outcastes should perform their *dharmas,* officiating at one another's sacrifices, teaching one another and getting married to one another. (BD 2.2.18)

There is a general preference that a *brāhmaṇa* should eat only food cooked and handled by another twice-born person, ideally another *brāhmaṇa* (GD 17.1 and MS 1.101). Even food given by *kṣatriyas* and *vaiśyas* is regarded with some suspicion (ĀD 1.18.9–10). There is a prohibition on all food that has been touched, prepared or given by *śūdras* (ĀD 1.16.22). Eating a *śūdra*'s leftovers is mentioned in the same breath as consuming human urine and excrement (ĀD 1.21.16–17).[16] If a *brāhmaṇa* eats the food of a *caṇḍāla* or an outcaste, he must perform arduous penance for three months, and has to be reinitiated (VD 20.17).[17] The consequences of eating the wrong food are dire indeed:

> A man whose body is nourished by the food of a *śūdra* does not find the upward path, even though he always recites the *Vedas*, offers sacrifices and murmurs prayers. (VD 6.28)

As we have seen, even the slightest indirect contact between a *brāhmaṇa* and a *śūdra* is avoided. How much more the intimate contact of sex. The lawmakers call down the direst punishments on offenders. Any *ārya* who has sex with a *śūdra* woman should be banished, while a *śūdra* who has sex with an *ārya* woman should be executed (ĀD 2.27.9), or his penis should be cut off (GD 12.2). If a *brāhmaṇa* woman has sex with a low-caste man, the king should have her publicly devoured by dogs (GD 23.14). A *brāhmaṇa* who has sex with a *śūdra* woman after eating at an ancestral offering plunges his ancestors into her excrement for one month (GD 15.22). "For one who drinks the saliva of a *śūdra*'s lips, who is tainted by her breath, and who has a son with her, no expiation is prescribed" (MS 3.19). That is, sex with a *śūdra* is a crime for which there is no atonement.

In conclusion, the brahmanical archive describes a society cleft by deep, dark, and threatening divisions among people of different *varṇas,* particularly between *brāhmaṇas* and *śūdras.* At least in the idealized world of normative texts, the *brāhmaṇas* went to great lengths of remove themselves from the ever-present threat of contamination. The *Pañcatantra* also reminds us of the profound and irreconcilable differences between various kinds of characters, specifically between predators and their prey. I am not suggesting that the *Pañcatantra* is "really" saying to *brāhmaṇa* boys, "You never should/play with the *śūdras* in the wood," but I believe that it functions discursively at a much more generalized and subtle level. The brahmanical archive provides the cultural context for the discourse on enmity and amity. It predisposes readers of the *Pañcatantra,* who are educated in the mores of the archive, to the idea that people have natural enemies among "outsiders" and natural allies among "insiders"; that some people are, by their very birth, inimical to one's interests; while others are born to be one's natural peers.

THE CULTURAL CONTEXT OF THE DISCOURSE OF DIVISION

The discourse of division as it manifests in the *Pañcatantra* is not an isolated phenomenon, but is part of a similar discourse in the broader brahmanical archive. The archive provides the cultural context for understanding *varṇa* and division, and for understanding the various aspects of the discourse that we identified in chapter 2: *svabhāva,* status and enmity.

As we have seen, the concept of *varṇa* is a central one. Despite the varying accounts of the origins of the *varṇas,* the archive is unanimous in designating them as the basic units of society. In the archive, it appears natural and normal that humans are deeply and sharply divided from one another. Here we find an analogy between the way the archive treats the concept of *varṇa* and the way in which *jāti* functions in the *Pañcatantra.* Just as the idealized brahmanical society described in the archive is divided into *varṇas,* so the fictional metasocieties of the *Pañcatantra*'s narratives are divided along the lines of *jāti.* As we have seen, an essential corollary to *varṇa* is the concept of *svadharma,* the idea that each *varṇa* has a divinely allotted "natural" role and attendant set of characteristics. This resonates through the *Pañcatantra* as the discourse of *svabhāva,* which confers an analogous set of characteristics on members of a given *jāti.* Hierarchy, another inherent aspect of the *varṇa* system, is constantly reiterated in the brahmanical archive. There is a deeply entrenched preconception that some sections of society are naturally entitled to power and privileged by birth, while others are destined to live in servitude on the social periphery. These concepts also exert a formative influence over the narratives of the *Pañcatantra,* where some species are naturally central and powerful, while others are peripheral and subservient.

In short, the brahmanical archive provides a cultural context, which is predisposed toward division, and in which the *Pañcatantra* may be understood. The *Pañcatantra* is just one element embedded within the greater discursive system that is represented in the brahmanical archive. The archive and the text exist in a mutually supportive and reinforcing relationship. They interpenetrate one another, and along with the creators of the text and its audiences, are woven together into a single system.

5

Conclusion

> The conditions for understanding this literature are the permanence, predictability, the common-sense of the social world, and by the very writing and reading of this and all other poetry—and this seems to be a crucial social effect—these conditions are made all the more permanent, predictable, and commonsensical. It is the very taken-for-grantedness of this world, for its part, that renders it invisible to readers like Ānanda; the sphere of social (or literary) convention was one they inhabited too deeply to see.
>
> —Sheldon Pollock, *The Social Aesthetic and Sanskrit Literary Theory*

In these concluding remarks, using the story of the indigo jackal as a metonymy for the discursive patterning of the *Pañcatantra* narrative as a whole, I will summarize the main findings of this investigation, and suggest some avenues for future research. I will also pose a number of general questions about the *Pañcatantra,* and offer a preemptive defense of my findings and methodology. While addressing the underlying themes of what these narratives in the *Pañcatantra* do and how they do it, I will provide a tentative answer to the key question of this inquiry, why did the indigo jackal fall?

The jackal, the other characters in the narratives that we have discussed, and indeed the creators and audiences of the *Pañcatantra,* all inhabit a world ordered by discourse that renders social phenomena "permanent, predictable, and commonsensical." The "social effect" of these narratives, as we have seen, is to strengthen these very perceptions. Discourse and narrative are conjoined in a mutually sustaining, dialectical relationship: discourse gives narrative its shape, form, and substance; narrative perpetuates and propagates that same discourse. Contingent constructs become part of the "taken-for-grantedness" of the social world, with the result that they become invisible. The Foucauldian approach enables us to draw out for investigation these previously obscure discursive phenomena. In short, it makes visible the otherwise invisible workings of discourse.

We have observed a parallel between the *jāti,* as the natural division of the forest realm, and the *varṇa,* its analogue in the idealized human society depicted in the hegemonic texts of the brahmanical archive. These are two complementary manifestations of a single discursive force: one in the meta-societies of the *Pañcatantra* narrative, the other in human society. The discourse that divides the animals of the forest into *jātis* is the same discourse that classifies humankind by *varṇas.* The discourse in the archive provides the basic framework for understanding the *jāti* of the forest. The hegemonic texts engender a predisposition to the idea of deep, unbridgeable divisions in society. All societies may be seen as ideally and naturally divided into mutually exclusive sects.

The jackal's demise was inevitable because it was subject to a discourse of division, and it was impelled by forces as irresistible, pervasive, and yet as apparently natural and taken-for-granted as gravity. These underlying forces shape not only the patterns of behavior of the jackal, but those of many other characters in these narratives.

As we have seen, the discourse as it manifests in the *Pañcatantra* attributes a set of characteristics to individuals based on their *jāti.* First, each is understood to have an essential nature, a *svabhāva,* which is characteristic of its kind. We saw how all jackals shared in an essential nature, a state or condition of existence, which was determined by their birth. Such a nature was innate and immutable. The indigo jackal's essential nature was such that, when he heard his fellows howl in the distance, he was unable to resist the compulsion to respond to them, even though this was the cause of his downfall. Not just the jackal, but all those lions, bulls, frogs, snakes, and herons were ultimately passive subjects of their respective essential natures, victims of their *svabhāvas,* despite their best attempts to be otherwise. When their natures reasserted themselves, all their artifice, all their futile efforts to change or conceal their inner dispositions, came unstuck.

We identified a parallel between the *svabhāva* attributed to the *jātis* of the *Pañcatantra* and the *svadharmas* which characterize the *varṇas* in the brahmanical archive. The concept of *svadharma* in the archive preconditions an acceptance of *svabhāva* in the text. These twin phenomena are, again, merely two sides of the same coin. Just as knowledge of *svadharma* derived from the hegemonic texts would sensitize a reader to the idea of *svabhāva,* so too would the discourse on *svabhāva* in the *Pañcatantra* reinforce the understanding of *svadharma.* In demonstrating how the indigo jackal failed to counteract his *svabhāva,* the text appears to reinforce the conservative social dictum that one cannot escape one's *svadharma.*

The second characteristic determined by the discourse of division is the individual's position in social space. Like *svabhāva,* the idea of an innate or natural status is also determined by one's birth. We saw how the jackal was, in every sense, a creature of the periphery, perpetually relegated to the outer edges of the social *maṇḍala.* We also saw how other characters—owls, camels and dogs—also labored under inherent inferiority, while lions and the other large carnivores, being naturally superior, occupied the center of the *maṇḍala.* In many contexts, we witnessed the failure of centripetal movements from the periphery toward the center, such as that attempted by the indigo jackal.

There is a sense in which these centripetal transgressions are punished, since the transgressors usually die. Yet, there is no single agent sitting in judgment; there is no court, no sentence. We are not necessarily witnessing open, coercive power in effect. The discourse is subtler than this: centripetal movement is not simply made to appear to be wrong, but is made to appear impossible. The jackal, the owls and the rest were not punished by any agent in particular, but in the course of events, the flowing tide of the narrative just "naturally" went against them. They fell victim to the transgression itself, not to a retributive god.

The idea of an inherent hierarchy among the four *varṇas* of orthodox brahmanical thought is, as we saw, an inalienable aspect of the discourse of division in the archive. One of the basic effects of the archive is to perpetuate that very hierarchy. Even the way in which the *varṇas* are listed seldom varies, and serves as a textual sign of their natural order. We are repeatedly reminded of the inherent superiority of the *brāhmaṇa* on the one hand, and on the other, of the inferiority of the *śūdra* and other outcastes. Here too we observed a close parallel between the social hierarchies of the fictional and human worlds. In this regard, the "social effect" of the *Pañcatantra* is also inherently conservative. The fall of the indigo jackal "proves" the impossibility of rising above one's station, and of living contrary to one's supposed nature; not just because such a move is illegal or immoral—it is simply "adharmic."

The third force dragging the jackal down is that aspect of the discourse of division that pertains to enmity and amity. The discourse holds that, as an aspect of one's birth, those of one's own kind are one's natural friends. Story 2-00 demonstrated that amity among members of different kinds may be possible, and indeed beneficial, but there are many potential enmities that can never be averted; for example, the "natural hostility" between predators and their prey. After the jackal's elevation to sovereignty, he caused those of this own kind to be "seized by their throats" and cast into exile. In doing so, he breached a fundamental tenet laid down by the discourse: that members of his own kind were his natural allies. This same force brought down all those other individuals who had attempted to form alliances with their "natural" enemies.

The idea that an individual has natural allies by birth, but even more, the idea that certain sections of society are naturally inimical to one's interests, runs deeply and widely through the archive. *Brāhmaṇas* are repeatedly exhorted to associate with their own kind, to eat what is their own and to wear what is their own. At the other end of the social spectrum, *śūdras, caṇḍālas* and other outcastes are also lumped together and relegated to the far side of the cremation grounds, where they are also enjoined to the company of one another. The idea that any form of physical contact, direct or indirect, with *śūdras* is naturally inimical for *brāhmaṇas* is a constant theme, particularly in the *dharma* texts. *Śūdras,* as a consequence of their low birth, have the potential to pollute a *brāhmaṇa,* to ruin the sacrifice or to render futile a Vedic recitation. The same discourse that produced the natural incompatibility of *brāhmaṇa* and *śūdra* provides a useful cultural backdrop for interpreting the natural enmity between those ill-fated dyads in the *Pañcatantra.*

I began this investigation by asking two questions: What does the *Pañcatantra* do and how does it do it? In regard to those sections of the narrative that I have explored, I will now summarize my answer to the first question. The various aspects of the discourse of division as they appear in the text and the archive are really just paired manifestations of the one discursive system. The same discourse drives both sets of phenomena. Just as I identified a dialectical relationship between discourse and narrative above, I suggest that a similar relationship exists between the discourse in the archive and the discourse in the text. The orthodox discourse provides the ground rules for the narratives; it gives them their broad outline and shape. It provides the cultural context for understanding the text. The forces emanating from the archive have molded and wrought the space in which the narratives exist. By filling the framework with narrative detail, the text feeds back into the discourse, underlining, reinforcing, and validating it. The net "social effect" of the discourse in the *Pañcatantra* is therefore inherently conservative.

Ultimately, the jackal had to fall because the *Pañcatantra* is what it is: an emanation of brahmanical power, a social manifesto, at once the product and the producer of orthodox tradition, one of whose effects is to perpetuate the privileged position of one section of society to the disadvantage of another. Its effect is to ensure that the cultural world in which it circulates remains "permanent, predictable and commonsensical." The effect of the regime of truth is to render invisible those practices which it employs to those ends. This, then, is what the *Pañcatantra* does.

Let us turn now to the second question: how does *Pañcatantra* achieve this effect? The jackal had to fall, and all those other narrative events had, of necessity, to reach their particular foregone conclusions, because the discursive forces which drove them followed their own internal logic. The narratives themselves can only exert a "social effect," and can only perpetuate the discourse, if that discourse has its own inherent validity.

We identified five attributes of the text that permitted it, and the discourse that pervades it, to function as "true." First, the discourse is enunciated in an authoritative voice. Even the fact that the narratives were written in Sanskrit, the "power language" of brahmanical culture, invested them with legitimacy. Second, we saw how the discourse and the *Pañcatantra* were universalized to create the impression that they applied equally to all places, times and audiences. Third, by associating itself with the body of authoritative treatises knows as *śāstras,* the *Pañcatantra* assimilated a quantum of the inherent and unassailable veracity that pertain to that genre. The *Pañcatantra* derives considerable veracity because it is widely regarded as a *nītiśāstra.* Fourth, we saw how the impact of the *Pañcatantra* might be reinforced by virtue of its position in a web of intertextual links. Stories found in this collection are repeated, not only in other literary works, but also in other media, such as the plastic arts. This process of constant repetition endows both narrative and discourse with an aura of credibility. Finally, we discussed the process of naturalization of the discourse. Social constructs are perceived in the natural world of the forest and are then cited in the narratives, as it were, as a means of validating those very constructs. The discourse of division instilled in the creators of the narratives certain preconceptions that colored their perception of the natural world. They employed their image of the realm of the forest to make certain points about human society; for example, that it is against nature and therefore impossible for individuals to attempt to change their natures, better their positions or betray their own kind. They drew corroborating evidence from the natural world to support these preexisting theses about the social world. The evidence they drew from nature is nothing more than a projection of the social phenomena they sought to validate in the first place.

The text creates the illusion that it infers deductively from nature in order to draw conclusions about society. The jackal's fall "proves" that peripheral individuals in human society cannot better themselves. In fact, the opposite is the case—the narrative is the product of deductive reflections on society. The jackal is caused to fall because this is how the creators of the story perceived human society. They, too, operated within the discourse of division, which stipulated that individuals could not alter their natal positions in the *maṇḍala,* etc. All the great authoritative texts of the brahmanical archive said so, the *Vedas* said so, the *Purāṇas* said so, the *Bhavagadgītā* said so. Disruption of the *varṇa* system would destroy the cosmic balance—*ṛta.* It would lead to the breakdown of society, to chaos and, ultimately, to the end of the world. Such reasoning underlies all those narratives in which the discourse of division appears to operate. This, ultimately, is why the jackal had to fall.

The five attributes which we have touched on here—the authoritative voice, universalization, the śāstric paradigm, intertextuality and naturalization—together constitute the regime of truth that allows the discourse to function. Building on the concepts of the śāstric paradigm and the naturalization of *varṇa* ideology in the *Vedas,* this study constitutes, I believe, a novel attempt to describe a regime of truth for Sanskrit narrative literature. It is, I hope, a first step toward defining what Foucault termed a "general politics of truth" for this field. To paraphrase him, we have begun to discern the types of discourse that the orthodox Sanskritic cultural universe accepted and made function as true. We have also begun to identify:

> the mechanisms and instances which enable one to distinguish true and false statements, the means by which each is sanctioned; the techniques and procedures accorded value in the acquisition of truth; the status of those who are charged with saying what counts as true. (Foucault 1977: 131)

We have now identified the elements and structures that comprise a regime of truth for the *Pañcatantra,* and we can see what gives its statements their validity and authority. Where might this idea of a Sanskritic regime of truth lead us? Having described this example from the field of *kathā* literature, we might ask how statements are sanctioned elsewhere. Is this same regime in force throughout *kathā* literature? Does it apply to some or all sections of the brahmanical archive? What procedures or structures, for example, give the epics the *Mahābhārata* and *Rāmāyaṇa* or the narrative mythologies of the *purāṇas* their veracity?

What novel elements might we expect to find in the regime of truth in a broader Sanskritic context? We might, for example, usefully examine the discourse of *ṛta.* This is a Vedic concept which expresses the natural order of things when *ṛta* prevails, everything is right in the world. For example, in the city of Ayodhyā, under the exemplary reign of Daśaratha, all the citizens were happy, righteous, and learned; no one lacked earrings, diadems, or necklaces; no lechers, misers, or agnostics were to be seen. More significantly;

> In the *varṇas,* which have the foremost as their fourth, all the people, honoring deities and guests, were long-lived, and resorted to *dharma* and truth. The *kṣatriya* accepted the *brāhmaṇa* as his superior, and the *vaiśya*s were subservient to the *kṣatriyas.* The *śūdra*s, delighting in their *svadharma,* served the [other] three *varṇas.* (Rām. 1.6.16–17).[1]

Wherever we find harmony and order in the Sanskritic literary universe, there too we see the four *varṇas* pursuing their allotted duties. Following one's *svadharma* is not merely an indicator of *ṛta,* it is also a cause of that state. Viewed in this light, *ṛta* is a highly political concept. The discourse of *ṛta* may be regarded as an aspect of the naturalization of brahmanical power, which would repay further study.

We might expect to find a certain degree of consistency in the way a brahmanical regime of truth is constituted, based perhaps on Vedic authority and essentially Vedic concepts such as *ṛta.* What happens when we step beyond that tradition and enter the discursive worlds of heterodox texts? What factors give statements their authority in the Buddhist, Jaina, Tantric, or Bhakti traditions, for example? Are the elements we identified above only relevant to the brahmanical archive, or do some of them carry over into heterodox traditions? Will we discover new elements in force in these other archives?

Our understanding of Sanskritic regimes of truth may cause us to reflect on how truth is constituted in our own epistemic space. If two statements are mutually contradictory, we usually maintain that they could not both be true. If we accept one as true, we must suspect the other, because we function within a regime of truth dominated by a particular species of logic. In contrast, mutual contradiction does not constitute invalidity for one or other contradictory propositions under a Sanskritic regime. In the above discussion, we saw several apparently incompatible accounts of the origin of the *varṇa* system. All these statements may function as true and exert power simultaneously, because they meet the criteria for truthfulness that are operational within that particular episteme. Both are underwritten by Vedic authority, and both are therefore true. The *Manusmṛti* and the other *dharma* texts are quite clear on this point: the *śruti* and *smṛti* are the ultimate yardsticks for measuring veracity. If a statement can be shown to be in conformity with these two, then it is demonstrably true. Manu give short shrift to logic, which we value so highly:

> The twice-born person who disregards these two [*śruti* and *smṛti*], because he relies on the teachings of logic (*hetuśāstra*), should be shunned by good people. He is an atheist (*nāstika*) and a reviler of the *Vedas.* (MS 2.11)

In post-Renaissance Western thought, logic has taken precedence over revealed truth; in this example of brahmanical thought the reverse is the case.

Turning now from regimes of truth, and the new directions in which these ideas might lead us, I will now make some general observations about the *Pañcatantra* itself. Pūrṇabhadra was a Jaina, yet he superintended the production of an orthodox brahmanical text. Is it not surprising that his heterodox hand left so few impressions on the page? Perhaps it is no stranger than the fact that the German scholar Hertel or the American Edgerton left so little of their own national imprint on their respective reworkings of the text. All three adopted and adapted a preexisting cultural monument, and all negotiated their own relationships with it, without necessarily imprinting their personalities on it. One can do little to infer authors' psychological states from their writings. There is, of course, no certain, tangible or causal relationship between what authors believe and what they write.

It always seemed to me that several topics were missing from the *Pañcatantra.* The question of who handles and prepares food, and the ever-present fear that food may be tainted, are constant preoccupations of the *dharma* texts (e.g., MS 4.205–225, 5.5–56; ĀD 1.16–19; GD 17; VD 14). What constitutes suitable food and with whom may one share it? In Story 2-00, the mouse and the crow dined together, but one nibbled on grains of millet, while the other pecked at a piece of buffalo meat which "resembled a *kiṃśuka* flower" (PT 132.27). The question of inappropriate commensality may underlie a passage in Story 1-14 "Lion and wheelwright" in which the king-of-animals, counter to his *"siṃhadharma,"* fed on "various kinds of special foods, beginning with sweetmeats, *aśokavartin* and foods flavoured with sugar, ghee, raisins and *caturjātaka*" (PT 81.13–15). The only reference to obviously polluted food is made with regard to Mother Śāṇḍalī's highly suspect sesame seeds in Story 2-03. Why does the *Pañcatantra* have so little to say about purity of food and commensality, when these issues loom so large in the law books? This question, I believe, warrants further reflection.

Similarly, why do we find so little in regard to marriage in the *Pañcatantra*? There are only a handful of passing references, including the remark made by the love-lorn artisan in Story 1-08 "Weaver as Viṣṇu," and the more substantial treatment in Story 3-13 "Mouse-maid will wed a mouse." In contrast, the question of whom one may marry is treated at some length in the brahmanical archive. Why such scant treatment here? Two possible explanations come to mind: first, perhaps marriage was not regarded as an important theme in narratives targeted at a young audience, not yet of marriageable age. Alternatively, perhaps because family elders made the arrangements, further reflection on marriage would be redundant. Neither of these explanations is, I admit, entirely satisfactory.

One of the major themes that we explored was the question of enmity and amity. We found plenty about enmity in the brahmanical archive to complement our findings in the *Pañcatantra,* but we found comparatively little about friendship. Perhaps the *Pañcatantra* dwells at such length on amity precisely to compensate for the lack of guidance on this subject in the archive. We can take this line of inquiry no further at this stage: it is sufficiently difficult to account for the presence of particular discourses in the *Pañcatantra,* let alone the absence of others.

Moving from these open-ended and perhaps unanswerable questions, I will now deal with some potential criticisms of this study and of the methodology that I have adopted. The first question has been raised on a number of occasions: Is it appropriate to apply a theoretical approach developed in Europe in the late-twentieth century to Sanskrit texts which evolved in India two thousand years earlier? How can one defend the application of Foucauldian theory to materials from another time and place? This question has arisen, it seems to me, from a misunderstanding of the relationship between tools and materials. Tools must be appropriate for the materials in question, but they need not be made of the same stuff. A theoretical approach is a set of tools—a way of framing questions. The application of contemporary theory to the *Pañcatantra* is simply a case of applying new tools to old materials. We might draw an analogy between this process and undertaking a ultrasound analysis of Egyptian mummies. Both enable us to examine preexisting materials in new ways—with new tools—and to conjure new understandings from old texts by doing so. After all, Foucault himself made effective use of classical European texts in writing his *History of Sexuality*.

Here is a second complaint. A Russian colleague took issue with my interpretation of a particular story in which I had identified *svabhāva* as a significant theme. He remembered that same story from his childhood, and said that it meant nothing of the sort to him. "We don't even have *svabhāva* in Russia," he said. This objection caused me much discomfort and reflection. In the end, I formulated my response in the following way. The creation of meaning is a process of negotiation between the author and the audience. A given text means different things to different people in different contexts. The way in which meaning is created from a text in the process of reading is at least partly culturally determined, and may take place within differing cultural contexts, with differing outcomes. Throughout this work, I have been trying to imagine what meanings the stories of the *Pañcatantra* may have produced when they were read by an audience whose worldview, expectations, and prejudices were conditioned by the brahmanical archive. To sketch a geography of the world-of-ideas in which the *Pañcatantra* exists, I have drawn parallels between the cultural stereotypes and archetypes found in the archive and those we found in specific narratives. My Russian friend's reading is a perfectly valid one, I assume, for a Russian audience. I have attempted to suggest readings of the *Pañcatantra* that would be equally valid for an inhabitant of the brahmanical literary world.

Third, could it be that these stories are about individuals and individual traits after all, and are not about social groups, *varṇas* or *jātis*. Being a party to the Orientalist obsession with caste, have I, like Procrustes, stretched some innocent narratives to fit a *jāti*-delimited bed, and truncated others?

To attempt to define an "either-or" meaning for the *Pañcatantra* would draw us into the same essentialist trap that has caught so many of my predecessors. We are no longer required to state that the *Pañcatantra* is "really about" individuals or that it is "really about" *varṇas*. There is now sufficient critical space for both of these meanings, and many more besides, to coexist. My reading of these stories from the *Pañcatantra*, one which highlights the discourse of division, is but one of many possible readings, but one which, I hope, is consistent with the evidence in the text and with what we know about Sanskrit literature in general.

Texts have no voice and cannot speak for themselves. I have consciously selected stories, passages, and phrases in order to build a particular case, to develop and elaborate an argument. I have applied my own subjective judgment over the inclusion or exclusion of each piece of evidence. I originally approached these stories with an open mind, not knowing at first what might come to light. As *jāti* began to emerge as a potentially fruitful line of inquiry, I collected and collated those passages that seemed to have a bearing on the topic.

A successful refutation of my approach would first need to overcome a number of significant challenges. Not the least of these is in regard to the indigo jackal itself. If these narratives were about individuals, and were not about groups, it must first be demonstrated that the implied pun on *varṇa*—meaning both "color" and "caste"—was unintentional. If the pun were to be allowed under any circumstances, then the jackal's change of color can only be understood as a metaphoric change of *varṇa*. If the *Pañcatantra* were about individuals and not about social divisions, *varṇa* can only mean "color" in this context, and does not—and indeed cannot—mean "caste." This would be a difficult position to defend.

Sometimes I also have also worried that this study might be seen as a throwback to the bad old days of Dumont, when caste was held to be the "essence" of Indian society. Have we not finally put the Western preoccupation with India as a "caste society" behind us? Is another book on the subject really necessary at this late stage? As I have said before, this study is about ideas, ideals, and ideologies, not about social or historical "realities." It is set in the world-of-ideas reflected in the brahmanical archive, of which the *Pañcatantra* is one small element. I am less concerned with the "reality" of *varṇa* and *jāti* in society—then or now—than with the function of the discourse that surrounds and underwrites these concepts in the texts. Perhaps enough has been written about caste, *varṇa* and *jāti* in Indian society, but discourses of division operate in all societies, affect us all and should concern us all. I imagine fondly that while this study may, in some small way, reveal something new about India, it may also show us something new about ourselves, our own societies and the discourses of division which we take for granted and regard as "commonsensical." I often think of Doniger's observation:

> the study of India stretches our understanding of what it is to be human and enriches our lives with the products of its imagination, so different from our own. (Doniger 1999: 955)

This book describes a world that is temporally, spatially, and culturally remote from our own. But perhaps these modest findings way serve to remind us of the ways in which discourses of division are formulated, articulated and inscribed within our own society, no matter how we are divided. The discourses that legitimize divisions—be they religious, ethnic, cultural, or gender-related—like those in the *Pañcatantra,* are so deeply ingrained in the fabric of society that the divisions themselves appear normal and natural. There is nothing inherently natural in culture; everything that we regard as social is ultimately contingent and constructed: these are perhaps the most valuable conclusions that we, as a contemporary audience, may draw from the fall of the indigo jackal.

Appendix 1

Core Stories of the *Pañcatantra* Family

The level of embedding is indicated by indentation from the left.

Story 0-00 *Kathāmukha:* Pañcatantra Frame-Story

Story 1-00 "Lion and Bull" (First *tantra*)
- Story 1-01 "Ape and Wedge"
- Story 1-02 "Jackal and Drum"
- Story 1-04a "Monk and Swindler"
- Story 1-04b "Rams and Jackal"
- Story 1-04c "Cuckold Weaver"
- Story 1-05 "Crows and Serpent"
  - Story 1-06 "Heron, Fishes, and Crab"
- Story 1-07 "Lion and Hare"
- Story 1-10 "Louse and Flea"
- Story 1-13 "Lion's Retainers Outwit Camel"
- Story 1-15 "Strand-Bird and Sea"
  - Story 1-16 "Two Geese and Tortoise"
  - Story 1-17 "Three Fishes"
- Story 1-25 "Ape, Glow-Worm, and Officious Bird"
- Story 1-26 "Good-Heart and Bad-Heart"
  - Story 1-27 "Heron, Serpent, and Mongoose"
- Story 1-28 "How Mice Ate Iron"

Story 2-00 "Dove, Mouse, Crow, Tortoise and Deer" (Second *tantra*)
Story 2-02 "Mouse and Two Monks"
Story 2-03 "Hulled Grain for Unhulled"
Story 2-04 "Too Greedy Jackal"
Story 2-09 "Deer's Former Captivity"

Story 3-00 "War of Crows and Owls" (Third *tantra*)
Story 4-07 "Ass in Tiger-Skin"
Story 3-02 "Birds Elect a King"
Story 3-02 "Elephant and Rabbit and Moon"
Story 3-03 "Cat as Judge between Partridge and Hare"
Story 3-04 "*Brāhmaṇa*, Goat, and Three Rogues"
Story 3-09 "Old Man, Young Wife, and Thief"
Story 3-10 "Ogre, Thief and *Brāhmaṇa*"
Story 3-12 "Cuckold Wheelwright"
Story 3-13 "Mouse-Maiden Will Wed a Mouse"
Story 3-16 "Frogs Ride a Serpent"

Story 4-00 "Ape and Crocodile" (Fourth *tantra*)
Story 4-02 "Ass without Heart and Ears"

Story 5-01 "*Brāhmaṇa* and Mongoose" (Fifth *tantra*)
Story 5-00 "Barber Who Killed the Monks"
Story 5-07 "*Brāhmaṇa* Builds Air-Castles"

Appendix 2

Summary of Stories in Pūrṇabhadra's *Pañcatantra*

Story 0-00 *Kathāmukha*

The *Pañcatantra* frame-story: King Amaraśakti engages the *brāhmaṇa* Viṣṇuśarman to educate his three dull-witted sons. Viṣṇuśarman composes the *Pañcatantra.*

Story 1-00 "Lion and Bull"

To improve his prestige, a jackal used deceit to encourage the friendship between a stray bull and a lion. When, under the influence of the bull, the lion neglected his duties, the jackal rued his actions, and used deceit to set the lion and bull against one another.

Story 1-01 "Ape and Wedge"

A monkey playing on a construction site pulled a wedge out of a half-split log; his testicles were crushed and he died.

Story 1-02 "Jackal and Drum"

A jackal supposed an abandoned war-drum to be a carcass full of fat. On tearing the skin and looking inside, he was disappointed to find it was only wood and skin.

Story 1-03 "Merchant and King's Sweep"

A lowly sweeper artfully exerted his influence over a king to revenge an insult by bringing about a powerful merchant's downfall and then causing his subsequent reinstatement.

Story 1-04a "Monk and Swindler"

A rogue who pretended to be a pious disciple robbed a mendicant of his wealth.

Story 1-04b "Rams and Jackal"

A jackal saw two rams crashing their heads together. He was so intent on licking up their blood that he was crushed between them and died.

Story 1-04c "Cuckold Weaver"

A go-between had her nose cut off by accident while trying to encourage one of her clients, a weaver's wife, to meet her lover.

Story 1-05 "Crows and Serpent"

To get rid of a cobra that lived in his tree, a crow stole a golden chain and dropped it into the snake's hole. When men came to retrieve the chain, they saw and killed the snake.

Story 1-06 "Heron, Fishes and Crab"

A heron tricked a crab and carried him off in its bill. Before the heron was able to eat him, the crab severed the bird's head with his nippers.

Story 1-07 "Lion and Hare"

A rabbit tricked a lion into thinking that his reflection in a well was a rival. The lion leaped into the water and drowned.

Story 1-08 "Weaver as Viṣṇu"

A weaver fell in love with a princess. He disguised himself as the god Viṣṇu and won her heart. Her father, the king, called on him to defend his kingdom. The real Viṣṇu was obliged to intervene to protect his reputation.

Story 1-09 "Grateful Beasts and Thankless Man"

A man rescued a tiger, a monkey, and a snake from a well, and they all repaid his kindness. He also rescued a goldsmith who betrayed him.

Story 1-10 "Louse and Flea"

A louse admitted a flea to the king's bed on the understanding that it would not bite the king until he was asleep. The flea bit the king prematurely and escaped, but the louse was discovered and killed.

Story 1-11 "Blue Jackal"

A jackal, accidentally dyed blue, declared himself king of the forest, and lorded it over the lions, and so on. One day, he heard other jackals howling in the distance and joined in. The other animals discovered his true nature and killed him.

Story 1-12 "Goose and Owl"

A goose formed a friendship with an owl. An archer shot an arrow at the owl, but hit the goose.

Story 1-13 "Lion's Retainers Outwit Camel"

By trickery, a jackal convinced a camel to offer itself as food to a lion.

Story 1-14 "Lion and Wheelwright"

A wheelwright befriended a lion in the forest, but when the lion's villainous entourage appeared, the wheelwright grew uneasy.

Story 1-15 "Strand-Bird and Sea"

A lapwing boasted that the ocean could not harm him, so the ocean stole his eggs to test him. The lapwing enlisted the help of other birds, Garuḍa, and even Viṣṇu, and the ocean was forced to return the eggs.

Story 1-16 "Two Geese and Tortoise"

A tortoise was rescued from a shrinking lake by two friendly geese. He held on to a stick with his jaws while the geese carried him in their bills. In spite of their warnings, the tortoise opened his mouth to speak and fell to his death.

Story 1-17 "Three Fishes"

Three fish in a pool learned that fishermen were approaching. One planned ahead, fled and survived. One employed a ruse and survived, the third did nothing and died.

Story 1-18 "Sparrow's Allies and Elephant"

A rutting elephant destroyed a sparrow's nest. The sparrow enlisted the help of a woodpecker, a fly, and a frog. The frog devised a plan by which the fly hummed in the elephant's ear, the woodpecker put out its eyes, and the frog lured it into a pit where it died.

Story 1-19 "Goose and Fowler"

An elderly goose warned his flock to remove a creeper growing on their tree. They ignored him, and eventually a hunter climbed up it and trapped them. They escaped by pretending to be dead.

Story 1-20 "Lion and Ram"

A lion was at first frightened of a feral ram, but when he saw it eating grass, he realized his mistake and killed it.

Story 1-21 "Jackal Outwits Camel and Lion"

A jackal tricked a camel into offering itself as food for a lion. He then tricked the lion into abandoning the carcass and ate it himself.

Story 1-22 "King, Minister, and False Monk"

A false ascetic tricked a king into believing that he could swap his body for a divine form and visit heaven. A loyal minister incinerated the ascetic in his hut.

Story 1-23 "Maid Weds a Serpent"

A couple gave birth to a snake, and gave it to a girl in marriage. The snake turned into a handsome young man and all were rewarded.

Story 1-24 "Gods Powerless against Death"

The gods wanted to save their own pet parrot from death, but even they could not avert fate.

Story 1-25 "Ape, Glow-Worm and Officious Bird"

A cold monkey was blowing on a firefly, hoping to make a real fire to warm itself. A bird tried to convince the monkey of the futility of its actions, but only succeeded in annoying it, and was killed.

Story 1-26 "Good-Heart and Bad-Heart"

A wicked merchant cheated a good merchant out of his portion of their shared wealth, but then accused the good merchant of the theft. He attempted to cheat the court by calling on a "tree-spirit." The good merchant exposed the fraud and was rewarded, but the wicked man was killed.

Story 1-27 "Heron, Serpent, and Mongoose"

A heron asked a crab for help to get rid of a snake that was devouring the heron's young. The crab suggested that the heron lure a mongoose to the snake's hollow, knowing that the mongoose would also kill the herons, the natural enemy of the crab.

Story 1-28 "How Mice Ate Iron"

A merchant left an iron beam as surety for a loan with the head of a guild. When he returned, the headman said that mice had eaten the beam. The merchant kidnapped the headman's son and told him that an eagle had carried off the boy. Both told their stories in court. The incredulous magistrates caused both boy and beam to be returned.

Story 1-29 "Good Makes Good, Bad Makes Bad"

A parrot had two offspring: one raised by a seer became kind, but the other raised by hunters became cruel and rude.

Story 1-30 "Wise Foe/Foolish Friend"

A robber gave up his own life to save his three intended victims. A king was accidentally killed by his own pet monkey.

Story 2-00 "The Dove, Mouse, Crow, Tortoise, and Deer"

A crow saw a trapped dove freed by a mouse. The crow befriended the mouse and took him to a tortoise. A deer arrived and was befriended by all three. The deer was then trapped by a hunter and they collaborated to free him. The tortoise was also caught and again they collaborated. All lived happily together.

Story 2-01 "Bird with Two Necks"

A *bhāruṇḍa* bird had one stomach and two heads. When one of its heads found some nectar, the other demanded half. When the first head failed to give any, the second ate poison and, sharing one stomach, both died.

Story 2-02 "Mouse and Two Monks"

Two monks attempted to stop a mouse from stealing their food.

Story 2-03 "Hulled Grain for Unhulled"

A dog urinated on some hulled sesame seeds, rendering them inedible. When their owner attempted to barter them for unhulled seeds her neighbor grew suspicious, thinking she would not want to swap them without a reason.

Story 2-04 "Too Greedy Jackal"

A jackal came across the corpses of a boar and a hunter, and began by eating the hunter's bow. When the bowstring snapped, the bow sprang up and killed him.

Story 2-05 "Mr. What-Fate-Ordains"

A merchant's son paid one hundred rupees for a book in which was written, "A man gets what he deserves." His father immediately evicted him, but by simply repeating this advice and allowing fate to take its course, he ended up marrying a princess and became heir-apparent.

Story 2-06 "Weaver and Stingy and Bountiful"

A weaver, who was fated to be poor, worked hard to earn money, but lost it twice. He was offered a boon and chose wealth. He was sent to observe two merchants, one mean and one generous. He observed that the latter fared better, and elected to become generous like him.

Story 2-07 "Jackal and Bull's Cod"

A jackal followed his wife's advice and waited in vain for fifteen years for a bull's testicles to drop off.

Story 2-08 "Mice Rescue Elephants"

Elephants on their way to drink trampled a colony of mice. The mice petitioned the elephant king to be compassionate, and promised to help him in future. The elephants later became trapped and the mice gnawed through the ropes to free them.

Story 2-09 "Deer's Former Captivity"

The deer told how he strayed from his herd, was trapped and suffered as a pet in a palace. He spoke in a human voice of his desire to return to the herd and was set free again.

Story 3-00 "The War of Crows and Owls"

A crow infiltrated the stronghold of his enemies, the owls, by posing as an ally. He later led the crows to the cave where they exterminated the owls.

Story 3-01 "Birds Elect a King"

The society of birds was about to consecrate an owl as their king, when a crow interrupted the ceremony and declared the owl to be unfit. Thus began the enmity between the two species.

Story 3-02 "Elephant and Rabbit and Moon"

A herd of elephants going to drink crushed a colony of hares. One hare, pretending to be the moon's ambassador, told the elephants that the moon intended to withhold its cooling rays and that the elephants would die because of their carelessness. The elephants retreated.

Story 3-03 "Cat as Judge between Partridge and Hare"

A partridge and a hare were arguing over ownership of a burrow. They took their case to a cat for adjudication. The cat lured them close with pious words and killed them.

Story 3-04 "*Brāhmaṇa*, Goat and Three Rogues"

Three rogues conspired to trick a *brāhmaṇa* into giving them the carcass of a goat.

Story 3-05 "Serpent and Ants"

A great snake was killed by a multitude of tiny ants.

Story 3-06 "Gold-Giving Serpent"

A *brāhmaṇa* who worshiped a snake was rewarded with one gold coin every day. The *brāhmaṇa*'s son attempted to kill the snake, thinking its hole would be filled with gold. The snake bit him and he died.

Story 3-07 "Gold-Giving Birds"

A flock of golden geese each shed a golden feather every six months, which went to the king as "rent." When a strange goose appeared, they drove him off. He complained to the king, who sent men to kill the geese, and they flew away.

Story 3-08 "Self-Sacrificing Dove"

A compassionate pigeon offered himself as food to a hunter. The pigeon's wife followed him into the flames. The hunter renounced his profession and sacrificed himself in a forest fire.

Story 3-09 "Old Man, Young Wife, and Thief"

A young wife was frightened into the arms of her old husband by a thief.

Story 3-10 "Ogre, Thief, and *Brāhmaṇa*"

A thief and a *rākṣasa* fell in together to rob and kill a *brāhmaṇa,* but argued about who should act first. The argument woke the *brāhmaṇa* who was then able to defend himself against both.

Story 3-11 "Prince with Serpent in Belly"

A princess, who said "You get what you deserve" to her father, was married off to a prince who had a snake in his belly. One day while the prince slept against an anthill, the snake emerged from his mouth. A second snake came out of the anthill where it had two pots of gold. The two angry snakes inadvertently revealed the means by which the other might be destroyed. The princess followed the snakes' instructions and won the honor and enjoyments "that she deserved."

Story 3-12 "Cuckold Wheelwright"

An unfaithful wife tricked her husband into believing that she really loved him while she carried on a liaison with her lover.

Story 3-13 "Mouse-Maiden Will Wed a Mouse"

A sage turned a mouse into a girl. When she grew up, she declined to marry the sun, a cloud, the wind and a mountain, but begged to marry a mouse.

Story 3-14 "Bird Whose Dung Was Gold"

A hunter caught a bird that produced droppings of gold. He gave it to the king, who, on the advice of a skeptical minister, released it: all came to regret their actions.

Story 3-15 "Lion and Wary Jackal"

A lion lay in wait in a cave to catch a jackal, but the jackal tricked it into revealing itself and ran away.

Story 3-16 "Frogs Ride a Serpent"

A snake tricked some frogs into riding on his back to win their confidence then ate them.

Story 3-17 "Cuckold's Revenge"

An unfaithful wife prayed to the image of a goddess how to make her husband blind, but her husband, who was hiding behind the deity, said, "Feed him butter and butter cake." She did so, and he pretended to be blind. When her lover came to her house, her husband killed him and cut off his wife's nose.

Story 4-00 "The Ape and the Crocodile"

A monkey dropped fruit for a crocodile to eat. The crocodile's wife craved the monkey's heart thinking it must be very sweet. The crocodile lured the monkey into the water but revealed his plan. The monkey then declared that he had left his heart in the tree. The crocodile took him back to the shore and he escaped.

Story 4-01 "Frog's Revenge Overleaps Itself"

A frog-king invited a snake into his well to eat his troublesome relatives. The snake ate all the frogs, and the frog-king only managed to escape by trickery.

Story 4-02 "Ass without Heart and Ears"

A jackal lured a donkey to a disabled lion to be killed for food. The lion sprang at the donkey but missed and the donkey escaped. The jackal convinced the donkey to return and it was killed by the lion, who went off to bathe. In the lion's absence, the jackal ate the donkey's ears and heart. When the lion returned, the jackal explained that the donkey must originally have had neither ears nor heart, otherwise it would never have returned.

Story 4-03 "Potter as Warrior"

A potter with a scar on his forehead was taken for a great warrior by a king. The king learned the truth and sent him away.

Story 4-04 "Jackal Nursed by Lioness"

A jackal was nursed by a lioness and grew up with her cubs. None of the young was aware of the difference in their backgrounds, until the lion cubs confronted an elephant, and the jackal ran away.

Story 4-05 "How False Wife Rewards True Love"

A *brāhmaṇa* pledged half his life to resuscitate his wife who had died suddenly. Later, she betrayed him, and he was able to recall his pledge and brought about her death.

Story 4-06 "Nanda and Vararuci as Slaves of Love"

A mighty king and a sagacious minister were reduced to neighing like a horse and shaving their heads in order to regain their wives' favors after a tiff.

Story 4-07 "Ass in Tiger Skin"

A laundryman set his donkey free in a field of grain, having covered it in a tiger skin so that it would be left alone. One day, the donkey heard a she-ass braying in the distance and answered it. The owners of the fields realized the donkey's true identity and killed it.

Story 4-08 "Adulteress Tricked by Paramour"

A plowman's wife ran off with a rogue who promised her good times and a new life. He deceived her, and in the end she lost her husband, lover, money, and clothes. Even a hungry jackal mocked her.

Story 4-09 "Ape and Officious Bird"

A monkey was caught in a storm. A small bird irritated the monkey by asking why it did not built a house. To punish the bird, the monkey climbed the tree and destroyed its nest.

Story 4-10 "Jackal's Four Foes"

A jackal found the carcass of an elephant. He warded off a lion with obsequiousness and a tiger with deceit. He induced a leopard to tear open the hide for him, and he fought off another jackal. He was then able to eat the carcass alone.

Story 4-11 "Dog in Exile"

A dog was forced by famine to venture to a foreign country. There he managed to find plenty of food, but was set on by other dogs. Preferring his own country, he returned.

Story 5-00 "Barber Who Killed the Monks"

A barber witnessed a merchant strike a magical mendicant who then turned to gold. Accordingly, the barber invited many mendicants to his home, but when he struck them, they died. He was arrested and punished.

Story 5-01 "*Brāhmaṇī* and Mongoose"

A woman saw her pet mongoose covered in blood and assumed that it had eaten her baby. She killed it, but then discovered that it had saved the baby from a snake.

Story 5-02 "Four Treasure-Seekers"

Four friends went to the mountains in search of wealth. The first was satisfied when he found some copper; the second was satisfied with silver; the third was satisfied with gold. But the fourth, driven by greed, proceeded further and was forced to endure the supernatural punishment of having a wheel perpetually grinding at his head.

Story 5-03 "Lion-Makers"

Three educated but impractical *brāhmaṇas* collaborated to bring a lion back to life, despite the warnings of their unschooled but worldly colleague. They ignored him, and were killed by the lion.

Story 5-04 "Thousand-Wit, Hundred-Wit, Single-Wit"

Two fish called Hundred-wit and Thousand-wit lived in a pond with a frog called Single-wit. When they learned that fishermen were coming, Hundred-wit and Thousand-wit planned to use their wits to escape. Both were killed, but Single-wit, who had escaped beforehand, survived.

Story 5-05 "Ass as Singer"

A donkey and a jackal were raiding a field of cucumbers at night. The donkey ignored the jackal's advice and began to bray and woke the owner of the field. The donkey was caught and punished.

Story 5-06 "Two-Headed Weaver"

A weaver, granted a boon by a sprite, wished for a second pair of arms and another head so that he could weave twice as quickly. His fellow villagers mistook him for a *rākṣasa* and killed him.

Story 5-07 "*Brāhmaṇa* Builds Air-Castles"

A penniless *brāhmaṇa,* daydreaming of a rosy future founded on a pot of barley meal, let fly with a kick, and broke the pot.

Story 5-08 "Ape's Revenge"

To avenge the destruction of his tribe, a monkey lured a king to his death in a lake.

Story 5-09 "Ogre, Thief, and Ape"

A *rākṣasa* in the form of a horse was stolen by a horse-thief. The *rākṣasa* mistook the horse-thief for a rival *rākṣasa* and was too terrified to eat him.

Story 5-10 "Blind Man, Hunchback, and Three-Breasted Princess"

In order to win a dowry of gold, a blind man, who had a hunchback for an attendant, married a princess with three breasts. The princess and the hunchback conspired to poison the blind man, but inadvertently cured his blindness. In attempting to punish them, the man accidentally knocked the woman's third breast back into her chest, and straightened out the hunchback's spine.

Story 5-11 "Ogre-Ridden *Brāhmaṇa*"

A *rākṣasa* jumped on the back of a *brāhmaṇa* who was wandering in the forest. The *brāhmaṇa* noticed that the *rākṣasa* had very soft feet, and asked why. The *rākṣasa* replied that he never let his feet get dirty. The *brāhmaṇa* led the *rākṣasa* to a lake, and when the *rākṣasa* entered the water, the *brāhmaṇa* ran away.

Notes

Chapter 1. Introduction

1. The earliest systematic attempt to document the international migration of stories from the *Pañcatantra* was undertaken by Benfey (1966 [1859]). His long introduction is credited with launching the science of comparative folkloristics. An abbreviated account is found in Jacobs's introduction to his edition of North's *Morall Philosophie of Doni* (Jacobs 1888). The spread of the stories was further described and elaborated by Hertel (1914). Edgerton provides a convenient summary (1924: 40–47). Penzer's notes in Tawney (1926) are also useful. Perhaps the clearest exposition of the spread of the *Pañcatantra* is found in the large fold-out table prepared by Edgerton in Tawney 1926, vol. 5 facing p. 242.

2. In the prelude to his "Wayside Inn," Longfellow describes "a Spanish Jew from Alicant": "And it was rumored he could say/the Parables of Sandabar,/and all the Fables of Pilpay,/or if not all, the greater part!"

3. The earlier Western authors usually remarked on the fact that the *Pañcatantra* ranked just behind the Bible in its ubiquity, while Jallad ranked it just behind the Qur'an (Jallad 2004: 19).

4. The spelling of both these names varies from source to source. I have followed Jallad 2004.

5. The number of pages in a given version provides only a general indication of comparative length, because the number of words on a page varies from book to book. It is useful, however, for comparing the relative lengths of the *tantras* within a given version.

6. On the *Bṛhatkathā* in general, see also Nelson 1978.

7. I note with interest that when a version of a text is too long, it is "contaminated" with "interpolations"; when it is too short, it has been "castrated" or "mangled."

8. Lanman wrote in his preface to the work: "Hertel's book, Das Pañcatantra, appeared only a short time before the outbreak of the world-war. The teaching-staff of the Gymnasium at Döbeln was reduced in number and the work of those left at home was correspondingly heavier. In December, 1914, Professor Hertel, while on a sick-bed, received his orders to join the colors. His latest letter to me is dated Borna (Saxony), February 9, 1915. It explains the situation as to the promised Introduction and Notes, and says that he

daily expects to be ordered to the front. If he returns to his wife and seven children and to the studies in which he has won such great distinction, he may yet prepare the Introduction and Notes so that they may be issued with the translation of the Tantrākhyāyika which I have undertaken. . . . [Footnote:] The printed sheets were shipped from Leipzig to Boston via Rotterdam, and by the Holland-America Line, about the middle of February, 1915, the beginning of the great activity of the German submarines. In spite of torpedoes and mines and other dangers of the long list given in the war-insurance policy, the sheets arrived safe in Boston about the first of April." (Lanman's preface, Hertel 1915: xii). I do not believe that Lanman's translation of the *Tantrākhyāyika* was ever published.

9. I am also indebted to Dr. Toke Lindegaard Knudsen for his assistance with the date.

10. I have chosen to use approximations because of the uncertainty associated with how the stories should be counted. For example, the three closely linked stories of self-inflicted injury (Stories 1-04a, 1-04b and 1-04c) could be counted as a single story or as three.

CHAPTER 2. THE DISCOURSE OF DIVISION

1. For classification of animals on the basis of the morphology of their feet, see Smith 1991.

2. In the version of this tale found in the *Hitopadeśa* (Hit. 1907ff), an old jackal among the exiles intentionally brought about the indigo jackal's downfall with a howl, knowing that the impostor would be unable to suppress his instinctive response.

3. On the question of purity and auspiciousness, see also Milner 1994: 51–52, 110–115.

4. Halbfass notes the existence of similar "horizontal" schemes of hierarchy consisting of "concentric circles of increasing distance from a dharmic centre" (Halbfass 1991: 349).

5. Sanskrit literature, being oceanic, naturally provides a counterexample for any given proposition. It is even possible to find an auspicious jackal if one searches carefully enough: "With one, two, three or four cries, a jackal would be auspicious, and similarly, with five or six, it is said to be inauspicious, and similarly, with seven it is auspicious. Otherwise, it would be a [portent of] failure" (AP 231.32–33).

6. This word appears as *cāṇḍāla* in some texts.

7. This interesting passage appears in the *Hitopadeśa:* "The wise person should unite with that which should be united with in this world. I am the food; you are the eater. How can there be affection [between us]? . . . Affection between prey and predator is the cause of disaster. The deer, caught in a net because of the jackal, was rescued by the crow." (*yad yena yujyate loke budhas tat tena yojayet* | *aham annaṃ bhavān bhoktā kathaṃ prītir bhaviṣyati* || . . . *bhakṣyabhakṣakayoḥ prītir vipatter eva kāraṇam* | *śṛgālāt pāśabaddho 'sau mṛgaḥ kākena rakṣitaḥ* || Hit. 301–304)

8. This is an example of the opposition between snakes and birds found in many cultures (Knipe 1966–67).

9. Damanaka was joined by a second jackal, Karaṭaka.

10. This denouement so alarmed the redactor of the *Hitopadeśa* that he appended the following words: "May the division of friends be confined to the camp of your enemies" (*suhṛdbhedas tāvad bhavatu bhavatāṃ śatrunilaye,* Hit. 1633). That is to say, he not only refused to not condone Damanaka's actions, but effectively condemned them. As we saw above, the Arabic version of the story, and hence all its European descendants, also condemn Damanaka.

11. Kumbhīpāka is "a hell in which the wicked are baked like potter's vessels or cooked like the contents of a cooking vessel" (MMW).

Chapter 3. The "Regime of Truth"

1. For Manu, according to Olivelle, "the lower classes of society" were a "an ever-present threat to the dominance of the upper classes" (Olivelle 2002b: 547).

2. The authoritative command to attend is not uncommon in Sanskrit literature. The initial dialogue between Manu and the seers ends (1.4) with Manu's command, "Listen!" (*śrūyatām*), . . . "I think the authentic voice of the author is heard in this imperious 'Listen!'" (Olivelle 2002b: 562). To supplement this Sanskritic example, in premodern England, public authority was delegated to the person of the town-crier, who uttered the cry "oyez" (OED: "Hear, hear ye"; a call by the public crier or by a court officer [generally thrice uttered], to command silence and attention when a proclamation, etc., is about to be made). Military and naval authority is manifest in pronouncements prefixed by the expression "Now hear this!"

3. In the Southern *Pañcatantra* and the *Hitopadeśa,* the court of King Amaraśakti was said to be in Pāṭaliputra, not Mahilāropya.

4. The Bay of Bengal is called the Southern Sea (*dakṣiṇasyodadhi*) in the *Skandapurāṇa* (SkP 2.2.6.3), providing a link between the ocean and "southerness."

5. For the significance of "the other side of the mountain" in the *Mahābhārata,* see Hiltebeitel 2001: 312–317.

6. *Nīti* is sometimes translated as "cunning" and "cleverness," both of which bear negative connotations. The word "Machiavellian" is often used in Western discussions of the *Pañcatantra.* In the Sanskritic view, the essence of *nīti* in these contexts is actually *buddhi* ("intelligence"), a positive attribute. This explains a fundamental difference in the way European commentators and the Indian audiences have viewed the *Pañcatantra.* Europeans have tended to see the *Pañcatantra* negatively as immoral, amoral or unmoral, whereas indigenous authors have seen it in a positive light.

7. For a study of the relationship between the *Arthaśāstra* and Manu see Olivelle 2004b.

8. John Barth, a master storyteller himself, discovered Indian *kathā* literature as an undergraduate while stacking library shelves at Johns Hopkins University. He remembers the *Pañcatantra* and the *Kathāsaritsāgara* as "Tales within tales within tales, told for the sake of their mere marvellousness" (Barth 1984: 9).

9. The patient reader could scan Bødker's *Indian animal tales: a preliminary survey* to find other examples of *Pañcatantra* stories in "oral" collections (Bødker 1991 [1957]).

10. In a radically different interpretation, Brodbeck argues a case for a "variable" *svabhāva* (Brodbeck 2004: 90).

11. Even the "natural" enmities listed by Hiraṇyaka are socially constructed and are culturally specific. The idea that lions and elephants are mortal foes, is, I suspect, a peculiarly Indian one.

CHAPTER 4. THE DISCOURSE OF DIVISION AND THE BRAHMANICAL ARCHIVE

1. See the bibliography in Doniger O'Flaherty 1981: 315–316; and Tull 1989.

2. I have been guided in this translation of the *Puruṣasūkta* by Doniger O'Flaherty 1981: 30–31.

3. When I try to visualize this act, "head" seems a better translation than "mouth."

4. For example, see the *Brahmāṇḍapurāṇa* (BAP 1.5.108), *Garuḍapurāṇa* (GP 4.34), *Kūrmapurāṇa* (KP 1.2.24–25), *Padmapurāṇa* (PP 1.3.127–130), *Skandapurāṇa* (SkP 2.9.24.41–42, 5.3.122.5–6, and 6.242.16), and *Viṣṇupurāṇa* (VP 1.6.6).

5. A similar passage is found in the *Padmapurāṇa* (PP 1.3.127–130).

6. In this translation, I have been guided by Dimmitt and van Buitenen 1978: 32.

7. Similar accounts are found in the *Nāradapurāṇa* (NP 1.43.53–59) and the *Vāyupurāṇa* (VāyP 8.154–164).

8. A similar comprehensive account is given in the *Gautamadharmasūtra* (GD 10.1–67).

9. I have been guided in the translation of this passage by Doniger and Smith 1991: 12–13.1. Similar passages of intermediate length are found in the *Agnipurāṇa* (AP 151.6–9), *Brahmapurāṇa* (BrP 117.1–14), *Mahābhārata* (Mbh 12.182.2–7), *Nāradapurāṇa* (NP 1.43.64–69); *Śivapurāṇa* (ŚP 13.2–6), *Skandapurāṇa* (SkP 6.242.19–32) and *Viṣṇupurāṇa* (VP 3.8.21–34).

10. Other short examples like this are found in the *Arthaśāstra* (AŚ 1.3.5–8), *Bhāgavatapurāṇa* (BP 3.6.30–34), *Kūrmapurāṇa* (KP 1.2.36–38), *Mahābhārata* (Mbh 12.73.6–8 and 12.285.20–21), *Mārkaṇḍeyapurāṇa* (MP 25.1–7), *Skandapurāṇa* (SkP 2.9.20.23–27), *Vasiṣṭhadharmasūtra* (VD 2.13–20), *Viṣṇupurāṇa* (VP 1.6.32–33), *Viṣṇusmṛti* (VS 2.1–14) and *Yājñavalkyasmṛti* (YS 1.118–120).

11. Doniger and Smith have described this escape clause as it is applied in the *Manusmṛti* (Doniger and Smith 1991: lii–liv). See also Rocher (1975).

12. See also MS 10.97.

13. In this and subsequent translations from the *Dharmasūtras* I have been guided by Olivelle. See also MS 11.224.

14. See also MS 4.140.

15. *Antyas* and *antyāvasāyins* are both classes of low-caste people.

16. On the general prohibition against eating food from a *śūdra*, see MS 4.211; VD 14.1–10 and 14.33.

17. While the archive presents ideals, exceptions are also made in deference to the demands of everyday life. Thus, a *brāhmaṇa* may accept food from a *śūdra* who is the tiller of his fields, a friend of his family, his cow-herd, his slave or his barber (MS 4.253). One must assume that without this element of flexibility the *brāhmaṇa* would go hungry.

Chapter 5. Conclusion

1. The *Skandapurāṇa* contains a similarly glowing description of Orissa (Utkala). Here, too, members of all four *varṇas* dutifully pursue their allotted roles (SkP 2.2.6.1–28).

Glossary of Sanskrit Terms

adharma	Unrighteousness, irreligion.
agnihotra	Sacred fire of the Vedic sacrifice.
arthaśāstra	Practical treatise on statecraft and governance.
ārya	"Noble," a member of one of the "twice-born" *varṇas* of *brāhmaṇa, kṣatriya* or *vaiśya.*
āśrama	One of the four stages in a *brāhmaṇa*'s life: student, householder, ascetic or forest-dweller.
brahman	Ultimate reality.
brāhmaṇa	Member of the first and highest *varṇa,* a priest.
caṇḍāla	Outcaste, a man of low, mixed descent (also *cāṇḍāla*)
daitya	Kind of demon.
dakṣiṇā	Fee or gift given to a *brāhmaṇa* for officiating at a sacrifice.
deva	Deity, god.
dharma	Traditional duties ascribed to a *varṇa,* righteous behavior, moral law.
guṇa	Elemental property, of which there are three: *tamas, sattva,* and *rajas.*
jāti	Of animals: kind, genus, or species. Of humans: caste, hereditary occupational grouping.
kathā	Story, fable, tale; the branch of Sanskrit literature to which the *Pañcatantra* belongs.
kathāmukha	Introduction, preface.

kṣatriya	Member of the second *varṇa,* a warrior.
maṇḍala	A symbolic circular figure representing the universe, with symmetrical divisions and figures of deities, and so forth at the center.
mantra	A sacred, mystical, or magical utterance.
nītiśāstra	Practical treatise on kingly conduct.
praśasti	Eulogistic metrical colophon.
purohita	King's domestic priest.
rājadharma	Idealized kingly conduct.
rājaguru	King's preceptor.
rākṣasa	Nocturnal demon which haunts cemeteries, disturbs sacrifices and eats people.
rajas	One of the three *guṇas:* energy.
rasa	Dominant character or sentiment of a cultural production.
sādhya	"Those who are to be propitiated": a class of divine being.
samādhi	State of union with creation attained through yoga.
śāstra	Authoritative religious or scientific treatise.
sattva	One of the three *guṇas:* purity.
siddha	Semidivine being of great purity and perfection, said to possess supernatural powers.
śloka	Poetic couplet, each line containing sixteen syllables.
smṛti	Texts "remembered" by human teachers; canonical texts other than the *Vedas.*
śruti	Texts which are "heard" from divine teachers; revealed sacred texts, especially the *Vedas.*
subhāṣita	"Spoken well or eloquently," maxim, gnomic verse.
śūdra	Member of the fourth and lowest *varṇa,* whose duty is servitude to the other three *varṇas.*
sūtra	Text consisting of "strings" of short sentences or aphoristic rules.

svabhāva	"Essential nature"; an individual's natural constitution or innate disposition.
svadharma	Occupations and conduct ascribed to each *varṇa,* for example, sacrifice for a *brāhmaṇa,* governance for a *kṣatriya,* and so on.
svayaṃvara	Event at which a *kṣatriya* woman chooses a husband from among a number of contenders.
tamas	One of the three *guṇas:* darkness.
tantra	One of the five chapters, books or sections which comprise the *Pañcatantra.*
vaiśya	Member of the third *varṇa,* whose traditional occupations are agriculture and trade.
varṇa	Originally "color," but traditionally translated as "caste" or "class." Idealized brahmanical society is divided into four *varṇas: brāhmaṇa, kṣatriya, vaiśya,* and *śūdra.*

Bibliography

Sanskrit Sources

Agnipurāṇa. Sharma, R. N. (ed.) 1985. *The Agnimahāpurāṇam*. Delhi: Nag Publishers.

Āpastambadharmasūtra. Olivelle, P. 2000. *Dharmasūtras: the law codes of Āpastamba, Gautama, Baudhāyana, and Vasiṣṭha*. Delhi: Motilal Banarsidass Publishers Private Limited.

Arthaśāstra. Kangle, R. P. (ed.) 1969. *The Kauṭilīya Arthaśāstra*. Delhi: Motilal Banarsidass.

Atharvaveda. Roth, R., and Whitney, W. D. (eds.) 1966 (1856). *Atharva Veda Sanhita*. Bonn: Ferd. Dümmlers Verlag.

Baudhāyanadharmasūtra. Olivelle, P. 2000. *Dharmasūtras: the law codes of Āpastamba, Gautama, Baudhāyana, and Vasiṣṭha*. Delhi: Motilal Banarsidass Publishers Private Limited.

Bhāgavatapurāṇa. Shastri, J. L. (ed.) 1983. *Bhāgavata Purāṇa of Kṛṣṇa Dvaipāyana Vyāsa, with Sanskrit commentary Bhāvārthabodhinī of Śrīdhara Svāmin*. Delhi: Motilal Banarsidass.

Brahmāṇḍapurāṇa. Sarma, K. V. (ed.) 1983. *The Brahmāṇḍa-Mahāpurāṇam*. Varanasi: Krishnadas Academy.

Brahmapurāṇa. Sharma, R. N. (ed.) 1985. *The Brahma Mahāpurāṇam*. Delhi: Nag Publishers.

Bṛhatkathāmañjarī. Shivdatta, M. M., and Parab, K. P. (eds.) 1982 (1931) *Bṛhatkathāmañjarī*. New Delhi: Panini.

Garuḍapurāṇa. Bhattacharya, R. (ed.) 1964. *Garuḍapurāṇam of Maharṣi Vedavyāsa*. Varanasi: The Chowkhamba Sanskrit Series Office. (The Kashi Sanskrit Series no. 165.)

Gautamadharmasūtra. Olivelle, P. 2000. *Dharmasūtras: the law codes of Āpastamba, Gautama, Baudhāyana, and Vasiṣṭha*. Delhi: Motilal Banarsidass Publishers Private Limited.

Hitopadeśa. Johnson, F. (ed.) 1864. *Hitopadeśa: the Sanskṛit text, with a grammatical analysis, alphabetically arranged.* Hertford (UK): Stephen Austin. London: W. H. Allen and Co.

Kathāsaritsāgara. Śarmā, K. N. (ed.) 1960. *Mahākavi Somadeva bhaṭṭa-vicarita Kathāsaritsāgara.* Patna: Bihāra-rāṣṭrabhāṣā-pariṣad.

Kūrmapurāṇa. Gupta, A. S. (ed.) 1971. *The Kūrma Purāṇa.* Varanasi: All-India Kashiraj Trust.

Mahābhārata. Sukthankar, V. S., et al. (eds.) 1933–1972. *The Mahābhārata.* Poona: Bhandarkar Oriental Research Institute.

Manusmṛti. Jolly, J. (ed.) 1887. *Mânava Dharma-śâstra: the code of Manu.* London: Trübner and Co.

Mārkaṇḍeyapurāṇa. Sharma, R. N. (ed.) 1984. *The Mārkaṇḍeya Mahāpurāṇam.* Delhi: Nag Publishers.

Nāradapurāṇa. Śāstrī, C. D. (ed.) 1985. *The Nāradīyamahāpurāṇam.* Delhi: Nag Publishers.

Nītisāra. Mitra, R. (ed.) 1980 (1849–1884). *The Nítisara, or the elements of polity, by Kamandaki.* Osnabrück: Biblio Verlag.

Nītiśataka. Kāle, M. R. (ed.) 1971. *The Nīti and Vairāgya Śatakas of Bhartṛhari.* Delhi: Motilal Banarsidass.

Padmapurāṇa. Śāstrī, C. D. (ed.) 1984. *The Padmamahāpurāṇam.* Delhi: Nag Publishers.

Pañcatantra (Pūrṇabhadra's recension). Hertel, J. (ed.) 1908. *The Panchatantra: a collection of ancient Hindu tales in the recension, called Panchakhyanaka, and dated 1199 A.D., of the Jaina monk, Purnabhadra.* Cambridge, Mass.: Harvard University. (Harvard Oriental Series vol. 11.)

Pañcatantra (*textus simplicior*). Kielhorn, F. (ed.) 1885. *Panchatantra I.* Bombay: Government Central Book Depot. (Bombay Sanskrit Series no. 4). Bühler, G. (ed.) 1886. *Panchatantra II and III.* Bombay: Government Central Book Depot. (Bombay Sanskrit Series no. 3). Bühler, G. (ed.) 1885. *Panchatantra IV and V.* Bombay: Government Central Book Depot. (Bombay Sanskrit Series no. 1.)

Rāmāyaṇa. Mehta, J. M. et al. (eds.) 1960–1975. *The Vālmīki-Rāmāyaṇa: critical edition.* Baroda: Oriental Institute.

Ṛgveda. Max Müller, F. (ed.) 1877. *The hymns of the Rig-veda in the samhita and pada texts.* London: Trübner and Co.

Ṛtusaṃhāra. Dwivedi, R. P. (ed.) 1990. *The Ṛtusaṃhāra of Kālidāsa.* New Delhi: Sahitya Akademi.

Śatapathabrāhmaṇa. 1987. *The Śatapathabrāhmaṇa according to the Mādhyandina recension.* Delhi: Gian Publishing House.

Śivapurāṇa. Singh, N. S. (ed.) 1986. *The Śivamahāpurāṇam.* Delhi: Nag Publishers.

Skandapurāṇa. Kṛṣṇadāsa, K. (ed.) 1986. *The Skandamahāpurāṇam.* Delhi: Nag Publishers.

Southern Pañcatantra. Hertel, J. (ed.) 1906. *Das südliche Pañcatantra. Sanskrittext der Rezension β mit den Lesarten der besten Hss. der Rezension α.* Leipzig: B. G. Teubner. (Der Abhandlungen der Philologisch-historischen Klasse der Königl. Sächsischen Gesellschaft der Wissenschaften Bd 24, no. 5.)

Śukasaptati. Tripāthī, R. (ed.) 1966. *Śukasaptati.* Varanasi: The Chowkhamba Sanskrit Series Office. (The Haridas Sanskrit Series no. 269.)

Taittirīyabrāhmaṇa. Mahadeva Sastri, A. (ed.) 1985 (1911). *The Taittirīya Brāhmaṇa.* Delhi: Motilal Banarsidass.

Taittirīyasaṃhitā. 1981. *Kṛṣṇa-yajurvedīyā taittirīya-saṃhitā.* Bahālgarh: Yudhiṣṭhira Mīmāṃsaka.

Tantrākhyāyika. Hertel, J. 1915. *The Panchatantra: a collection of ancient Hindu tales in its oldest recension, the Kashmirian, entitled Tantrakhyayika. The original Sanskrit text, editio minor, reprinted from the critical editio major which was made for the Königliche Gesellschaft der Wissenschaften zu Göttingen.* Cambridge, Mass.: Harvard University. (Harvard Oriental Series vol. 14.)

Vāmanapurāṇa. Gupta, A. S. (ed.) 1968. *The Vāmana Purāṇa with English translation.* Varanasi: All India Kashiraj Trust.

Vasiṣṭhadharmasūtra. Olivelle, P. 2000. *Dharmasūtras: the law codes of Āpastamba, Gautama, Baudhāyana, and Vasiṣṭha.* Delhi: Motilal Banarsidass Publishers Private Limited.

Vāyupurāṇa. Singh, N. S. (ed.) 1983. *The Vāyumahāpurāṇam.* Delhi: Nag Publishers.

Vetālapañcaviṃśati. Emeneau, M. B. 1967 (1934). *Jambhaladatta's version of the Vetālapañcaviṅśati.* New York: Kraus Reprint Corporation. (American Oriental Series vol. 4.)

Viṣṇupurāṇa. Sharma, R. N. (ed.) 1985. *The Viṣṇumahāpurāṇam.* Delhi: Nag Publishers.

Viṣṇusmṛti. Krishnamacharya, V. (ed.) 1964. *Viṣṇusmṛti with the commentary Keśavavaijayantī of Nandapaṇḍita.* Madras: Adyar Library and Research Centre.

Yājñavalkyasmṛti. Ācārya, N. R. (ed.) 1985. *Yajnavalkyasmrti.* Delhi: Nag Publishers.

Other Sources

Appadurai, A. 1986. "Is homo hierarchicus?" *American Ethnologist* 13 (4): 745–761.

Artola, G. T. 1957. "Pañcatantra manuscripts from South India." *The Adyar Library Bulletin* 21 (3–4): 185–262.

Barth, J. 1984. *The Friday book: essays and other nonfiction.* Baltimore and London: The Johns Hopkins University Press.

Barthes, R. 1981. Theory of the text. In: Young, R. (ed.) *Untying the text: a post-structuralist reader.* Boston, London and Henley: Routledge & Kegan Paul: 31–47.

Benfey, T. 1966 (1859). *Pantschatantra: Fünf Bücher indischer Fabeln, Märchen und Erzählungen.* Hildesheim: Georg Olms Verlagsbuchhandlung

Bickell, G. 1876. *Kalilag und Damnag: alte syrische Übersetzung des indischen Fürstenspiegels.* Leipzig: F. A. Brockhaus.

Blackburn, S. 1996. "The brahmin and the mongoose: the narrative context of a well-travelled tale." *Bulletin of the School of Oriental and African Studies* 59 (3): 494–507.

Bødker, L. 1991 (1957). *Indian animal tales: a preliminary survey.* Helsinki: Academia Scientiarum Fennica. (FT Communications no. 170.)

Bourdieu, P. 1991. *Language and symbolic power.* Cambridge, UK: Polity Press.

Brodbeck, S. 2004. "Calling Kṛṣṇa's bluff: non-attached action in the *Bhagavadgītā.*" *Journal of Indian Philosophy* 32: 81–103.

Bronkhorst, J. 1996. Sanskrit and reality: the Buddhist contribution. In: Houben, J. E. M. (ed.) *Ideology and status of Sanskrit: contributions to the history of the Sanskrit language.* Leiden: E. J. Brill: 109–135.

Brown, W. N. 1919. "The Pañcatantra in modern Indian folklore." *Journal of the American Oriental Society* 39: 1–54.

Brown, W. N. 1931. "The sources and nature of *pūruṣa* in the Puruṣasūkta (Rigveda 10.91)." *Journal of the American Oriental Society* 51 (2): 108–118.

Condylis-Bassoukos, H. 1995. *Stéphanitès kai Ichnélatès, traduction grecque (XIe siècle) du livre Kalīla wa-Dimna d'Ibn al-Muquffa' (VIIIe siècle): étude lexicologique et littéraire.* Leuven: Peeters.

Culler, J. 1981. *The pursuit of signs: semiotics, literature, deconstruction.* Ithaca, New York: Cornell University Press.

Derrett, J. D. M. 1968. *Religion, law and the state in India.* London: Faber and Faber.

Desai, V. N., and Mason, D. 1993. *Gods, guardians, and lovers: temple sculptures from North India A.D. 700–1200.* New York: The Asia Society Galleries.

Dimmitt, C., and van Buitenen, J. A. B. (eds.) 1978. *Classical Hindu mythology: a reader in the Sanskrit Purāṇas.* Philadelphia: Temple University Press.

Dirks, N. B. 1987. *The hollow crown: ethnohistory of an Indian kingdom.* Cambridge: Cambridge University Press.

Doniger, W. 1999. "Presidential address: 'I have Scinde': Flogging a dead (white male orientalist) horse." *Journal of Asian Studies* 58 (4): 940–960.

Doniger, W. 2004. "Diverse views of diversity, or, interdisciplinary cross-cultural eclecticism." http://www.liberalarts.wabash.edu/cila/docs/pbk2_doniger.pdf.

Doniger, W., and Smith, B. K. 1991. *The laws of Manu.* London: Penguin Books.

Doniger O'Flaherty, W. 1981. *The Rig Veda: an anthology.* Harmondsworth: Penguin Books.

Dubois, J.-A. 1826. *Le Pantcha-Tantra ou les cinq ruses: fables du Brahme Vichnou-Sarma.* Paris: J. S. Merlin.

Dumont, L. 1970. *Homo hierarchicus: the caste system and its implications.* London: Weidenfeld and Nicolson.

Edgerton, F. 1924. *The Panchatantra reconstructed: an attempt to establish the lost original Sanskrit text of the most famous of Indian story-collections on the basis of the principal extant versions. Vol. 2. Introduction and translation.* New Haven: American Oriental Society. (American Oriental Series vol. 3.)

Edgerton, F. 1926. *Vikrama's adventures, or, the thirty-two tales of the throne.* Cambridge, Mass.: Harvard University Press. (Harvard Oriental Series vol. 26.)

Eichinger Ferro-Luzzi, G. 1997. "The polythetic network of Tamil folk stories." *Asian Folklore Studies* 56: 109–128.

Falk, H. 1978. *Quellen des Pañcatantra.* Wiesbaden: Otto Harrassowitz.

Foucault, M. 1972. *The archaeology of knowledge.* London: Tavistock Publications.

Foucault, M. 1977. Truth and power. In: Gordon, C. 1980. *Power/knowledge: selected interviews and other writings 1972–1977: Michel Foucault.* New York: Pantheon Books: 109–133.

Fritze, L. 1884. *Pañcatantra (textus simplicior).* Leipzig: Otto Schultz.

Ganguli, K.M. (trans.) 1993 (1883–1896). *The Mahabharata of Krishna-Dwaipayana Vyasa.* New Delhi: Munshiram Manoharlal Publishers Pvt Ltd.

Ganguly, D. 2001. Hierarchy and its discontents: caste, postcoloniality and the new humanities. Canberra: The Australian National University. [PhD thesis].

Geib, R. 1969. *Zur Frage nach der Urfassung des Pañcatantra.* Wiesbaden: Otto Harrassowitz.

Goldman, R. P. 1984. *The Rāmāyaṇa of Vālmīki: an epic of Ancient India. Vol. 1. Bālakāṇḍa.* Princeton, New Jersey: Princeton University Press.

Haksar, A. N. D. (trans.) 2000. *Shuka Saptati: seventy tales of the parrot.* New Delhi: HarperCollins Publishers India.

Halbfass, W. 1991. *Tradition and reflection: explorations in Indian thought.* Albany: State University of New York Press.

Hämeen-Anttila, V. 2003. *Some notes on the origin of the frame-story device in Sanskrit literature.* [Paper presented at 12th World Sanskrit Conference, Helsinki, July 2003.]

Hertel, J. 1904. *Über das Tantrākhyāyika, die Kaśmīrische Rezension des Pañcatantra. Mit dem Texte der Handschrift Decc. Coll. VIII, 145.* Leipzig: B. G. Teubner. (Der Abhandlungen der Philologisch-historischen Klasse der Königl. Sächsischen Gesellschaft der Wissenschaften Bd 22, no. 5.)

Hertel, J. 1906. *Das südliche Pañcatantra. Sanskrittext der Rezension β mit den Lesarten der besten Hss. der Rezension α.* Leipzig: B. G. Teubner. (Der Abhandlungen der Philologisch-historischen Klasse der Königl. Sächsischen Gesellschaft der Wissenschaften Bd 24, no. 5.)

Hertel, J. (ed.) 1908. *The Panchatantra: a collection of ancient Hindu tales in the recension, called Panchakhyanaka, and dated 1199 A.D., of the Jaina monk, Purnabhadra.* Cambridge, Mass.: Harvard University. (Harvard Oriental Series vol. 11.)

Hertel, J. 1909. *Tantrākhyāyika: die älteste Fassung des Pañcatantra.* Leipzig and Berlin: B. G. Teubner.

Hertel, J. 1912a. *The Panchatantra-text of Purnabhadra: critical introduction and list of variants.* Cambridge, Mass.: Harvard University. (Harvard Oriental Series vol. 12.)

Hertel, J. 1912b. *The Panchatantra-text of Purnabhadra and its relation to texts of allied recensions as shown in parallel specimens.* Cambridge Mass.: Harvard University. (Harvard Oriental Series vol. 13.)

Hertel, J. 1914. *Das Pañcatantra: seine Geschichte und seine Verbreitung.* Leipzig and Berlin: B. G. Teubner.

Hertel, J. 1915. *The Panchatantra: a collection of ancient Hindu tales in its oldest recension, the Kashmirian, entitled Tantrakhyayika. The original Sanskrit text, editio minor, reprinted from the critical editio major which was made for the Königliche Gesellschaft der Wissenschaften zu Göttingen.* Cambridge Mass.: Harvard University Press. (Harvard Oriental Series vol. 14.)

Hiltebeitel, A. 2001. *Rethinking the Mahābhārata: a reader's guide to the education of the Dharma King.* Chicago and London: The University of Chicago Press.

Hocart, A. M. 1925. "*The Panchatantra Reconstructed,* F. Edgerton." [book review]. *American Anthropologist* 27 (3): 467–469.

Hooykaas, C. 1929. *Tantri, de middel-javaansche Pancatantra-bewerking.* Leiden: A. Vros.

Huilgol, V. 1987. *The Pañcatantra of Vasubhāga: a critical study.* Madras: New Era Publications.

Jacobs, J. 1888. *The earliest English version of the Fables of Bidpai, "The Morall Philosophie of Doni" by Sir Thomas North, whilom of Peterhouse, Cambridge.* London: David Nutt.

Jahn, M. 1999. "Narratology: a guide to the theory of narrative." http://www.cx.unibe.ch/ens/cg/genres/pppn.htm.

Jallad, S. S. 2004. *The fables of Kalilah and Dimnah.* London: Melisende.

Kale, M. R. 1998 (1896). *Hitopadeśa of Nārāyaṇa.* Delhi: Motilal Banarsidass Publishers Private Limited.

Keith, A. B. 1920. *A history of Sanskrit literature.* London: Oxford University Press.

Keith-Falconer, I. G. N. 1885. *Kalīlah and Dimnah or the fables of Bidpai: being an account of their literary history, with an English translation of the Later Syriac version of the same.* Cambridge: Cambridge University Press.

Klokke, M. J. 1991. The tortoise and the geese: a comparison of a number of Indian and Javanese literary and sculptural versions of the story. In: Chandra, L. (ed.) *The art and culture of South-east Asia.* New Delhi: International Academy of Indian Culture and Aditya Prakashan: 181–198.

Klokke, M. J. 1993. *The Tantri reliefs on ancient Javanese candi.* Leiden: KITLV Press. (Verhandelingen van het Koninklijk Instituut voor Taal-, Landen Volkenkunde 153.)

Knipe, D. M. 1966–67. "The heroic theft: myths from Ṛgveda IV and the ancient Near East." *History of Religions* 6: 328–360.

Kristeva, J. 1980. Word, dialogue, and novel. In: Roudiez, L. S. (ed.) *Desire in language: a semiotic approach to literature and art by Julia Kristeva.* New York: Columbia University Press: 64–91.

Lacôte, F. 1908. *Essai sur Guṇāḍhya et le Bṛhatkathā.* Paris: E. Leroux.

La Fontaine, J. 2001. *La Fontaine's Fables.* London: Everyman Publishers plc.

Lamb, C. 1954 (1833). *Last essays of Elia.* London: J. M. Dent & Sons Ltd.

Leidy, D. P., and Thurman, R. A. F. 1997. *Mandala: the architecture of enlightenment.* London: Thames and Hudson.

Lerner, M., and Kossak, S. 1991. *The lotus transcendent: Indian and Southeast Asian art from the Samuel Eilenberg Collection.* New York: The Metropolitan Museum of Art.

Levi, S. 1886. *La Bṛhatkathāmañjarī de Kshemendra.* Paris: Imprimerie Nationale.

Lévi-Strauss, C. 1963. *Structural anthropology.* New York and London: Basic Books.

Lüthi, M. 1970. *Once upon a time: on the nature of fairy tales.* Bloomington and London: Indiana University Press.

Macdonell, A. A. 1924. *A practical Sanskrit dictionary.* London: Oxford University Press.

Macdonell, A. A. 1955 (1927). *A Sanskrit grammar for students.* London: Oxford University Press.

McHoul, A., and Grace, W. 1993. *A Foucault primer: discourse, power and the subject.* Melbourne: Melbourne University Press.

MacIntyre, A. 1988. *Whose justice? Which rationality?* Indiana: University of Notre Dame Press.

Maten, E. P. 1980–81. "In quest of the original Pañcatantra. A methodological discussion." *Indologica Taurinensia* 8–9: 241–252.

Milner, M. 1994. *Status and sacredness: a general theory of status relations and an analysis of Indian culture.* New York and Oxford: Oxford University Press.

Monier-Williams, M. 1995 (1899). *A Sanskrit-English dictionary. Etymologically and philologically arranged with special reference to cognate Indo-European languages.* Delhi: Motilal Barnarsidass Publishers.

Nelson, D. 1978. "*Bṛhatkathā* studies: the problem of an ur-text." *Journal of Asian Studies* 37 (4): 663–676.

Nietzsche, F. 1974 (1887). *The gay science, with a prelude in rhymes and an appendix of songs.* New York: Vintage Books.

Olivelle, P. 1997. *Pañcatantra: the book of India's folk wisdom.* Oxford and New York: Oxford University Press.

Olivelle, P. 2000. *Dharmasūtras: the law codes of Āpastamba, Gautama, Baudhāyana and Vasiṣṭha.* Delhi: Motital Banarsidass Publishers Private Limited.

Olivelle, P. 2002a. Meat-eaters and grass-eaters: an exploration of human nature in Kathā and Dharma literature. In: Rosen, S. J. (ed.) *Holy war: violence and the Bhagavad Gita.* Hampton, Virginia: Deepak Heritage Books: 99–116.

Olivelle, P. 2002b. "Structure and composition of the *Mānava Dharmaśāstra.*" *Journal of Indian Philosophy* 30: 535–574.

Olivelle, P. 2004a. *The law code of Manu.* Oxford: Oxford University Press. (Oxford World Classics.)

Olivelle, P. 2004b. "Manu and the *Arthaśāstra*: a study in śāstric intertextuality." *Journal of Indian Philosophy* 32: 281–291.

Panigrahi, K. C. 1961. *Archaeological remains at Bhubaneswar.* Bombay: Orient Longmans.

Patil, C. S. 1997. "Panchatantra sculptures in India and abroad." *Asia Prashant* 4 (1–2): 46–62.

Peterson, P. (ed.) 1986 (1887). *Hitopadeśa by Nārāyaṇa.* Delhi: Bharatiya Book Corporation.

Pollock, S. 1985. "The theory of practice and the practice of theory in Indian intellectual history." *Journal of the American Oriental Society* 105 (3): 499–519.

Pollock, S. (trans.) 1991. *The Rāmāyaṇa of Vālmīki: an epic of Ancient India. Vol. 3. Araṇyakāṇḍa.* Princeton: Princeton University Press.

Pollock, S. 1998. "The cosmopolitan vernacular." *Journal of Asian Studies* 57 (1): 6–37.

Pollock, S. 2001. "The social aesthetic and Sanskrit literary theory." *Journal of Indian Philosophy* 29: 197–229.

Pollock, S. 2002. "Introduction: working papers on Sanskrit knowledge-systems on the eve of colonialism." *Journal of Indian Philosophy* 30: 431–439.

Pollock, S. (ed.) 2003. *Literary cultures in history: reconstructions from South Asia.* Berkeley: University of California Press.

Rajan, C. (trans.) 1993. *Viṣṇu Śarma: the Panćatantra.* New Delhi: Penguin Books India.

Renou, L. 1957. *Vedic India (Classical India Vol. 3).* Calcutta: Susil Gupta (India) Pvt Ltd.

Richman, P. (ed.) 1991. *Many Rāmāyaṇas: the diversity of a narrative tradition in South Asia.* Berkeley: University of California Press.

Rocher, R. 1975. Caste and occupation in classical India: the normative texts. *Contributions to Indian Sociology (NS)* 9 (1): 139–151.

Rocher, R. 1993. British Orientalism in the eighteenth century: the dialectics of knowledge and government. In: Breckenridge, C. A., and van der Veer, P. (eds.) *Orientalism and the postcolonial predicament: perspectives on South Asia.* Philadelphia: University of Pennsylvania Press: 215–249.

Roudiez, L. S. 1980. Introduction. In: Roudiez, L. S. (ed.) *Desire in language: a semiotic approach to literature and art by Julia Kristeva.* New York: Columbia University Press.

Ruben, W. 1959. *Das Pañcatantra und siene Morallehre.* Berlin: Akademie-Verlag.

Ryder, A. W. (trans.) 1925. *The Panchatantra.* Chicago: The University of Chicago Press.

Santoso, S. 1971. "The islamization of Indonesia/Malay literature in its earlier period." *Journal of the Oriental Society of Australia* 8 (1–2): 9–27.

Sattar, A. 1994. *Tales from the Kathāsaritsāgara.* New Delhi and New York: Penguin Books.

Schmidt, R. [1901]. *Das Pañcatantram (Textus ornatior): eine altindische Märchensammlung.* Leipzig: Lotus-Verlag.

Schulthess, F. 1982 (1911). *Kalīla und Dimna: die altsyrische Version des indischen Fürstenspiegels (Pantschatantra) oder Bidpai's Fabeln.* Amsterdam: APA-Philo Press.

Shamasastry, R. 1951. *Kauṭilya's Arthaśāstra.* Mysore: Sri Raghuveer Printing Press.

Sharma, A. 1978. "The Puruṣasūkta: its relation to the caste system." *Journal of the Economic and Social History of the Orient (Leiden)* 21 (3): 294–303.

Sivaramamurti, C. 1977. *The art of India.* New York: Harry N. Abrams.

Sjöberg, L.-O. 1962. *Stephanites und Ichnelates: Überlieferungsgeschichte und Text.* Stockholm: Almqvist & Wiksell.

Smith, B. K. 1990. "Eaters, food, and social hierarchy in ancient India: a dietary guide to a revolution of values." *Journal of the American Academy of Religion* 58 (2): 177–205.

Smith, B. K. 1991. "Classifying animals and humans in ancient India." *Man,* New Series 26 (3): 527–548.

Smith, B. K. 1994. *Classifying the universe: the ancient Indian varṇa system and the origins of caste.* New York and Oxford: Oxford University Press.

Snead, S. 1989. *Animals in four worlds: sculptures from India.* Chicago and London: The University of Chicago Press.

Speyer, J. S. 1908. *Studies about the Kathāsaritsāgara.* Amsterdam: Johannes Müller.

Stchoukine, I. 1929. *La peinture indienne a l'époque des Grands Moghols.* Paris: Librairie Ernest Leroux.

Sternbach, L. 1960. *The Hitopadeśa and its sources.* New Haven: American Oriental Society. (American Oriental Series vol. 44.)

Sternbach, L. 1971. *The Kāvya-portions in the Kathā-literature (Pañcatantra, Hitopadeśa, Vikramacarita, Vetālapañcaviṃśatikā and Śukasaptati): an analysis. Vol. 1. Pañcatantra.* Delhi: Meharchand Lachhmandas.

Stoler Miller, B. 1991. "Presidential address: Contending narratives—the political life of the Indian epics." *Journal of Asian Studies* 50 (4): 783–792.

Stoler Miller, B. 1994. The imaginative universe of Indian literature. In: Stoler Miller, B. (ed.) *Masterworks of Asian literature in comparative perspective.* Armonk (NY) and London: M. E. Sharpe: 3–14.

Sumitra Bai, B. N., and Zydenbos, R. J. 1991. The Jaina Mahābhārata. In: Sharma, A. (ed.) *Essays on the Mahābhārata.* Leiden: E. J. Brill: 251–271.

Tawney, C. H. 1926. *The ocean of story: being C. H. Tawney's translation of Somadeva's Kathā Sarit Sāgara (or Ocean of Streams of Story).* London: Chas. J. Sawyer.

Thapar, R. 1966. *A history of India. Vol. 1.* Harmondsworth, UK: Penguin Books Ltd.

Thiel-Horstmann, M. (ed.) 1991. *Rāmāyaṇa and Rāmāyaṇas.* Wiesbaden: Otto Harrassowitz.

Thompson, J. B. 1991. Editor's introduction. In: Bourdieu, P. *Language and symbolic power.* Cambridge, UK: Polity Press: 1–31.

Tull, H. W. 1989. *The Vedic origins of karma: Cosmos as Man in ancient Indian myth and ritual.* Albany: State University of New York Press.

Van Damme, G. 1991. *De jakhals in de Oudindische Pañcatantra.* Brussels: Paleis der Academiën. (Verhandelingen van de Koninklijke Academie voor Wetenschappen, Letteren en Schone Kunsten van België, Klasse der Letteren, Jaargang 53, Nr. 141.)

Venkatasubbiah, A. 1934. "The Pañcatantra of Vasubhāga." *Indian Historical Quarterly* 10: 104–111.

Venkatasubbiah, A. 1965. "A Tamil version of the Pañcatantra." *Adyar Library Bulletin* 29 (1–4): 74–143.

Venkatasubbiah, A. 1967. "A Javanese version of the Pañcatantra." *Annals of the Bhandarkar Oriental Research Institute* (*ABORI*) 47 (1–4): 59–100.

Venkatasubbiah, A. 1969. "The *Pañcatantra* version of Laos." *Adyar Library Bulletin* 33 (1–4): 195–283.

Vogel, J. P. 1962. *The goose in Indian literature and art.* Leiden: E. J. Brill.

von Mankowski, L. 1892. *Der Auszug aus dem Pañcatantra in Kshemendras Bṛihatkathâmañjarî.* Leipzig: Otto Harrassowitz.

Winternitz, M. 1967 (1889). *History of Indian literature. Vol III, Part II (Scientific literature).* Delhi: Motital Banarsidass.

Witzel, M. 1987. On the origin of the literary device of the "frame story" in old Indian literature. In: Falk, H. (ed.) *Hinduismus und Buddhismus, Festschrift für Ulrich Schneider.* Freiburg: Hedwig Falk: 380–414.

Yule, H., and Burnell, A. C. 1968 (1886). *Hobson-Jobson: a glossary of colloquial Anglo-Indian words and phrases, and of kindred terms, etymological, historical, geographical and discursive.* London: Routledge & Kegan Paul.

Zoetmulder, P. J. 1974. *Kalangwan: a survey of old Javanese literature.* The Hague: Martinus Nijhoff.

Index